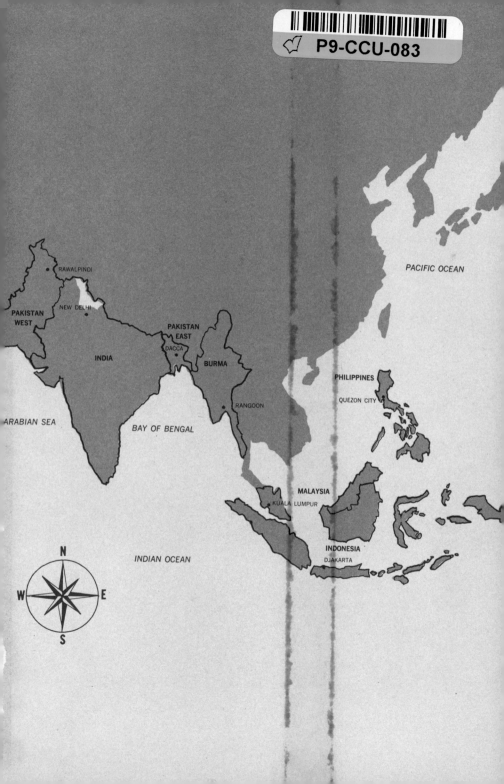

P9-CCU-083

PACIFIC OCEAN

PAKISTAN
WEST

RAWALPINDI

NEW DELHI

INDIA

PAKISTAN
EAST

DACCA

BURMA

RANGOON

ARABIAN SEA

BAY OF BENGAL

PHILIPPINES

QUEZON CITY

MALAYSIA

KUALA LUMPUR

INDONESIA

DJAKARTA

INDIAN OCEAN

N

W   E

S

LEADERS
OF
NEW
NATIONS

LEADERS OF NEW

DOUBLEDAY & COMPANY, INC.

NATIONS

LEONARD S. KENWORTHY

and ERMA FERRARI

illustrated by MICHAEL LOWENBEIN

GARDEN CITY, NEW YORK

PICTURE CREDITS

Wide World Photos: pages 2, 92, 106, 128, 224, 246, 270, 290, 310,
and 336
UPI: pages 30, 48, 66, 156, 180, and 202

AUTHOR'S NOTE

Shortly after World War II I started collecting material about the new nations. Soon my filing cabinets were bulging with clippings from newspapers and magazines. Then I took two trips around the world. On one of them I met and interviewed the leaders of many new nations, and several of them permitted me to tape-record part of the interviews.

All this background was used in writing the first edition of *Leaders of New Nations,* published in 1959. To this new edition four chapters have been added—the chapters concerning Balewa, Kenyatta, Nyerere, and Senghor. Also, the material which appeared in the earlier edition has been brought up to date.

In the work on this edition I have had the able assistance of Erma Ferrari. She has done the writing on the new chapters and has revised the old chapters.

We both hope that through this book you will become better acquainted with some of the leaders of our three billion neighbors and begin to understand the successes and failures of the new nations in our closely knit modern world.

LEONARD S. KENWORTHY

CONTENTS

AFRICA SOUTH OF THE SAHARA

NYERERE
OF TANZANIA

Far up on the slopes of the majestic Mount Kili-manjaro a snowstorm was raging. In the cold, dark stillness, a young army lieutenant kept a lonely vigil, waiting for the hour of midnight. The young lieutenant's name will probably never appear in the history books, but he was to play a significant role that night in a thrilling drama for which all of Tanganyika had long been preparing. Three hundred miles to the southeast, in the capital city of Dar-es-Salaam, seventy thousand people had crowded into the National Stadium. They also waited for midnight, when they, too, would play their roles in the same national drama.

At last the time came. On the rugged slope of Mount Kilimanjaro the young lieutenant raised the flag of Tangan-yika, then lit a torch that shone bravely and symbolically through the storm. Simultaneously, the crowd in the National Stadium greeted with a mighty roar their country's flag as it rose triumphantly to welcome a new day for Tangan-yika. As they saluted their flag, the people of Tanganyika remembered that the same flag was waving gallantly on Mount Kilimanjaro. They remembered, too, the prophetic words of their Prime Minister spoken two years earlier.: "We the people of Tanganyika would like to light a candle and put it on top of Mount Kilimanjaro to shine beyond our borders, giving hope where there was despair, love where there was hate, and dignity where before there was only humiliation."

The man of the hour on that Day of Independence in December 1961 was the young Prime Minister, Julius Nyerere. In appearance he was not impressive—small in stature, quiet, almost shy at times, disliking ostentation, and without personal vanity. But of him the retiring British Governor General of Tanganyika said, "This is no ordinary man." The Governor General knew whereof he spoke. Julius Nyerere is indeed no ordinary man. By what route had a young lad from a remote village of Tanganyika come to the highest position his country could bestow?

Kamborage Nyerere was well born. His father was a chief of one of Tanganyika's tribes, the Zaraki. Being the son of a chief doubtless gave Kamborage some status with his playmates, but his father's position did nothing for the family finances. The family was miserably poor. Nor could the boy aspire to become a chief himself someday, for the position would be inherited by the eldest son, one of his half-brothers.

Butiama, the home village, was situated on the hot plains that border that vast inland sea, Lake Victoria. The Nyerere family comprised the entire village. The father's several wives and their large families (Kamborage was one of twenty-six brothers and half-brothers) made up what in some countries would be considered a clan, and the group of thatched-roof huts which housed the families created the village. Other similar villages of the Zaraki tribe were scattered throughout the plains.

The sale of skins and hides from sheep, goats, and cattle provided the family income, and Kamborage and his young brothers tended the precious livestock on the pasture lands just outside the village.

Life was not tedious for young boys on the Tanganyika plains, however. For one thing, exotic animals, familiar to Western children only in zoos and circuses, were a common sight not many miles from the home village. Crocodiles and hippos slept on the surface or churned the shallow waters of the lakes. Flocks of pink flamingos turned their feeding places into pools the color of delicate sunsets. Ostriches and grazing animals in the thousands roamed the plains. The giraffe was and is so common to Tanganyika that it was made the national emblem. As a matter of fact, the great variety and numbers of the wild animals which inhabited the Serengeti Plains not far from Kamborage's home village led the government some years ago to establish Serengeti as one of two large game reserves where the big game of Tanganyika is protected from poachers and safaris of hunters.

During the long African evenings, the children of the village listened in respectful and interested attention to the village storyteller, whose tales taught the rising generation the history and traditions of their tribe. On special occasions they watched as their elders danced to the rhythmic thumping of the tom-toms to celebrate the installation of a chief, or a wedding, or the planting or reaping of the crops. After the dancing, the children joined heartily in the general feasting on rice cakes, oranges, bananas, and, when the fathers could afford it, meat. When the children reached the age of fifteen or sixteen, they would be taught the dances and would take part in the ceremonies. Some fortunate boys would learn to play the drums.

Today Nyerere remembers that he learned in his home village something more important than dancing and tribal history. "I witnessed democracy at work in its purest form," he says. He saw the chiefs sitting under a big tree and talking over the problems of governing the tribe until they came to an agreement without bloodshed.

Lake Victoria, the second largest body of fresh water in the world, was to furnish the background for the next period of Kamborage's youth. At twelve years of age, he set out one day with other boys of the village for the government school twenty-six miles away at Musoma, a small but busy port on Lake Victoria. He was clothed in little more than a piece of old cloth, and clutched in his hand a small amount of money with which to buy something more suitable in the way of school clothes when he reached Musoma. Twenty-six miles was not a long distance for an African boy to go to school. Some boys walked incredible distances back and forth between home and school, leaving home before daylight and returning late in the evening.

The shy young student did so well in his studies at Musoma that he was able to crowd the four years of the curriculum into three. His extracurricular education was equally successful. It is not difficult to imagine with what interest this young lad from a remote village watched the steamers from other ports on the lake coming into Musoma to unload and take on cargo and passengers. His active mind must have wondered about the places from which the steamers had come. Someday he would find out. He watched the fishermen bringing into the docks their gaily painted boats or dugout canoes to unload their catches of the popular tilapia, the fish for which Lake Victoria is famous. Kamborage's horizons were widening fast in school and out. He remembers vividly the shock with which, during these first schooldays, he viewed for the first time two very strange objects, an automobile and a white man.

It was during his student days that Julius (he was given the name Julius at his baptism) began to question the government under which his people lived. He had been born very shortly after the close of World War I, probably about 1921. In World War I Germany lost Tanganyika, which it had ruled since 1885, and the League of Nations made it a British mandate. Julius grew up under the British regime. There was a British Governor, and serving under him were British provincial commissioners.

A central Legislative Council consisted of Europeans and Asians, but no Africans. The Africans were represented by Europeans, the British excuse for this being that there were no educated Africans available.

At least Britain's governing policy was less harsh than Germany's had been. She returned to the local chiefs, from whom the Germans had stripped all power, some of their governing privileges. They could make certain laws for their area, and they could try small crimes in native courts. For this service the British paid the chiefs a small salary.

But Julius had learned from his schoolbooks that the United States had won its independence from Britain, and he asked himself, "Why are we different? Why should we not have independence too?" Independence was to come to Tanganyika while Julius Nyerere was still a young man, but no one, British or Tanganyikan, would have believed it during his schooldays, or that this young student would himself be the prime factor in winning that independence.

At the completion of his work at the Musoma school, Julius went to Tabora to attend Tanganyika's only secondary school. At the time, he may not have been aware of the importance of that city in his country's history. Tabora was the goal of the earliest invaders of the East African inland. Hundreds of years before Julius' arrival in Tabora, Arab caravans had pushed their way from the east coast on the Indian Ocean through the bush country and across rivers and streams, with the help of native porters, to Tabora. The arduous trek took several months. The Arabs were looking for precious ivory and for men to carry it back to the coast and their waiting dhows. The unfortunate men whom the Arabs seized or bought from local chiefs not only served as porters on the return trip, but were sold as slaves when they reached the coast. A modern railroad now follows the route of the original Arab traders from Dar-es-Salaam on the eastern coast to Tabora.

It was the Arab merchants who settled in Tanganyika and married African girls who brought the Moslem religion to the country. The mixture of Arabic and African languages that they spoke became the Swahili language of East Africa today.

Lured by stories of riches in Tanganyika, Belgian explorers reached Tabora in 1879 after a long and difficult journey from the coast. Then the Germans came and gradually got control of the entire country by means of devious methods of land purchase. Through the years all the explorers of Tanganyika headed first for Tabora and made the town their headquarters.

In World War I, much of Tanganyika, especially the Tabora area, became a battleground. The fighting was chiefly between the Germans who held the country and the Belgians who wanted it back. The people suffered from the military invasions, and ten thousand Tanganyikan men served as *askaris,* or scouts, for the Germans. Eventually, Tabora was captured by the Belgian Army.

Now, to this city, steeped in the history of his forefathers, Julius came to continue his education. He spent six years at the Tabora school, which was strictly English, run like the exclusive "public" schools of England. Julius made good grades, but, as one of his teachers explained, he never became the head of his class because he resisted discipline. This is understandable. The shift from the unfettered world of his childhood to the rules and regulations of an English school could not have been easy.

From Tabora, Julius left his native land for the first time to go north to the University College of Makerere in the town of Kampala, Uganda. University College was affiliated with the University of London, and was at that time the only university in existence between Egypt and South Africa. In other words, it was the only one in the entire length of the continent. At Kampala, the commercial center of Uganda, Julius' horizons continued to expand, as he observed the new world about him and read widely. More and more the social injustices suffered by his people at the hands of the foreign white men became of paramount concern. He was not at the time bothered so much by the colonial system as such, as by the lack of opportunities afforded his people to better themselves. He now describes his feelings at the time as the "politics of complaint" only. He learned that his father's generation had been ruthlessly conquered and exploited by the Germans, and had finally been forced to give in to Bismarck's armies. His own generation had known only British rule, and had for the most part accepted it without question. In 1946, at the end of two years at the university, Julius received his diploma. He won at least one distinction, first prize in a literary competition for his essay on "An Application of John Mill's Arguments for Feminism as Applied to the Tribal Societies of Tanganyika." Julius had been studying Mill's "The Subjection of Women," which had been radical in its day. This was indeed revolutionary talk for a young African. But it did not faze Julius, who characteristically studied Mill's ideas in terms of his own people.

Now Julius was ready for the career he had chosen, teaching. A political role was not in his mind. Never in his most imaginative youthful dreams did he envision his land as independent within the space of sixteen years, and himself as head of its government.

World War II had ended, and the United Nations had been organized. Tanganyika had become a trust territory of Great Britain rather than a mandate. This meant, according to the UN charter, that Great Britain was to manage Tanganyika for the "good of all the people" until such time as the Tanganyikans were ready for complete self-government. To the young teacher, this was an exciting time in which to live and to teach the future leaders of his country.

A devout follower of Roman Catholicism, to which faith he had become converted while a student, Julius turned down the offer of a more lucrative teaching position in order to return to Tabora to teach biology at St. Mary's Mission School. Four of his students there were one day to become members of his cabinet. The years at St. Mary's were happy, and his qualities of leadership began to emerge. Some years earlier, British civil servants in Tanganyika had formed a social club for Africans which they called the Tanganyikan Association. Julius now started a branch in Tabora. As secretary, he made new friends and escaped frequently from the routine of a strictly academic atmosphere. And he became engaged to the girl of his choice. Even in the field of romance he demonstrated his non-conformist tendencies, since his fiancée was of another tribe. This raised some eyebrows, but no serious criticism.

Soon larger opportunities came in the form of a scholarship to the University of Edinburgh in Scotland. Once again Julius was a "first," this time the first Tanganyikan student to attend a British university.

Three years at Edinburgh gave the young man a Master's degree in history, a much expanded, first-hand knowledge of the world of the white man, a growing awareness of the lack of privilege of his people, a mustache on his lip, and a Scotch burr on his tongue!

The teacher was not yet ready to leave his chosen vocation, and when, in 1952, he returned home, he accepted a position at St. Francis High School outside the capital city of Dar-es-Salaam, the beautiful port city on the Indian Ocean. His prospects were good for a comfortable, rewarding career in education. He was one of the very few educated young men in Tanganyika, and the future looked bright. But the very studies that had prepared him for that career likewise had awakened his conscience and nurtured his ambitions to help his people. History had taught him that other subjected peoples had fought for and won their freedom. Economics had taught him that economic systems helped to maintain some people, like his own, in bondage, while other people reaped and enjoyed the fruits of the earth. He had seen freedom and democracy in Britain. He saw neither in Tanganyika.

His first efforts on behalf of his people were mild, but clever. When he became the president of the local Tanganyikan Association, he made plans for the club which were far removed from those that its founders had had in mind. He rewrote the club's constitution to give it a political objective, and at its annual conference in 1954, the delegates renamed the organization the Tanganyika African National Union (TANU). Thus, on July 7, 1954, was born the first nationalist movement in Tanganyika, in a wave of enthusiasm that never subsided during the years that followed.

Now the young schoolteacher had to make a choice. Would it be schoolteaching and security, or politics and insecurity, not to say personal danger? Troubled, but already sure in his own mind of the decision he must make, he went to the principal of St. Francis. "Teaching and politics do not mix," the priest told him, and urged him to remain in the academic field. But the young man had made his own decision. He would devote his life to ridding Tanganyika of foreign government and improving the lot of his people. "By this time the goal was clear," he recalled. "I had had three years in which to think. I had given up the 'politics of complaint' and was going to tackle the roots of the problem of colonialism."

TANU would be his vehicle. No longer the shy student, he had become a zealous, almost fiery orator. Sending his bride back to Musoma, the town of his primary school days, he and a few companions set out in a Land Rover to traverse the country. This was a new type of safari. Its purpose was not big-game trophies, but independence for Tanganyika in the shortest possible time. Nyerere remembers clearly the license number of the Land Rover, for he had it indelibly impressed upon his mind when, during the rainy season, he and his companions repeatedly tugged, pushed, and pulled the car through the deep mud of rough roads.

Everywhere the Land Rover stopped, crowds of people gathered to listen. Some thought Julius a wild dreamer. No nation south of the Sahara (except Ethiopia and Liberia, which had been self-governing for many years) was independent of foreign rule. This young agitator, they warned, was headed for trouble, probably imprisonment by the British authorities. But others listened and responded more optimistically. The common language, Swahili, was a big help in getting the message to the people in every area and of every tribe. Nyerere emphasized always that tribal loyalty must give way to national loyalty or there could never be a united Tanganyika.

There had been some progress in self-government under the British. For example, in 1945 there were only two Africans on the Legislative Council. In 1955, there were fifteen. Africans also were allowed to make speeches in the legislature in the Swahili language.

But such slow progress was unacceptable to Nyerere. He wanted no half measures. The time for complete independence was now.

"No colonial power, however benevolent, has the slightest right to impose its rule on another people against their will," he stated. And the people shouted their agreement. *"Uhuru! Uhuru!"* ("Freedom! Freedom!")

The British government could not long ignore TANU and its dynamic young leader. They considered Nyerere an agitator and troublemaker. TANU meetings were broken up and in some areas banned. On every possible occasion the government tried to discredit TANU and its leaders. However, the organization not only survived, it grew at a phenomenal pace. By the end of the first year, chapters of TANU had been organized across half of Tanganyika. The following year it had covered the country, and the number of its members was in the thousands.

In 1955, Nyerere made his first visit to the United States. He came as a representative of TANU to the United Nations and addressed the Trusteeship Council, since Tanganyika was a trust territory of Great Britain. He expressed the hope that very soon the Trusteeship Council would meet to discuss and approve Tanganyika's membership in the UN. The gifted young advocate created a favorable and enduring impression as an able, sincere spokesman for his people.

In 1956, Nyerere came to the UN again. This time he spoke before the General Assembly and he made four bold requests: a target date for Tanganyika's independence; intermediate dates for constitutional reforms leading to independence; universal suffrage in the elections that were to take place two years hence (the law required literacy and other qualifications for voting); and the lifting of restrictions that had been imposed on TANU and the ban that prevented him from making public speeches.

Possibly to appease Nyerere, the Governor nominated him in 1957 as a temporary member of the Legislative Council to take the place of an absent member. He stayed in the Council four months only, for he quickly became aware that the British had no intention of listening to any proposals for independence. His letter of resignation was forthright. "Your Excellency," he wrote to the Governor, "your government has consistently and for the most unconvincing reasons, rejected every proposal that I have made in the Legislative Council. . . . I have given everything that it was in my power to give, and what I have given has been rejected. The spirit is not there. I would feel that I am cheating the people and cheating my own organization if I remained on the Council, receiving allowances and attending sundowners as an Honourable Member, giving the impression that I was still of some service on the Council when in fact I know that I am useless. I have, therefore, no alternative but to tender my resignation."

When Tanganyika's first election was held in 1958, TANU candidates gained all thirty seats of the Council. In the 1960 election, TANU members won all the African seats. By this time, there were fifty African seats in the Council, ten European, and eleven Asian. The Asians in Tanganyika are the Arabs and the Indian traders and shopkeepers. Over the years, the Indians had moved westward from India to East Africa and settled there. The Arabs live largely in the rural areas and the Indians in the large towns and cities.

The rapid growth of TANU was not the result of any pie-in-the-sky promises by Nyerere. He warned that hard work and sacrifice were the price of freedom. The slogan *Uhuru* was expanded to *Uhuru kazi* (Freedom and Toil).

Several major factors had contributed to Nyerere's popularity and political success. First, of course, was his personal ability and capacity for hard work. When he had entered politics, Tanganyika had no other leader with the education, qualities of leadership, and ideas for his country's future that Nyerere possessed. His oratorical gifts served him well in promoting TANU, and in TANU he built one of the best-organized and most effective political movements on the African continent.

Second, Tanganyika was populated largely by Africans. There was no "white settler" problem, as in Kenya, for example. A basic doctrine of Nyerere has always been the protection of minority groups. He has not tolerated the intimidation of any opposition. Speaking before the Tanganyika National Assembly on one occasion he stated, "My friends talk as if it is perfectly all right to discriminate against Europeans, Arabs, and Indians, and only wrong when you discriminate against black men. The crime in the world today is the oppression of man by man."

Third, TANU held strong appeal for the large groups of clerks, teachers, war veterans, trade unionists and members of co-operatives, all of similar economic backgrounds, and all outside any active association with the old tribal organizations. As a matter of fact, the powerful co-operative movement in Tanganyika served as a base for Nyerere's TANU party. TANU represented politically what these workers had been looking for, and Nyerere successfully wooed tribal chieftains as well.

Finally, Julius Nyerere is a personable man, an asset to a politician in any country. Although naturally somewhat retiring, he has a delightfully wry and penetrating sense of humor, and a sharp wit which he uses both to put people at their ease in private conversation and to make a point in public speeches. He is not one to take himself too seriously. Relaxed and informal, he prefers to dress in slacks and gay sport shirts. He wears native costumes only on very special occasions. The cane he often carries was presented to him by the picturesque, proud Masai tribe of northern Tanganyika.

Although Nyerere was consistently impatient and unyielding in his demands for Tanganyika's independence, at the same time "he calls forth a lot of happiness," one of his friends aptly remarked. As a matter of fact, a quotation from the psalmist that he has sometimes used at conferences reflects his own conciliatory attitude: "Behold, how good and pleasant it is for brethren to dwell together in unity."

As the year 1959 came to a close, an important meeting of the Legislative Council took place in Dar-es-Salaam. As the Council members emerged from the Capitol, they faced several thousands of people gathered outside awaiting the news. Sir Richard Turnbull, the Governor, announced that Tanganyika would receive internal self-government in 1960. At the Governor's announcement, the celebration began. The people of Tanganyika knew to whom the credit belonged for this promise of freedom. Throwing a garland of flowers about Julius Nyerere's neck, they lifted him to their shoulders and began a procession through the streets of the capital city. Ten thousand Africans ignored the blazing heat as they danced and sang to the beat of drums in a parade of victory. Then Nyerere was transferred to an open car at the head of the parade. From this vantage point he waved a palm frond, the African symbol of peace, and grinned at the crowds that lined the streets.

His writings and speeches at the time reflected his wisdom:

> As Tanganyika becomes self-governing, we want our growth as a nation to be rapid, our credit to stand high, and our independent status to be a beacon of hope to our brothers who are still struggling for justice in other parts of Africa. We know we need help, but, when we say that, we do not mean we want charity. We want, and we intend, to help ourselves and to build Tanganyika by our own efforts.

Early in 1960, the United States got another look at the leader of Tanganyika. Nyerere came to this country on a five-week visit as a guest of the State Department and, as he said, "to see the United States and talk about Tanganyika." He was characteristically frank both with Africanists in this country, many of whom were not in sympathy with his moderate attitude toward Europeans, and with our government which, he said, had "missed the boat" on its African policy, but which was now becoming more aware of its opportunities in Africa.

The engaging visitor addressed many public meetings, spoke over the radio, and made television appearances. Mrs. Roosevelt interviewed him on a National Education Television program. He also received during this visit an honorary degree of Doctor of Laws from Duquesne University.

In the fall of that year, a second general election was held in Tanganyika. The TANU candidates won seventy of the seventy-one seats in the Legislative Council, a resounding victory. The Governor thereupon asked Nyerere to form a government and to become the country's Chief Minister. Two days later, the Governor broadcast to the people as the head of their government, and shortly thereafter he and Nyerere appeared before a mass meeting of thirty thousand people in Dar-es-Salaam. The green and black flag of TANU flew above the platform as the crowd sang "God Bless Africa," a song that was later to be chosen Tanganyika's national anthem.

Within a few months, Tanganyika had a new constitution, the result of the careful planning of a Constitutional Conference, and the country became autonomous, with Nyerere its first Prime Minister. The date for complete independence was set for December 9, 1961.

At one minute past midnight on that day, the British Union Jack was lowered in complete darkness in the National Stadium, which had been built for the occasion. A few minutes later the flag of Tanganyika was flying in its place in the glow of lights and a burst of fireworks. At the same time, up in the north, the young lieutenant was raising the flag atop Mount Kilimanjaro and lighting the freedom torch.

The United States government immediately recognized Tanganyika and elevated the Consulate General at Dar-es-Salaam to the status of an embassy. On December 14, Tanganyika became the one hundred fourth member of the United Nations.

The new constitution of Tanganyika was completely democratic. Under its provisions, the Prime Minister filled important positions with those whom he felt to be the best equipped for the jobs. He did not use any second best because they were Africans, as he might well have been tempted to do. Two of his cabinet members were Europeans, and one an Indian. He summarized his domestic policy as "a war on poverty, ignorance, and disease."

But to many enthusiastic Tanganyikans independence meant a decent house, a good job, schools for their children, and medical care—immediately. Through some magic, they thought, their new government would meet these pressing needs. Despite Nyerere's warning to the contrary, too many were inclined to sit back and wait for miracles. TANU itself fell into a slump. Nyerere quickly diagnosed the trouble and made an extraordinary decision. Barely seven weeks after independence, for which he had worked so zealously, Nyerere resigned as Prime Minister, to the consternation of Tanganyika and the outside world. Foreign observers were quick to pass judgment. They knew that there was opposition from less patient Tanganyikans to Nyerere's policy of moderation toward Great Britain. Nyerere's resignation was the first crack in a collapsing government, they said. But they did not know their man. Nyerere had resigned to reorganize and strengthen a weakening TANU, which had become an organization without definite purpose or platform. To bolster it and to help his people understand what independence demanded of them he must get to them directly and personally. Power and display at the top would not do it. Once again, he must take the road leading to Tanganyika's towns and villages. And this he did, sometimes swinging a symbolic pickax, pleading with the people to work harder. "The war against ignorance, poverty, and disease is *our* war. It can only be won by our own sweat and toil."

Before Nyerere's resignation, a three-year development plan had been inaugurated, as recommended by the World Bank. It called for the expenditure of $67,000,000, a relatively small sum with which to make a start on the appalling problems of the country. Its major objectives were agriculture, water supplies, road building, and education. Said the Prime Minister, "Even if I devoted all of that to peasant agriculture, it would amount to only about twelve dollars per family per year. How can you raise the standard of living with that kind of money? And what about hospitals, roads, and schools? . . . The only way we can raise capital is through our own physical efforts, by increasing production. . . . Self-help is our only salvation. This is my task, to show my people the way. This is why I resigned."

The problems of Tanganyika were and are similar to those of all underdeveloped countries, "ignorance, poverty, and disease," as Nyerere expressed it. The three terms are almost synonymous, at least they overlap so much that one cannot be met without tackling the other two simultaneously. But Tanganyika has some important native products which it can eventually use to pull itself up toward economic stability. The major aim, Nyerere clearly saw, was to see that the people received their full share of profits from the products they produced, and to increase that production enormously in the quickest possible time.

The economy of the country is based largely on agriculture, although until recently only 9 per cent of the land was cultivated. And unless the tsetse fly, which carries the fatal cattle disease sleeping sickness, is wiped out, two-thirds of the land will remain virtually closed to cultivation. Another deterrent to land cultivation is lack of water. This must be remedied through systems of irrigation. Moreover, much of the land that is cultivated is devoted to the production of grains and other food crops for local consumption on a subsistence basis. These crops provide no money income. In 1961, a severe drought, followed by floods, ravaged the land and caused near-famine conditions.

Tanganyika's chief export crop is sisal, a fiber used in rope. Its cultivation was introduced by the Germans, and now Tanganyika is the world's leading producer. Other export crops are coffee and cotton, followed by some less important items, including hides and skins, tea, tobacco, and sugar. From a small beginning, the production of sisal increased to a tonnage valued at millions of dollars in 1964. Although by far the largest amount of sisal is grown on plantations by private enterprise, a slowly increasing proportion is now being produced by Africans, 3 per cent in 1964. The reason for this slow rate of production by Tanganyikans is of course the large amount of capital necessary to carry on the enterprise. The production of cotton has also increased in recent years, and here the picture is different. Practically the entire crop is raised by African farmers, advised by government experts. The crop is taken to Dar-es-Salaam and sold at auction.

The co-operative movement in Tanganyika since 1925 has been among the strongest in the world. The co-operatives have hundreds of thousands of members. The largest co-operatives market the cotton, coffee, and tobacco crops. Many smaller co-operative farms, from eighty to one hundred acres each, were established under the Three-Year Development Plan. Other co-operatives sell seed and agricultural implements to farmers. There are also highly successful co-operative savings banks and educational centers.

Diamonds, gold, and mica are the chief mineral products. The Mwadui Diamond Mine, in the region west of Lake Victoria, discovered in the late 1930s by a Canadian adventurer and geologist, J. T. Williamson, is one of the richest in the world. In 1959 it was purchased jointly by the Tanganyika government and a diamond syndicate of South Africa. In 1964, the value of diamond exports had increased to nearly 7 million pounds sterling, or about one and a half billion dollars.

Nyerere's government embarked early on a road-building program, including reconstruction of existing roads so that they would withstand the severe periods of rain when too many of the country's roads wash out. The roads are either tarred or all-weather gravel roads.

Of course the government had to have money, a great deal of money, to make these improvements, to build schools, hospitals, clinics, airports, electrical plants, and to train technicians and other workers. It must have seemed to Julius Nyerere that he was on an endless merry-go-round as he tackled one set of problems only to run into interminable new ones. But he persevered with phenomenal courage, wisdom, and energy. Constantly he emphasized the necessity for hard work and sacrifice on the part of Tanganyikans. Foreign investments were encouraged through attractive concessions, and the World Bank contributed financial aid, as did the United States and Great Britain. Through heavy taxation, individuals and businesses of Tanganyika supported their government's efforts. In 1965, Britain withdrew its promise of financial aid to the country's economy, because Nyerere had broken off diplomatic relations with Britain over the question of policy toward Rhodesia. When the Prime Minister had resigned in 1962, he had stated, "I really had no ambitions to be Prime Minister. . . . I am prepared to spend the rest of my political career organizing my party."

But the people of Tanganyika had no intention of letting the man whose efforts had achieved independence for them in so short a time retire to mere party leadership. To them Nyerere was and is as reliable as Mount Kilimanjaro itself. In November 1962, a presidential election was held in Tanganyika. It was a foregone conclusion that Julius Nyerere was marked for victory. He did no campaigning, finding the idea distasteful. "An election campaign," he explained, "is not traditional African practice; it is one we have inherited from the Europeans. It smacks of pride, vanity, and sometimes stubbornness. A man standing before the public outlining his good qualities, this is a shameful thing." There is no reason to doubt the sincerity behind his words. Nevertheless, it is true that Nyerere did not need to do any formal campaigning at this time. He had, indirectly, intentionally or not, been campaigning for months as he covered the country rebuilding TANU. His opponent did campaign, but his was a lost cause. Nyerere won the election by an overwhelming vote. The former Prime Minister, Kawawa, who had carried on Nyerere's government policies faithfully and well, became Vice-President.

Despite his victory, all was not smooth sailing politically for the new President. A struggle for political power developed on the labor front, allegedly led by a former High Commissioner of Labor in London, an African who had returned to Tanganyika during the election to lead an opposition party, the People's Democratic Party. A former head of the Tanganyika African Railway Union, this malcontent looked for support among the labor unions. He accomplished little, but temporarily he stirred up a good deal of trouble.

Meantime, the work of building a nation and promoting

the general welfare of its people continued under the new President and his helpers. Not one giant step forward but a number of giant steps was the dream of the President. A practical program of self-help was announced, in keeping with Nyerere's policy of encouraging, in fact demanding, hard work and self-help on the part of the Tanganyikans. For example, peasants who lived on isolated strips of land were urged to resettle in villages. The object of this was to develop community life so that local social services in the villages, including education, medical aid, and water systems, could meet the needs of more people.

Local development committees planned worth-while self-help projects by building on the old tribal tradition of voluntary communal labor and utilizing this labor to perform essential community tasks. Action groups went about the local community to see that everybody did what had been assigned to him and report to the government on each crop-raising and building scheme. The government planned for marketing products and supplying needed materials.

Great emphasis was laid on local democracy. All chiefs were induced into resigning their administrative functions, although they were permitted, if the tribal members consented, to retain their title for ceremonials. These chiefs are today performing with distinction in such offices as regional commissioner, industrial arbitrator, and chairman of local boards.

In 1967, Nyerere nationalized the banks and many industries of the country.

An important new ministry was created in Tanganyika, the Ministry of Youth and Culture. The young men are inducted into national services of many varieties. "When those boys go back after their period of service," the head deputy of the new Ministry explained to Parliament, "they will no longer be, for example, Zanakis [members of Nyerere's tribe] but Tanganyikan members of one nation." One spectacular service of this youth corps was performed in 1963, when an unusually large crop of cotton in one area could not be taken care of locally. The farmers broadcast for help, and six hundred volunteer pickers were rushed to the area. With transport and rations supplied by the government, the cotton crop was saved by the youth corps.

Some fortunate young people from the United States have played a real part in the development of this new nation. As members of the Peace Corps, the first group of twenty-eight young men went to Tanganyika in 1962. Their project covered an area of over 350,000 square miles and consisted of building or rebuilding secondary farm-to-market roads that would withstand the heavy rains which turned them into lanes of deep mud. Better roads were one of the country's most pressing needs. The young people lived in the villages, and for the most part by the same standards as the natives, with whom they made good friends, for Tanganyikans are outgoing people. The Peace Corps was well received and considered very worth-while by the government. In 1966, there were 360 Peace Corps workers in the country.

Another group from the United States went to East Africa in 1961 as teachers. More than one hundred secondary school teachers first spent a year in college in Uganda and then went into the three countries, Kenya, Uganda, and Tanganyika, to help ease the teaching load and thus make it possible for more children and young people to go to school. The experience was so mutually profitable that it would be difficult to say who learned the most, the young people from the United States or the teachers and children of Tanganyika.

The flow of students and teachers between the two countries is not all in one direction. Under the African Scholarships Program of American Universities, qualified students from Tanganyika receive scholarships covering all expenses for four years of study in the United States in almost every field.

To conservationists around the world one of the most rewarding and inspiring occasions to take place in Africa in recent years was a conference on wildlife conservation held at Arusha, near the Serengeti Plains, in September 1961. The active support of Julius Nyerere gave strong impetus to the conference. In more forthright and stronger terms than Africans had ever used, the Arusha Manifesto, signed by Nyerere and two of his ministers, announced a new government policy of conservation. To back up the Manifesto, the announcement was made at the same time that the budget of the Wildlife Department would be increased 40 per cent.

For many years the magnificent wildlife of Africa had been despoiled by hunters, both white men and Africans. This was particularly tragic in Tanganyika, truly a wildlife paradise. Elephants were slaughtered in huge numbers for ivory only. Rhinoceroses were shot for their horns or merely because unintelligent sportsmen thought they looked ugly. Antelope were wantonly killed for a small amount of food or simply for the pleasure of killing. Zebras, wildebeests, giraffes, gazelles, elands, and many other beautiful animals, roaming the plains in vast numbers, could not outrun the sportsman's bullets. During World War I, the warring armies also took their toll of wildlife. Had it not been for the size of Tanganyika and the prodigious number of wild animals that were inaccessible, they would have been nearly decimated.

After World War II, the Serengeti National Park was established, and Lake Manyara National Park somewhat later. In addition, there are now several game reserves. The Wildlife National Training School was opened at Mweka to train East Africans to serve as park wardens and game wardens. These were important preliminary steps in a conservation policy, but not nearly adequate to stem the destructive inroads of hunters, including poachers, whose activities were even harder to check. The need was for a vital concern on the part of the Tanganyikan government, and that concern materialized in Nyerere, who recognized its wildlife as one of the assets of his country. Today, more and more people go to the reserves of Tanganyika to see the animals, not to shoot them, and these include hundreds of African children who live in areas that the animals do not inhabit. The children of Tanganyika are being taught a new respect for this precious national heritage.

Its wildlife is important to Tanganyika not only esthetically, but economically, for the tourist trade is a heavy source of national income, and the country's animals and birds are a big attraction. In a recent year, the tourist trade brought about six million dollars into Tanganyika.

Tanganyikans know how to have fun, and they make the most of national holidays, which have sober significance for them as well. April 2 is Union Day, for on that day, in 1964, the coral island of Zanzibar, on the east coast of the country, united with Tanganyika to form the republic of Tanzania, a name formed from the first syllables of the names of the two countries. Zanzibar had been granted self-government in 1963 and complete independence later that same year. In January 1964, the African majority party ousted the Arab minority party, thus deposing the sultan, who fled the island, and elected their own President. He later became the first Vice-President of Tanganyika. President Nyerere recommended the union of the two countries, but, characteristically, he made it clear that the decision was for the people themselves to make. "As President of the Republic I can make recommendations to you, but it is for you to consent or to disagree. . . . You will debate it. . . . The Union is a serious matter, deserving your most deep consideration." In April, the United Republic of Tanzania was created, with Julius Nyerere as President. As did many other government heads, President Johnson sent a message of congratulation. "On behalf of the government and people of the United States, I send you warmest congratulations upon the birth of the United Republic of Tanganyika and Zanzibar. This African initiative to create the union of the two states will be viewed by friends of Africans the world over as a beacon in Africa's drive toward self-determination and unity."

The Union is not complete, however. Each state has its own political party and its own army. Many Communists from Zanzibar came to the mainland after the so-called Union and perhaps paved the way for the heavy Chinese assistance program in Tanzania. This Communist assistance to Tanzania has worried the neighboring states of Kenya and Uganda, who see in it a threat to East Africa.

Independence Day is also a gala holiday, but the National Festival, which takes place in July and continues for a week, is the highlight of celebrations for the Tanzanians. "Nobody sleeps or works during the National Festival," a young Tanzanian commented to a visitor. There are parades, fireworks, elaborate trade fairs, and every kind of holiday activity. The bazaars and outdoor markets in Dar-es-Salaam and other cities are at their colorful best. During the National Festival, Nyerere travels over the country in his personal plane, visiting every community he can. Members of his cabinet also traverse the country as his representatives. There are few areas that at least one and often several government representatives do not visit during the Festival.

Julius Nyerere, as evidenced by his accomplishments for Tanzania, is a man of superior gifts. One of these is his ability to galvanize people into astonishing activity. And his interests go far beyond politics. He is, for example, proud of his native language, and in his "spare moments" he translates Shakespeare into Swahili. He has finished the translation of *Julius Caesar* and hopes to find time to translate other plays.

The Nyerere home is a modest concrete house in Dar-es-Salaam, some distance from the State House. To save precious time, it is necessary for the President to drive back and forth between home and office. His vacation retreat is a lodge at Lake Manyara where he occasionally is able to escape from the heavy duties of his office for a holiday with his family.

The serious observer of Tanzanian life today is impressed by two outstanding characteristics, which reflect Nyerere's basic objectives, around which all other objectives, economic and cultural, are built. These are the widespread programs of self-help carried on by the people in their own communities, many of them small villages, and the relative absence of racial tension and animosity. Nyerere has his own inimitable, charming way of expressing these objectives to the people. "We Tanzanians cannot pat ourselves on our nine million backs and think to ourselves that all is over, since we will make nothing of Tanzania and we will set no example to the world unless it be by our renewed efforts of hard work for ourselves and kindness toward others."

KENYATTA
OF KENYA

A romantic land of mud-hut villages, picturesque tribes dancing to the haunting beat of tom-toms, lakes of pink flamingos, and lions, elephants, giraffes, and zebras roaming freely across the landscape under majestic, snow-capped Mount Kenya—this is the image of Kenya that on-location movies, shown in color on a wide screen, have projected around much of the world.

There is indeed great beauty in Kenya, but the beauty of his country was not what impressed young Kamau Ngengi as he tended his father's herds in the pasture lands of Ichaweri. For even at an early age, this precocious boy was beginning to question the presence of the British settlers in his homeland and to wonder how long his tribesmen, the Kikuyu, would tolerate foreign domination.

It was only a few years before Kamau's birth that the great powers of Europe, meeting at the Berlin Conference on African Affairs in 1884–85, had carved up the African continent and divided it among them. Kenya had been handed to Britain. Almost at once, the Imperial East Africa Company was formed with a royal charter giving it a trade monopoly throughout the vast area, which included both Kenya and Uganda. In 1895, the British government made "peace treaties" with various tribes and established the "British East African Protectorate." Now the question was how to make the best use of this potentially wealthy territory. Obviously, settlers must be encouraged to come and farm the fertile lands. So through a system of land allotments, very large plantations in the best areas were

made available to immigrant farmers. There must also be modern transportation facilities to move people and goods. The answer seemed to be a railroad, to be built from the east coast of Kenya on the Indian Ocean, across to Lake Victoria and into Uganda.

The building of this 600-mile railroad was an extraordinary feat. It required first an enormous surveying job, as there were no maps of the area, then the building of bridges over swamps, and the laying of tracks across deserts, up mountains, and down again into the valleys. Work was sometimes hindered by rainy seasons that made any progress almost impossible, serious diseases that disabled the workmen, and the hostility of some of the native people, who quite naturally were disturbed at such an unfamiliar if not terrifying intrusion. Indians were brought in to augment the native labor forces. The railroad was finally built at a cost of $15,000,000, an enormous amount of money at the time, and on its completion British farmers poured into Kenya.

For the most part the settlers who came were hard workers and good farmers. They had the patience and courage to meet many of the same types of hardships that faced the American frontiersmen who went to the West. They wrestled with the soil, experimented with crops, and built prosperous farms on land which they had every right, from the point of view of their government, to assume was theirs.

By the end of World War II, the population of Kenya consisted of three distinct groups: the wealthy white landowners at the top, the Indian and Arab shopkeepers and tradesmen who made up the middle class, and the native Africans, the great majority, at the bottom.

So it was that the young Kamau saw the best land in what came to be known as the White Highlands owned and successfully farmed by foreigners, while his own people could barely raise enough to eat on their small, tsetse-fly-infested plots. As he and the other young herdsmen played their games with one eye on the cattle they were tending, Kamau may well have dreamed of someday doing something about this near-serfdom of his people. For he saw a system very much like forced labor, which drove many Kenyan workers from their own lands to work on the farms of the settlers.

Meantime, Kamau received the education provided by his tribe for its boys and girls. The educational system of the Kikuyus was not built around books and school buildings. There were none of either. All teaching came from the parents or other adults selected for the purpose, and was acquired within the home and its immediate surroundings. Boys and girls learned the history of their tribe and its people through legends told by their parents and other story-tellers, and through songs and dances. The mother of the family taught the children the laws, customs, and etiquette of the tribe and community. This she did, not through direct instruction, but through folklore, legends, and example. Respect for and obedience to the tribal laws and customs were serious business, and those who broke these ancient codes were punished.

Health education, although woefully inadequate to meet the needs of a land plagued by disease and malnutrition, was taken seriously. To keep them physically fit the boys were taught wrestling, sparring with sticks and shields, and weight-lifting. Both boys and girls were instructed in the medicinal use of plants and herbs and in personal hygiene.

On the practical side, Kamau's father, a farmer, taught his son to use a digging stick, called a *moro,* with which to turn the soil. He learned to identify and number his father's herds, not by counting them, but by observing their color, type of horn, and other physical characteristics.

To observe accurately and to remember details were important skills, to be cultivated seriously. After a reasonable period of training, the tribe tested the boy by confronting him with a mixed herd and asking him to select his father's animals. His report was made to a watchful examiner, to whom only a perfect score was acceptable. "During my boyhood," Kenyatta wrote of his own youth, "my special task in the family was to look after our cattle, sheep, and goats. Therefore I had to go through this training, and afterward taught my brothers."

Memory training was applied also to the identification of forest paths and animals, a practical skill for a boy growing up in wild country.

His stepfather described the boy as clever, playful, and ambitious. He was also often lonely, despite the fact that he had a large family and many playmates. He spent hours alone in the forests near his home. Possibly ambition and restlessness prompted him one day, when he was ten years old, to leave his cattle unattended and run away from home. He was headed for school.

Formal education in Kenya at the time was provided only by the mission schools, and Kamau found his way to the Church of Scotland Mission in Kikuyu. There his European education began, and there he was operated on and cured of a serious spinal condition. At the mission school, too, he was duly baptized and christened with the name Johnstone Kamau. The school combined formal education and vocational training. Kamau was put into the carpentry division, and he was introduced to the mysteries of mathematics, English, and the Bible.

After a few years, the boy became restless and dissatisfied, and once again he ran away, this time to Nairobi, twenty miles away, the principal town of Kenya, through which the railroad passed on its way to Lake Victoria. Nairobi was the center of colonization activities in Kenya, and it was run on modern European lines. Naturally it was the objective of all ambitious young Kenya Africans. Nairobi might have been dubbed "the corrugated-iron city," sprung up in a wilderness of grasslands. The railroad buildings which predominated were of corrugated iron, as were the public buildings and the homes of the employees, the stores and shops along Victoria Street, and the houses of the English officials up on the hill. It was a busy, ugly, European town.

Racial animosity was rampant in the cities—a few hundred Englishmen against several thousand Africans, and both Englishmen and Africans against a few thousand Arab and Indian shopkeepers, who were highly useful to them but whom they tended to resent. The Europeans were supreme. There was little opportunity for a young man, even one with some European education, to make much of his life. So Kamau found himself uncomfortably suspended between two very different cultures, the tribal culture of his homeland and the British.

Little is known of his early years in Nairobi, but he became a leader among the young Africans in the city and socially popular. The fancily embroidered belt (*kinyata*) that he wore won him the nickname Kenyatta. Thereafter he was to be known as Jomo Kenyatta, and under that name to become a world figure. It soon became apparent that his physical stature, for he had grown into a giant of a young man, was matched by the extraordinary quality of his mind.

Opportunities for a Kikuyu to hold office were non-existent under British rule, which had organized the government of Kenya into three inflexible divisions. First, there was the *location,* a group of villages or other small area, headed by a local chief. This chief was the only native leader in the government. Several locations comprised a *district*, with a British District Commissioner in charge. Several districts, in turn, made up a *province*, with a British Provincial Commissioner as head. Over the entire country was the Governor, appointed by the ruling monarch of Britain, assisted by a Council of Ministers, all British.

Despite the restrictions imposed upon them, the spirit of nationalism was rising among the Kikuyu people, and in this movement Kenyatta found an important place. In 1928, he became General Secretary of the Central Association, the first formal nationalist movement in East Africa. The objective of the Association was to get back from the foreign intruders the land that had belonged to the Kikuyu people. But Kenyatta's dreams went far beyond that objective. His burning ambition was to unite all of Kenya into an independent nation. To a less dedicated and courageous person this would have loomed as a formidable or even fantastic idea. To begin with, one man pitted against the British Empire was hardly an even match. There was also the almost insurmountable barrier of the tribal culture of Kenya. The rivalry was keen and bitter, involving cattle-stealing and tribal wars.

For centuries, the only government in Kenya was that provided by the tribal chief, with sometimes a council of elders. Although the British replaced this tribal setup, tribal loyalties are still strong, and vast numbers of the people think of themselves first as members of their particular tribe, of which they are extremely proud, and only secondly as citizens of Kenya. When Kenyatta first entered public life, the tribal culture was even stronger than it is today.

Kenyatta's own tribe, the Kikuyu, live around Mount Kenya. They comprised about 20 per cent of the population of Kenya, or nearly two million people. The Kikuyu are considered the most advanced and industrious tribe, partly because they have lived at the crossroads of exploration and trade routes and have for many years had contact with various other cultures. But a good deal of credit for their educational and political advancement belongs to Kenyatta. Very early in his career, for example, he set up schools for the Kikuyu children. At the time, this was a new and explosive idea. Certainly the British government did not look with enthusiasm on such a proposal. And Kenyatta's dream did not stop with elementary education. Teachers must be provided through teacher-education institutes. This shocked the British authorities even more. They were interested in education for Africans only for the purpose of training clerks for government service. There were troublesome practical questions to be answered. Would fathers want their children to acquire knowledge quite different from and possibly in contradiction to that imparted by tribal custom and tradition? Where would the schools meet? Who would pay for them?

Partly to further the cause of tribal schools, Kenyatta entered politics by way of the Kikuyu Central Association in 1925. This was an outgrowth of the Young Kikuyu Association, formed a few years earlier to fight for justice for the Kenyan farm laborers, who were heavily taxed, forbidden to grow coffee (a valuable crop), and had no representation in government. These were only a few of their grievances. Meanwhile, the number of British farm owners was constantly increasing. In the three years following World War II, eight thousand new settlers took up land in the White Highlands.

But lack of educational opportunities for his people was only one small part of the vast problem confronting a man with the vision for his country that Kenyatta held. How could one unite and develop a country whose people were divided into various closely knit tribes, whose land, with almost no natural resources, was three-fifths unproductive desert, where ways of earning a living were limited to the most primitive forms of agriculture, with few crops that could be sold for money, and whose people were victims of what Kenyatta himself says are still their worst enemies—poverty, ignorance, and disease? But this seemingly bleak outlook was only a challenge to Kenyatta, who welcomed what he called "stimulating discouragement" and held to his dream.

First, he must become personally acquainted with the people. He would start within his own tribe, the Kikuyus. As General Secretary of the Central Association, he started and edited the first Kikuyu journal, *Muig wathania.* Of course, few people could read his paper, but the few who could were influential, and the news of his plans also spread fast by word of mouth. In the interests of his paper, Kenyatta traveled all over the Kikuyu country, talking with everyone he met, young and old, and listening to their problems.

Kenyatta soon came to the conclusion that to win victories for his people he must go to a higher court. He believed the British Colonial Office in London would be more sympathetic than the British officials in Kenya, so in 1929, he persuaded the Kikuyu Central Association to send him to London.

In London, Kenyatta was not permitted to see the Colonial Secretary in person, but he nonetheless achieved a great victory for his people: permission to found and run their own schools. At the same time he made full use of his opportunities to meet as many people as possible and to learn as much as he could from everyone. He was aided and advised by many people, including a Church of England missionary and Kenya's former Director of Public Works, who had retired to England. He visited Moscow, and, with letters of introduction from Moscow, he went to Berlin and Hamburg. In Hamburg he attended the International Negro

Workers' Congress. Everywhere he was enthusiastically welcomed.

At the end of eighteen months, his money having run out, Kenyatta returned home to continue his work there. His visit had taught him a great deal, and had raised his prestige in Kenya. His daughter recalls "the crowds of people who used to visit him at home."

Kenyatta soon realized, however, that, much as his people tried to help themselves, any real progress was impossible without the co-operation of the British government. At the end of a year, he returned to London, again under the sponsorship of Kikuyu Central Association. This time he was to stay away from his homeland for fifteen years. His experience and accomplishments during that period are a measure of the energy, perseverance, and talents of the man. In the interests of freedom for Kenya, he presented petition after petition to the Colonial Office, wrote letters to newspapers, talked to everyone he met, and made speeches in Trafalgar Square to any passersby who would stop to listen. He helped to organize the Pan-African Federation, and in the city of Manchester formed the Pan-African Congress.

His extracurricular activities were even more spectacular. For a time he shared a flat in London with Paul Robeson, the American singer, and appeared with him in a movie of Edgar Wallace's *Sanders of the River*. This short but successful venture into the theatrical world opened new doors. Segments of London society, intrigued with the performance of this dramatic African in native dress, invited him to their cocktail parties, which he attended in his impressive native costume, the better to propagandize on behalf of his people.

Kenyatta studied English seriously in a Quaker religious education center in the city of Birmingham. He later enrolled at the London School of Economics, majoring in anthropology. "He was able to make valuable contributions to class discussions," his professor wrote, "giving us illuminating sidelights, inspired by the inside knowledge of an African." Certainly Kenyatta's familiarity with the ancient tribal life of Kenya brought what must have been fascinating first-hand knowledge to classes interested in primitive cultures. Kenyatta knew his people, and it was a rare privilege to have such a source in the classroom. One result of Kenyatta's studies in anthropology was his authorship of a distinguished book, *Facing Mount Kenya,* an account of African tribal society which ranks high in anthropological literature.

He continued to travel widely in Europe, speaking and writing for Kenyan independence. His reasonable attitude was impressive. "Africans are not hostile to Western civilization as such, but they are put in an intolerable position when the European invasion destroys the very basis of their old tribal way of life, yet offers them no place in the new society except as serfs."

During World War II Kenyatta worked as a laborer on English farms in Sussex, where his fellow workers gave him the nickname "Jumbo" because of his size. Amid all this activity he found time to court and marry an English girl.

Kenyatta's talents and good humor won him friends and audiences everywhere. Persons who worked with him on the Sussex farms recall his liking for the works of Rudyard Kipling, an unlikely poet to win friends for the anti-colonial cause, pro-Empire as he was, but whose verse Kenyatta nevertheless liked to quote. His readings from Shakespeare's *Othello* were also popular.

Shortly before returning home, Kenyatta wrote and published a pamphlet, *Kenya, Land of Conflict,* in which he warned that if the English settlers in his country did not agree to radical reforms, revolution would break out. His prophecy proved to be correct.

At home again, Kenyatta became president of the Kenya African Union. This organization was the outgrowth of a new movement for independence among the Kikuyus. Because of the high respect in which he was held, and aided by his gift of oratory and his untiring zeal, Kenyatta was able to unite the eager young Kenyans and their cautious tribal elders in the common cause of independence. He was also able to bring other tribes into the movement, until in 1951 the Kenya African Union claimed 150,000 members. The meetings sponsored by the Union were attended by thousands when Kenyatta addressed them. The Kikuyu people had advanced too far to submit to constant frustration and denial of privileges. Many of them were alert, educated young men. Outstanding leaders had arisen among them, but they could advance no further politically, socially, or economically.

Kenyatta's demands of the British government on behalf of his people seem reasonable in retrospect. He pressed for African voting privileges in local elections, the abolition of color discrimination, and, of course, the return of the rich farmland of the Highlands to the people to whom it historically belonged. But the British government would have none of this. It was not thinking of independence for Africa and Kenyatta's ideas seemed radical in the extreme. Serious trouble lay ahead for Kenyatta.

As principal of the independent Kikuyu Teacher Training College, Kenyatta became more and more influential, and the English settlers became more and more uneasy. They saw their security threatened. Their fears grew, until finally they demanded that Kenyatta be exiled from Kenya. At the same time they made a grave accusation, namely that the Mau Mau terrorists were acting through the Kenya African

Union. The Mau Mau was a secret society that overran Kenya in the early 1950s. Its methods were violent and ruthless, including terrorism and murder. The British claimed that Kenyatta was the mastermind behind the Mau Mau movement. Kenyatta denied this, and stated publicly:

> I want you to know the purpose of KAU. It is the biggest purpose the African has. It involves every African in Kenya, and it is their mouthpiece which asks for freedom. . . . True democracy has no color distinction. It does not choose between black and white. . . . He who calls us the Mau Mau is not truthful. We do not know this thing Mau Mau. . . . KAU is not a fighting union that uses fists and weapons. . . . Remember the old saying that he who is hit with a rangu returns, but he who is hit with justice never comes back.

His protests and declarations of innocence proved futile. Most of the white men of Kenya looked upon him as a devil incarnate. Early in the morning of October 20, 1952, the police came to his home to find him dressed and waiting for them.

In a tiny agricultural village school in central Kenya, as far from the public limelight as possible, Kenyatta, no longer a young man, stood trial for fifty-eight days with five other men for leading the Mau Mau. The difficulties for the defense lawyers who were, with one exception, Africans and Indians, were appalling. The only hotel was twenty miles away, and was for whites only. The lawyers had to be guarded by police, to protect them from violence.

The courtroom scene somewhat resembled a shot from a movie of the American Old West. The magistrate sat at the teacher's desk. A portrait of his British Queen hung on the wall behind him. Among the spectators the men, dressed in shorts and wearing wide-brimmed hats, had brought their revolvers. The women settled down with their knitting. All eyes were on Kenyatta as he entered the room, dressed in his usual brown corduroy trousers, a brown suede jacket, a russet-colored shirt, a beaded belt. His bright blue eyes shone from his bronze skin with the intensity of marbles, "almost hypnotic in their effect," one spectator said.

Kenyatta's defense was spirited, witty at times, and courageous. He was unflinching before the sarcasm of the prosecuting attorneys. He described the new form of slavery that had been introduced by the white man. "While formerly a man could walk and feel like a man, we were subjected to the humiliation of the color bar." "That must be terrible!" the prosecutor interrupted contemptuously. In the end, and almost inevitably, Kenyatta and his fellow defendants were found guilty. In his last speech, Kenyatta maintained his innocence and added:

> "We look forward to the day when peace shall come to this land and when the truth shall be known that we, as African leaders, have stood for peace . . . we stand for the rights of the African people, that Africans may find a place among the nations."

Standing to hear his sentence, Kenyatta addressed the court. "We have not received justice. None of us would condone the mutilation of human beings. We have families of our own."

The sentence was seven years at hard labor in a desolate desert post in the north of Kenya. As a result of Kenyatta's imprisonment, guerilla warfare broke out and heightened terrorism swept the country. When British troops came in, they met resistance from the Kenyan people, and what amounted almost to a civil war ensued.

During the years of Kenyatta's imprisonment he suffered frustration, physical hardship, and terror. He grieved for the interruption of his work, and he and his fellow prisoners lived in constant fear lest their food be poisoned by their guards. At night the prisoners lay awake until completely exhausted trying to ward off snakes and scorpions which ran rampant around them. At one point Kenyatta was made to dig what he was told would be his own grave.

There are many who believe in retrospect that Kenyatta's punishment was the result of the fear of the Mau Mau that was widespread in Kenya and that Kenyatta was sacrificed in an effort to break up the Kenya African Union. Many believe he was innocent, but Kenyatta will probably always be a controversial figure.

During Kenyatta's imprisonment, the Kenya African Union was banned by the British government, but some progress had been made in winning some political rights. The African community was given eight seats in the Legislative Council, the British governing body, and African political parties were permitted to organize, in local districts only. At this time the Kenya African National Union (KANU) was formed, and Kenyatta was elected president, in absentia. It soon became the strongest political party in Kenya. The second party was the Kenya African Democratic Union (KADU).

Six months before the sentence of seven years was to end, the African members of the Kenyatta Legislative Council started a campaign for the immediate release of the man they still considered their leader. He was removed by the British to another post in the desolate north country, but was given a small cottage to live in and even an allowance with which he could purchase approved newspapers and magazines. Meantime, the campaign for his immediate release increased in intensity. Young men marched through cities and villages shouting *"Uhuru na Kenyatta!"* (Freedom and Kenyatta!) The KANU party won an important election, but refused to form a government until Kenyatta was released. In August 1959, the British Colonial Secretary announced in the House of Commons that Kenyatta was to be moved to a place just outside the city of Nairobi and released.

A spectacular welcome awaited Kenyatta's return to his home. The house itself had been torn down by the British and the property turned into an experimental farm. But for several weeks thousands came to the site, on foot or in hired trucks, as though to a shrine, bringing gifts of the only things they had to give—pigs, goats, cows, sheep, and baskets of corn. Their cheers of welcome testified to their loyalty to the man whom, after seven years of absence, they still considered the leader of their country.

Out of prison, Kenyatta refused to expend precious energy on bitterness and revenge. "The past is dead," he said. "It is the future that is living."

As president of his party, which was now a strong political force in Kenya, Kenyatta flew to London to press for independence. In an interview with the London *Times*, he expressed his philosophy of government:

"We do not think in tribal terms. . . . Our aim is not to select a man because he is black or brown, but on his capability. . . . We have no room for dictatorship in Kenya. We believe in democratic government." Today, Kenya has a completely non-racial society.

Eventually, after bitter disputes between the two rival parties in Kenya, the British Colonial Secretary led the way in gradually setting up a coalition government with a parliament of two houses. Kenyatta became Minister of State, responsible for economic planning, possibly Kenya's most pressing need. At least, the British government was anticipating independence. They moved, step by step, to give Kenya more independence, and they did an intelligent job, leaving, among other things, many well-trained workers and leaders who would serve the new country well.

Independence Day in Kenya is celebrated on December 11, for on that day, in 1963, Kenya became independent. Kenyatta became first Premier, then President of his country. As President, he faces enormous problems. The masses of the people of Kenya are poor and ignorant. Disease takes a heavy toll. Tribal loyalties are strong. Some Kenyan politicians with less wisdom than Kenyatta would help themselves to land legally owned by Europeans and Asians. Kenyatta holds them in check.

Communism is a constant threat, but with this philosophy Kenyatta has no patience, for he sees it for what it is. Speaking to several thousand people who had come to Nairobi to hear their President he said: "It is naive to think that there is no danger of imperialism from the East. . . . It is a sad mistake to think that you can get more food, more hospitals or schools by crying 'Communism.' To us, Communism is as bad as imperialism."

In 1966, in what seemed to be a move to curtail Communist influence, envoys from four Communist embassies were expelled from Kenya, along with two Communist journalists. The country was divided into forty-one districts, with a party convention organized in each district, the better to keep in touch with all the people. Eight vice-presidents were appointed, ostensibly to give the people more representation, but this move was widely interpreted as a means of upsetting the power and influence of the left-wing vice-president, Oginga Odinga, who headed a radical opposition group.

Kenya's birth rate is one of the highest in the world. The number of young people entering the job market each year is too large for the economy to take care of. Consequently, unemployment is alarmingly high. Many of these young people have not been trained for work on the farms, where they are needed. They drift toward the cities, where they become disillusioned and discontented. Many better-trained university graduates, equipped for civil service, see their way blocked by older, sometimes less competent Africans, or by Europeans who remain in positions of power. This situation creates one of Kenyatta's major problems.

Kenyatta holds out to his people no quick and easy solutions to their country's difficulties. He is frank to say again and again that unity and hard work are the only remedies. Under his tutelage the Kenyans are building schools, hospitals, clinics, roads, industries, and farms.

The private building industry is booming with non-government projects, including new houses. A five-year development plan calls for private investments of more than $90,000,000 a year, much of it drawn from outside Kenya. Both the United States and Great Britain maintain generous aid programs for Kenya. Tourism, one of Kenya's biggest sources of income, has increased enormously in recent years and brings needed money into the country as the tourists are attracted to the "world's largest zoo." Nairobi is the safari headquarters of East Africa.

Kenya coffee now leads the world's market, and its bacon is becoming famous, too.

Most important, the political stability of Kenya is a beacon in a generally troubled and unstable Africa. To a large measure this is the result of Kenyatta's wise leadership.

The President's house with its typical conical-shaped thatched roof is in the community of his boyhood, Ichaweri. His family is made up of his second wife, the daughter of a tribal chief, and four children, to whom he is devoted. He is up very early, and is likely to be working in his rose garden long before the village is astir. He grows corn, bananas, and coffee on the estate. Often, while the President cultivates his garden, one of his aides discusses with him the day's plans. At 8:15, his aides and bodyguards accompany him thirty miles by car to the capital city of Nairobi, where the hard work of the day begins. A fresh bouquet of roses is always on his desk, and he is likely to have another blossom in the lapel of his jacket. Driving to the State House in Nairobi, a visitor passes along wide and tidy streets bordered with willow and eucalyptus trees. Bird-of-paradise plants are ablaze with color. Neon signs, traffic lights, efficient policemen, buses, small skyscrapers built by foreign investors who believe in Kenya, big hotels, and a major railroad give evidence that Nairobi is a modern city, the commercial center of East Africa. Here Kenyatta heads his country's government.

Kenyatta's greatest effectiveness has always been in reaching the people by going to them himself. On weekends, he often tours the country, visiting villages, inspecting schools and clinics, and talking to individuals and to crowds who are always eager to listen to their President. Advance notice is given of his coming, and the occasion is likely to be a combination of carnival and serious discussion of problems. Speaking in Swahili, Kenyatta encourages, scolds, praises, as needed. His success with the masses of the people across the country has been an important base of his power. His costume is always the same—corduroy pants, likely to be rumpled, and a brown jacket. He carries a walking stick with a buffalo tip, and a fly whisk of a zebra's tail, with which he gestures frequently. Always he ends his speeches with the rallying cry, *"Harambee!"*, a loggers' call meaning "Let's all work together." And the enthusiastic crowds shout back, *"Harambee!"*

BALEWA
OF NIGERIA

The first faint light of dawn would soon bring into shadowy outline the sprawling city of Lagos. At this early hour, all was quiet in the Nigerian capital. No planes roared into the airport, no autos honked, and no bicycles moved through the streets. Shortly, the outdoor markets would be bustling. Now they were empty and still. In their squalid, tin-roofed houses, the poor of Lagos were asleep. So were the rich, in their pleasant homes along quiet, tree-lined streets. Down in the lagoon, big ships waited silently at their docks and small craft bobbed noiselessly about.

Few of the people of Lagos were aware that the pre-dawn stillness of their city was ominous. But a tragedy was in the making as a small band of soldiers moved stealthily along the marina toward the house of the Prime Minister. Entering the official home, the soldiers quickly and quietly did what they had come to do, and with the coming of day, the city of Lagos awoke and, unaware, went about its business.

By mid-morning the rumor was spreading that the Prime Minister was missing, and some of the more knowledgeable people of Lagos were expressing their fears for his life. Soon the sad news was flashed across the world. On January 15, 1966, the Prime Minister of Nigeria, Sir Abubakar Tafawa Balewa, had been kidnapped. A few days later, a passing motorist spotted his mutilated body lying off the highway, thirty miles from the capital, obviously the victim of murder.

What had brought an honest, dedicated, scholarly man to such a tragic end? The passing of time may bring complete

answers to that question. Among the answers will be Nigeria's
tribal and linguistic divisions, the sharply separated geo-
graphical-political regions of the country, and the temperament of the Prime Minister himself.

In order to appreciate the magnitude of the task that
governments of the new African nations face, and why they
have sometimes seemed to fail, one must understand the
nature of the ancient tribal civilization of Africa. In Nigeria,
for example, there are more than two hundred fifty tribes.
They vary in size, but each tribe numbers thousands of
people, and the four largest are over four million each. The
tribes differ in their origins—centuries ago they migrated
from various parts of Africa—in their language, and in their
ways of life. Some tribal groups live in small towns and
villages, some in larger towns and cities, and some are no-
madic. In all African countries, membership in a particular
tribe is a source of intense loyalty. In recent years, there has
been no fighting between tribes, but fierce rivalries still exist.
Even in those nations that have won their independence,
most citizens think of themselves first as members of a particular tribe, and only second as citizens of their country.
This situation is not favorable to forming and carrying
on a successful central government behind a united nation.

In addition to tribal divisions, Nigeria has four sharply
defined geographical regions which grew up around the tribes.
These are the Northern, Eastern, Western, and Midwestern
regions, and they were once politically semi-autonomous.
When Nigeria became a British protectorate in 1914, the
British set up four distinct regional governments in these
areas. Since there was no central government, these political
divisions were self-governing. When independence came to
Nigeria, its constitution permitted these regional governments
to continue. Each had its premier, parliament, civil service,
and police. The regions differ in their tribal composition,

in the economic opportunities available to their people, and in their consequent achievements. These regional divisions, like the tribal organization, encourage rivalry and mutual suspicion. The Northern Region, for example, although the most populous, is the most educationally and economically underprivileged. The North has always feared that it would be dominated by the other regions, and the other regions have, in turn, feared the political power of the North's nearly thirty million people. The North outvotes all other regions at the polls.

There are also distinct and fundamentally different religious groups in Nigeria—the Moslems, the Christians, and the animists.

Despite these separations that seemed to discourage any thought of a united Nigeria, at the end of World War II a few Nigerians began to dream of independence for their country, but in the far distant future. They did not have to wait long, however, for the British government, under pressure from rising young Nigerians, granted Nigeria some self-government in 1946 and established a central legislature for all of Nigeria. By 1951, the legislators were being elected by the Nigerians. Step by step, region by region (except in the North, where the Premier discouraged it), self-government became a reality. On October 1, 1960, Nigeria became an independent nation within the British Commonwealth. The first Prime Minister was Sir Abubakar Tafawa Balewa. What background did he bring to the staggering problems of Nigeria, and how well equipped was he to tackle them?

To answer that question we must go back to a remote village in the Northern Region, Tafawa Balewa, where Abubakar Tafawa Balewa was born in 1912. The name of the village of his birth became, according to custom, a part of his own name. His father was a butcher and a local government official. He was a Moslem, as are most of the people of the Northern Region, and although poor, he had high ambitions for his son. The boy went first to the village school which his father, as a member of the local government, had been instrumental in building. He then went on to the Bauchi Provincial School. He was a superior student and found time to excel at track and cricket as well. At sixteen he graduated from the Katsina Training College, of which he was later to become a director. He was headed for a teaching career, and his first position was in the Bauchi Middle School, where he taught geography, history, and English. He was to look back on this period of his life as one of its happiest, for he liked young people and enjoyed teaching them. Eventually he became headmaster of the school.

The young teacher might have remained happily at Bauchi for many years had not a friend made a slighting remark one day to the effect that no Northerner had ever passed the examination for a Senior Teacher's Certificate. Piqued by this remark, Balewa took the examination and passed it easily, whereupon the University of London Institute of Education granted him a scholarship for further study. He was so successful as a teacher that he won the Ministry of Education's Teacher's Proficiency Certificate, and on his return home held many high positions as teacher and supervisor.

Balewa's London education was more than academic. He saw a free people, making democracy work. "I returned to Nigeria with new eyes," he later wrote. "I had seen people who lived without fear, who obeyed the law as part of their nature, and who knew individual liberty."

As a student of history, Balewa was naturally interested in government, and his own country provided a ready-made laboratory in which to work. He played a significant role in establishing the Northern People's Congress (NPC) as a political party. It had formerly been a cultural group. This was a fortunate move, for whether he realized it at the time or not, the NPC was to make Balewa's climb up the political ladder faster and easier. On its first ticket as a party, the NPC elected him to the Northern House of Assembly, and the following year to the Federal House of Representatives. Now for the first time the North had a voice in the central government, and the voice was a powerful one. Balewa's fellow legislators and his constituents found him friendly, modest, scholarly, and quietly efficient. He was a brilliant debater in the legislature. His eloquence was such that he came to be known as "The Golden Voice of the North." Although early in his career he was mainly interested in his home region, he soon was working for a united Nigeria. He saw clearly the overwhelming needs of his country, but he believed in gradual reform, not in revolutionary upheavals.

Balewa was selected to be one of Nigeria's representatives at the opening of the Festival of Britain in 1951. While there he was invited to Buckingham Palace to be presented to the royal family, who were charmed by this tall, dignified man in his flowing blue-green robe and white turban. He was later knighted by the Queen and thereupon became Sir Abubakar Tafawa Balewa, an honor in which he took modest pride. He received other honors in Britain. He was made a Knight of the British Empire and then Commander of the British Empire. His consistently friendly attitude toward Great Britain was later to be seized upon by some of his political enemies and used as a weapon against him.

When Balewa, in 1952, became a member of the federal cabinet as Minister of Public Works, he was privileged to attend several international conferences on mutual problems. One of these conferences took him back to London to discuss with the British government constitutional changes for its Nigerian protectorate.

His next position in the cabinet was that of Minister of Transport. In that capacity he made his first visit to the United States, where he studied water transport problems, particularly of the Ohio and Mississippi rivers. Once again, his intelligence and charm brought Balewa friends and honors. New Orleans made him an honorary citizen of the city.

Balewa was greatly impressed by the United States, especially by the success with which a united democracy had been created by people of many different races and national origins. He wrote to a friend, "Until now I never really believed Nigeria could be one united country. But if the Americans could do it, so can we."

As Minister of Transport he set to work at once improving Nigeria's transportation facilities, an urgent need. He extended the Apupa Wharf at Lagos, opened new entrances to delta ports and to the Niger and Benine rivers, creating points of access to the interior of Nigeria for ocean-going ships.

When, in 1957, Nigeria became the Federation of Nigeria, Balewa was appointed by the British to be the first Prime Minister. The federal form of government meant that the four geographical regions, like the states that make up the United States, would share some legislative powers with the central government. Balewa was then leader of the majority political party in the North, the Northern People's Congress, and his major task was to prepare the country for complete independence, which was promised for 1960.

The first meeting of the Nigerian Parliament over which the new Prime Minister presided was an exciting and colorful affair. The head of the local Lagos government was there, resplendent in a purple robe and a helmet-shaped crown of gold beads. One powerful tribal chief made his entrance clad in a bright blue satin blouse, a skirt with a train ten yards long, and on his head a straw boater decorated with feathers two feet high. These flamboyant costumes did not reflect any carnival spirit within the legislature. On the contrary, they were evidence of the high importance the representatives attached to the occasion. The Prime Minister, wearing on his robe the red ribbon of a Commander of the British Empire, stood before these leaders who came from many tribes and from all regions of their country and pleaded for unity among them all in the interests of a united nation. He pledged to work for complete independence for Nigeria by 1960.

His pledge and the promise of Great Britain were honored, and on October 1, 1960, as drums rolled, guns saluted, and the enthusiastic people of Lagos danced through the streets, the green and white flag of Nigeria rose over the capital in place of the Union Jack which had flown there for a hundred years.

An exciting national election had taken place just before independence, in 1959. There was universal adult suffrage in the Eastern and Western regions and in the Lagos area and male adult suffrage in the North. Voters were not required to be literate, and most of them proudly cast their secret ballots in boxes marked with symbols representing the various parties—an elephant, a star, a hoe, a palm tree, a cock. Ballots were carried from the remotest regions by whatever means were available, including helicopter, camel, and canoe, to the nearest telegraph office. The NPC won the election, and as leader of the victorious party, Balewa became the first Prime Minister of an independent Nigeria.

One of the Prime Minister's first official duties brought him to the United States a second time. On this occasion he arrived in New York as head of his country's delegation to the United Nations, and on October 7, 1960, Nigeria became the ninety-ninth member of that world organization. In the afternoon of that day, Balewa took his seat in the Assembly. A few minutes later, he mounted the rostrum and addressed the Assembly. In a stirring speech he dealt with some of the problems of Africa and of Nigeria. "The most serious problem seems to be that in itself political independence is totally inadequate if it is not accompanied by stability and economic security, and genuine personal liberty. . . . We in Nigeria honestly believe in the principles of the United Nations . . . as we gratefully take the place to which you have invited us, we feel an immense responsibility to the world which you represent."

The delegates to the General Assembly listened attentively and applauded vigorously at the close of an eloquent speech which reflected sincerity and wisdom. Obviously, Nigeria was in good hands.

And so Prime Minister Balewa returned home to face a task of staggering magnitude. He brought ability, training, experience in government, scholarship, and dedication to the job of uniting and governing a people with enormous problems of almost every variety. What assets could he count on?

First, the fact that Balewa was from the Northern Region, where the largest number of Nigerians live and which therefore has the most votes, was in his favor as he worked toward uniting tribes and regions. His own tribal membership was also in his favor. He was from the small Geri tribe. He did not, therefore, symbolize to the Nigerians of other regions the powerful Northern tribe, the Hausas, whom they feared. One of his first moves as Prime Minister was to form a coalition government in an attempt to unite opposing political parties and assuage tribal and regional rivalries.

Second, Nigeria had come to independence gradually and peacefully. The Nigerian people were not scarred and embittered by a war to win their freedom. The British had been wise, on the whole, in transferring political leadership to the Nigerians region by region. Consequently, thousands of educated, responsible people, with an industry and vitality characteristic of Nigerians, were prepared to serve their country. Self-government was not new to Nigerians. Many had already found their places in political life. This situation was a helpful one.

Another asset to the new government was complete freedom from racial conflict in the nation. There were only a few thousand Europeans living in Nigeria, so there was no "white settler" problem to be dealt with, as in some other parts of Africa.

Materially, Nigeria was fortunate compared to other African countries. Her valuable agricultural resources include yams, sweet potatoes, and oil palms growing in abundance in the rich soil of the plains. Farther north, peanuts are grown successfully. Pyramids of bags filled with peanuts are a common sight in the northern shipping centers, where this crop provides much of the income. Grazing lands support cattle, horses, and sheep. There are many productive farms in the Jos Plateau, in the center of the plains country. The palm oil from the plains is in great demand for use in the manufacture of margarine, glycerine, soap, medicine, and explosives. Cocoa, cotton, and hides are other income-producing products.

Nigeria has large deposits of tin and of columbite, a rare metal which is used for making steel that will withstand high temperatures and is therefore much in demand for the construction of jet engines. Ninety-five per cent of the world's known deposits of columbite are in Nigeria.

With its large population of energetic, intelligent people, Nigeria has a potentially large labor supply for industry.

Although underdeveloped educationally, as are all countries just emerging from foreign rule, by 1957 Nigeria had made an impressive start on an educational program. The British had established a national university in Ibadan, with a large campus and well-equipped buildings. The College of Arts, Sciences, and Technology is in Zaria, with branches in other parts of the country. A University College Teaching Hospital and Nursing School was located in Ibadan, and several technical institutes in other areas. Elementary schools were first run by the missionaries to Nigeria, but from 1955 to 1957 the governments in the Western and Eastern regions started free education for all boys and girls. At present, elementary education is a long way from being universal, but about a quarter of the people of Nigeria can read and write, and this is a high percentage for a new African nation.

All the above advantages worked in favor of the new Nigeria. The Civil Service and the judiciary systems, established by the British, were efficient. But the problems the Prime Minister faced were enormous.

Nigerians are poor. Their per capita yearly income is less than one hundred dollars. In most of the villages the men till their small plots of land with hoes, as generations have done before them. Even the methods of the specialized farmers are for the most part old and inefficient. They are unable to earn even the small amount of money that would make life easier and more pleasant.

During the British regime in Nigeria some industries had been established, but the important products like cotton, tin, and columbite were exported at profits for the English alone. Nigerians received few benefits from their work as miners and farmers. Now they were demanding that their raw materials be produced and processed by Nigerians for the Nigerians. Many and diverse industries must be established to create thousands of jobs and produce much-needed products. And there must be improved harbors and more roads and railroads throughout the country over which these products could be moved.

Efforts to treat and conquer the dreaded diseases of leprosy, sleeping sickness, yaws, river blindness, and malaria had been woefully inadequate. Nigeria desperately needed doctors, nurses, public health agencies, clinics, and facilities for health education for the people.

Hundreds of schools on all levels must be built to educate Nigeria's children and young people.

It would take huge amounts of money, wise planning, and many trained technicians, teachers, engineers, and other skilled personnel to tackle the most pressing of Nigeria's problems. Where would a leader start, and with what?

The Prime Minister was keenly aware of the job to be done by Nigeria for itself. In 1962 he wrote,

> To the leaders and people of Nigeria, this event [independence] was a grim reminder of the fact that, for the first time in our history as a single unified state, we now have to fend for ourselves, and to sustain and consolidate our unity and freedom. We have to give real meaning to this freedom by making it an instrument for a better and more prosperous life for our people. . . . A federal system of government is always full of problems and difficulties, but so is democracy, because the art of persuasion is much more difficult than a dictatorship though in the long run more rewarding and satisfying.

The year before independence, the National Economic Council had planned for a National Development Plan for 1962–68. The plan was prepared with extreme care and was scrutinized by experts and advisers from foreign countries. It was widely publicized throughout Nigeria, approved by the regional governments, and generally praised by the Nigerian people. The plan gave highest priority to agriculture, industry, and technical education. Because over four-fifths of the population of Nigeria depend on agriculture, its economy must depend upon more and better crops. These, in turn, depend upon better-trained farmers, farm machinery, and the availability of fertilizers. New industries would provide jobs and money and needed products.

The National Development Plan would cost millions of dollars, half of which the Nigerian government hoped would come from the investment of foreign capital in their country, and from loans and grants. Many of these hopes were realized as foreign investors found evidence of wisdom and good will in the new Nigerian government.

To attract foreign investment, Nigeria permitted new industries to operate for two to five years without payment of taxes. The federal and regional governments provided industrial estates for the new enterprises.

Bit by bit, Nigeria's economy improved. Small industries were established. Four hundred eighty-two new companies registered in Nigeria in 1965 alone. Crops in many areas improved and increased, natural gas was produced in larger and larger quantities, and, very important, rich oil lands were discovered, making Nigeria today the twelfth largest oil exporter in the world, and superseding cocoa as the country's chief export. In 1965 a large oil refinery was opened near Port Harcourt. The federal and regional governments constructed thousands of miles of new roads.

But disunity and discontent among the people were problems that the Prime Minister and his fellow leaders seemed unable to cope with. As in most of the new countries, many Nigerians looked for quick miracles from their government. Still plagued by the lack of housing, unemployment, extreme poverty, deficiency of schools in many areas, and all the other miseries that they had known all their lives, while those in high places seemed to be getting rich, they blamed the government. "Nothing has changed except the color of the rich man emerging from the back seat of his car," was a typical bitter comment. Grave charges and ugly incidents increased. For example, the government was accused of squandering millions of dollars on industrial factories, built under contracts with overseas firms with no concern about whether such contracts were viable. Many of the factories, it was claimed, were built in inaccessible areas, far from essential raw materials but within a politician's home territory. Bribery was rampant, almost a way of life in business and government circles. Nigeria's Finance Minister, Chief Festus Okotie, was known as the "King of Bribery."

What is called "nepotism" in Western countries accounted for some of the inflated contracts. Such nepotism is deeply rooted in African culture. As soon as a man comes into a position of power, he is expected to assume the support of all his needy relatives. These are likely to include not only his immediate family but scores of cousins, uncles, and aunts. To an African it would be unthinkable to turn any of them away. Hiking the figure of a contract is one way to finance such a burden. Everyone is aware of the situation, and such overt "graft" is less reprehensible to an African than to neglect one's family.

Balewa's personal life was above reproach. He was a devout Moslem, whose daily routine as Prime Minister began with prayers at 6:30 in the morning. In his office at 8:15, he worked until 2:15 in the afternoon, then went home for more work until bedtime. The "Alhaji" that sometimes appeared before his name meant that he had made a pilgrimage to Mecca. He regarded this pilgrimage as a high point in his life. But he was ecumenical in his sympathies. When, for example, he was made a Commander of the Order of the British Empire, he asked a Roman Catholic friend, the Archbishop of Lagos, a native of Minnesota, to be his sponsor. The office of Prime Minister never went to his head. He had few interests except his work and his reading, although he took an occasional trip to his farm where he raised a small herd of cattle. If he had a hobby, he commented to an interviewer, it was astronomy, which he found fascinating.

As is the Moslem custom, Balewa's wife never appeared with him in public, but he was devoted to her and to their sons and daughters.

The Prime Minister was at heart more of a philosopher than a politician. He was possibly too mild and tolerant to engage in the tough political fights that would have established him as the unquestioned leader of Nigeria. Instead, the real power seemed to lie in the hands of two of his friends and political allies, Sardauna ("Prince") of Sokoto, Premier of the Northern Region, and Akintolo, Premier of the Western Region. Neither of these men was as interested in a united Nigeria as in his own region and his personal power.

"I shall send my lieutenant to Lagos and rule from the North!" the autocratic Sardauna once boasted, and his actions seemed to be bearing out the threat. For example, in October 1965, when the Western Region held its general election, there was very active opposition to Premier Akintolo within his own party. But Akintolo was the Sardauna's man. He consequently sent his henchmen into the region to engineer vote-rigging of the most flagrant sort. Many leaders of the opposition were thrown into prison, and the election was steam-rollered in favor of Akintolo and his representatives to the federal legislature. As a result of such abuse of power, killings, house-burnings, and general rioting broke out in the

Western Region, but Prime Minister Balewa did not interfere.

When his government was asked in Parliament for figures on the disorders in the Western Region, he delayed a reply until after the Commonwealth meeting and then gave out figures that many responsible leaders believed had been greatly lowered to deceive him. In this atmosphere the Sardauna is said to have planned to take over the federal government in Lagos and the national police by "northernizing" the high command. His plan was thwarted by his death from machine-gun bullets at the hands of the same military group that later kidnapped and assassinated the Prime Minister himself.

Another crisis from which Balewa turned away arose at the University of Lagos, whose highly respected Vice-Chancellor, Dr. Eni Nkoku, was dismissed, it was claimed, for reasons of tribal jealousy. Pressure was brought to bear upon the Prime Minister to intervene, but he made no move. His motives were probably honorable, but he did not state what they were and lost the support of some of the finest of Nigeria's future leaders.

The above are examples of Balewa's inaction at critical times, which was interpreted by his enemies and many of his friends as evidence of weakness or lack of judgment. Many thoughtful Nigerians, though deploring his violent death, nevertheless were relieved when the military took over. They believed this drastic step was the only way to thwart a coup by the Sardauna of Sokoto.

It is easy to be critical of the governments and leaders of new countries, forgetting the bitter struggle, the jealousies, the blunders that characterize all new nations, most of them with far fewer problems than the nations of Africa. In our own country, there was bitter jealousy for years between the small and large states, and animosity or indifference toward a federal government. Some states refused to send their militia outside their borders; at least one state declared itself "free and independent" of any central government, and this long before the secessions of the Civil War period. It is hard today to believe that an interested and sympathetic observer of the United States wrote in 1781, "Every prognostic that can be formed from a contemplation of their mutual antipathies and clashing interests, their difference of governments, habitudes, and manners, plainly indicates that the Americans will have no center of union among them, and no common interest to pursue, when the power and government of England are removed."

True to his philosophy of patience, Balewa would doubtless say to his country as it undergoes turmoil and tragedy in its continued struggle for political and economic stability, "The art of persuasion is difficult, but in the long run rewarding. Let us work in peace for a united Nigeria. If the Americans could do it, so can we."

NKRUMAH
OF GHANA

One day in May 1945, a group of passengers stood on the deck of a ship sailing out of New York harbor and gazed at the Statue of Liberty. It was a thrilling experience for all of them, but for one member of the group it was especially meaningful. This was a thirty-six-year-old African from the Gold Coast who was leaving the United States after ten years of study and work. As he looked at the Statue of Liberty, it seemed to him that her arm was raised in a personal farewell, and he made this vow to himself: "You have opened my eyes to the true meaning of liberty. I shall never rest until I have carried your message to Africa."

Less than twelve years later that vow was fulfilled. On March 6, 1957, independence was granted by the British to the Gold Coast, and it became the new nation of Ghana, the first country in black Africa to gain independence. In the center of the festivities on that independence day was the man who had made the vow to bring liberty to Africa. He had been a great fighter for the freedom of his part of the African continent, and now he had been selected as the first Prime Minister of the new country. Kwame Nkrumah was the most important leader of contemporary Africa south of the Sahara, a most remarkable person.

Kwame Nkrumah was born into the Akan tribe in the small mud-hut village of Nkroful, in the southwest corner of what was then the Gold Coast. The baptismal record in the local Roman Catholic church gives his birth date as September 21, 1909. But he was named Kwame, the name

given to all boys born on Saturday, so his birth date must have been September 18, 1909.

When he was three, he and his mother moved to the village of Half Assini to join his father, who worked there as a goldsmith. The journey of fifty miles had to be made on foot, so it was a slow, tiring trip.

Kwame was the only child of this marriage, but his father had other wives and so Kwame had several half-brothers. Polygamy was common in the Gold Coast, and a man was expected to have more than one wife. Polygamy produced more hands to do the work of the household, fields, or shops. To help make this situation work out smoothly, the first wife often helped to select the other wives, with whom she would have to live and work for the rest of their lives.

This meant that there were about fourteen members of the Nkrumah family living together. In addition, there were often visiting relatives. Local custom dictated that any relatives who came should be housed and fed no matter how long they stayed. Hotels were unheard of, and hospitality was high in the scale of values of the Akans, as of other Africans.

The Nkrumahs were poor people. There were no toys for the children, but they had plenty of playground space. There were the sea, the lagoon, and the bush or forest.

Kwame, however, preferred to play alone. He would wander into the forest and spend hours observing the birds and animals and listening to their songs and calls. Sometimes he would catch a bird or animal and take it home as a pet.

These wonderful times in the woods soon came to an end, however. Kwame's mother had not been able to go to school, but she was determined that her son should have this privilege. Kwame liked his school, and gladly raised chickens to earn money for fees and books and supplies.

After eight years of schooling, he became a pupil-teacher. He was not very old, but others had begun teaching at seventeen, so why shouldn't he? He was not very tall either, so he stood on a box when he wanted to write on the blackboard. Nor did he have much formal education, but he was well educated by African standards in those days.

The principal of the Government Training College in the capital city of Accra considered Kwame a good teacher, and urged him to continue his education. Kwame did so, first at the Government Training College and then at Achimota College, located near Accra.

At Achimota the young student met a man named Aggrey, one of the best-educated men of his day in all of West Africa. He had studied and taught in the United States for several years before being asked to become vice-principal of the new college of Achimota, a very high post then for an African. He was a man of tremendous vitality and enthusiasm and a gifted orator. His mission in life was the reconciliation of races. As he often said, "You can play a tune of sorts on the white keys and you can play a tune of sorts on the black keys, but for harmony you must use both the black and the white." Eventually Achimota took as its symbol a piano keyboard with its white and black keys, and this crest hangs over the entrance to the main building of the college.

Aggrey died soon after, but he left a lasting impression on the young Nkrumah, in whom he had instilled first the idea of African nationalism and second the desire to go to the United States to study.

In his years at Achimota, Kwame Nkrumah took part in sports and amateur dramatics, helped to form the Aggrey Students' Society, and worked to build a beautiful campus out of the forest in which the school had been built. He graduated from Achimota in 1930 and spent the next few years teaching.

His first job was in a Roman Catholic school at Elmina, where he taught the youngest children. Here he founded a teachers' association. Then he moved on to become head teacher in a Catholic school at Axim. In his spare time he organized a literary society among the students. In 1933 he was appointed teacher in the Roman Catholic seminary at Amissano, the first person from the Gold Coast to be asked to teach novice priests. While there he considered becoming a priest himself, but finally rejected the idea.

Meanwhile, Nkrumah had come under the influence of two other powerful men. One was Wallace Johnson, a citizen of Sierra Leone and the first labor organizer in West Africa. The other was Nnamdi Azikiwe, a Nigerian by birth, who was then editor of a newspaper in the Gold Coast. Both were fervent leaders in the nationalistic movement which was just beginning to appear in West Africa. Azikiwe was American-educated and he encouraged Nkrumah to go abroad for further study.

In 1935 Nkrumah stowed away on a boat bound for Lagos, Nigeria, to visit a relative who he thought might help him financially in his plan to go to the United States. He was successful, and returned to the Gold Coast to say good-by to his relatives and friends. "May God and your ancestors guide you," his mother said as she bade her son farewell.

Nkrumah went first to England, where he was able to get a visa for the United States. He arrived in New York in October 1935, and went on to Lincoln University, west of Philadelphia. Lincoln was the first institution to offer higher education to Negroes, and it was the school Azikiwe and other Africans had attended. Nkrumah had very little money

left when he arrived at the college, but he was allowed
to stay, and throughout the year he was able to supplement
his scholarship aid with work around the college. Later he
preached almost every Sunday in some Negro church. In
the summer he worked on ships.

In 1939 he graduated from Lincoln University with a
Bachelor of Arts degree. In the class yearbook his professors
made these comments upon his work:

> Biology—Strongly individualistic
> German—Loved controversy
> History and Philosophy—Ace Boy
> Physics—Noticeable but not spectacular
> Sociology—Purposive

Not content with a Bachelor's degree, Nkrumah continued
his work at Lincoln and received a Bachelor of Theology
degree in 1942. Meanwhile, he had begun commuting to
Philadelphia to study at the University of Pennsylvania,
where he received a Master of Science degree in 1942, a
Master of Arts degree in 1943, and started work for his
doctorate.

Soon he was appointed lecturer in political science at
Lincoln University. During this period at Lincoln he was
elected president of the African Students Organization of
America and Canada. Although he was already a nationalist,
his discovery at this time of the works of Marcus Garvey,
the Jamaican Negro who was working and writing for a
free and independent Africa, sparked his interest. He was
fascinated by Garvey's work, *The Philosophy and Opinions
of Marcus Garvey.*

During these ten years in the United States, Nkrumah
made a special point of studying the operation of voluntary
organizations in politics and in race relations. Someday, he

felt sure, the knowledge would be of tremendous value to him.

He also read widely, especially on politics—the works of the German philosopher Hegel and the German political philosopher Marx, the Italian political leader Mazzini, the Russian political leader Lenin, and scores of others.

In addition, Nkrumah tried his hand at writing himself. His idea was to put on paper his thoughts about freedom and political organization. These were published later under the title *Towards Colonial Freedom.*

Nkrumah's stay in the United States was not always easy or even pleasant. He had some bitter experiences. Money was scarce, and he had to save every penny that he could on food and lodging. He peddled fish in Harlem to earn a few dollars. He sometimes rode the subway all night by paying one fare and staying on the train as it shuttled back and forth from Harlem to Brooklyn, thus saving money on lodging. On one occasion he and a friend tried to spend the night in the waiting room of the railroad station in Philadelphia, but the police had other ideas and they had to retreat to the benches in the park.

In the United States, Nkrumah ran into race prejudice. His first of many such encounters was in Baltimore where he asked a waiter in a restaurant at a bus stop for a glass of water. Ignoring his request, the waiter said to him curtly, "The place for you, my man, is the spitoon outside."

As he looked back upon the twelve years he had spent in the United States and England he said, "Those years . . . were years of sorrow and loneliness, poverty and hard work." But he added that he would never regret them, "because the background they provided has helped me to form my philosophy of life and politics."

In 1945, Nkrumah went to England to continue his studies.

He enrolled in Gray's Inn to study law and arranged to attend lectures at the London School of Economics.

On the side he attended all kinds of political meetings and took part in many conferences and discussions on African affairs. Interest in the cause of freedom and independence of the African colonies was keen among the African students in London, and Nkrumah was now in his element. He was especially active in the West African Students' Union, of which he later became vice-president. This organization proved to be a training ground for many future leaders in Africa.

Perhaps the event of most importance to him during his months in England was the Fifth Pan-African Congress held in Manchester. This Congress brought together many of the leaders of the New Africa. It was a thrilling experience for the young man who was to be the leader of Ghana. For weeks he was busy as co-secretary of the organization committee. Plans were made to win independence in Africa through the organizing of mass parties and "positive action."

Again he ran across race prejudice, especially in his search for a place to live. He finally was able to rent a room in a shabby lodging house in the East End of London. But Nkrumah was happy with the general freedom of movement and expression he found in London. "There was nothing to stop you getting on your feet and denouncing the whole of the British Empire," he said. All in all, he found England an exciting place.

Back home in the Gold Coast, the movement for more control of their government by Africans was growing. Ever since 1900 there had been some kind of organized opposition to English rule in such groups as the Aborigines Rights Protection Society and the West African Congress. But in recent years the movement had taken on new life. And now it had taken a new turn, demanding a part in the government of the Gold Coast. Several things accounted for these changes. One was the fact that more people from the Gold Coast had studied abroad and had learned about the rights of human beings in other countries, particularly England. A second factor in the change was the wartime service of Gold Coast citizens abroad, where these young men had seen people working for independence or for more rights under colonialism. A third factor was the growing middle class in the Gold Coast. Merchants in particular were becoming more and more resentful of foreign control in commerce and industry. Then, too, the world-wide fight against colonialism had its influence. India, Pakistan, Ceylon, Burma, and other nations were winning their independence.

In the Gold Coast a new organization, called the United Gold Coast Convention, had been formed by a group of intellectuals, including Dr. Joseph Danquah, who was to be Nkrumah's valued friend and adviser for many years. They needed a young, energetic secretary who could bridge the gap that divided the lawyers and merchants who had formed the organization from the masses. Kwame Nkrumah had been recommended to them, and they asked him if he would take the job.

This seemed to be the chance Nkrumah had been waiting for. He knew that the men who controlled the United Gold Coast Convention were more conservative than he, but at least he could try to work with them. So in November 1947, he dropped his studies in London and returned to Africa.

No sooner had he begun his work in the Gold Coast than trouble broke out. A group from the Ex-Servicemen's Union had staged a demonstration and, in a clash between them and the police, two of the former soldiers were killed and five other Africans wounded. Although Nkrumah was not involved in this affair, he was arrested and his belongings searched. Among the few possessions which he had was an unsigned Communist Party card which he had used to attend meetings in London. This was used against him in an attempt to prove that he was a Communist Party member or at least a Communist sympathizer.

He and five other leaders of the United Gold Coast Convention, including Dr. Danquah, were sent to the Northern Territories prison. There Nkrumah spent six weeks in solitary confinement. Eventually he was released.

It was obvious that he and the leading members of the UGCC differed in their ideas about their organization and about the future of the Gold Coast. Nkrumah was more radical than his bosses and wanted to work for complete independence rather than for more representation in the government. He broke with the UGCC in the summer of 1949 and formed his own organization, called the Convention People's party, dedicated to complete self-government. On its executive committee were many of the men who later would form the cabinet of the government of Ghana.

This break with the elder group stirred up a great deal of bitterness. Most bitter of all was Dr. Danquah. Some of his feelings toward Nkrumah were expressed in this statement to a visitor to Ghana some years later:

> Nkrumah is selfish. With wiles and tricks he stole power. We sent for that man to come and help us. Then, while pretending to work for us, he secretly built up his following within our ranks. Ruthlessly he split the national front, then made a filthy deal with the British. . . . One day he said that he wanted national freedom and the next day he compromised with the British.

Nkrumah had long ago made his choice between two types of revolution. One was the violent type; the other the non-violent. Although as a very young man he had been radical and impatient with delay, he had never been a violent revolutionary. Eventually he decided upon a "revolution" patterned after the non-violent resistance movement led by Gandhi in India. To this movement in his own country he gave the name "Positive Action."

Positive Action included strikes and boycotts as the most effective weapons of people against their rulers. A nation-wide boycott against British products took place in 1949 in the Gold Coast, and for his part in this movement Nkrumah was arrested in 1950 and held in a filthy prison for several months. However, he was able to smuggle communications to his friends outside, and so keep in touch with the party.

Meanwhile, the British had sent a commission to the Gold Coast to try to ease the tension there. Their main recommendation was that a general election be held in 1951 to select members of the Legislative Assembly.

Elections were a new experience for almost everyone, and a tremendous educational campaign had to be conducted to prepare the people of the Gold Coast for this event. For those who could read, a half million leaflets were prepared in the six main languages of the Gold Coast. Charts and maps and wall newspapers were prepared and distributed throughout the country. The radio was used to explain the election. Mobile units were dispatched to all parts of the nation. Those who could read were enlisted to instruct the illiterate.

On election day people were handed ballots with the names of candidates and the symbols of the parties they represented, a device used especially for the illiterate. Mahogany ballot boxes for all the parties were placed in the polling booths, and people dropped their ballots into one of these boxes. In order to insure that no one voted twice, the thumb of each person voting was inked with an indelible purple stain.

The result was a landslide victory for Nkrumah's Convention People's party. Many voters did not even know the names of the opposition candidates, but they knew the name of Nkrumah, and they knew the symbol of his party, the red rooster.

The British Governor of the Gold Coast at that time was Sir Charles Arden-Clarke. He was an old hand at colonial administration and an example of British colonialism at its best. Despite the fact that Nkrumah had been in prison nine months, the Governor called him to the palace and asked him to form a government. In his new setup Nkrumah was to be known as Chief Minister and Leader of Government Business. Shortly after he took office, however, his title was changed to Prime Minister, though he did not have as much power as a Prime Minister had in England or in other Commonwealth countries.

Nkrumah had come a long way in a short time. In 1948 he had returned to the Gold Coast as an unknown student who had spent the last twelve years of his life abroad. Now he was the Prime Minister.

What power did he have that made him rise so fast? What qualities did he possess which made him the popular leader of his nation? What talents had he developed which made it possible for him to reject the leadership of older men in the Gold Coast and launch his own party, and push or pull it to power?

There is no easy answer to these questions. For centuries people have debated whether the times make the man or whether the man makes the times. There is truth in both theories. Certainly there is some kind of interaction between the leading men and the period of history in which they live.

Let us look first at the period of history in which Nkrumah's rise took place. We have already mentioned that many people in the Gold Coast were dissatisfied with the status quo. They were restless, ready for change.

In this period of world history, Britain had begun to see that her best policy for survival as a global power was to free her colonies as quickly as possible, hoping that they would remain in the Commonwealth of Nations out of economic necessity, friendship, and gratitude. Since World War II, she had already freed India, Pakistan, Burma, and Ceylon, and all but Burma had remained in the Commonwealth. The pattern had been set in Asia. Now the British hoped that this same approach might work in Africa.

The Gold Coast was fortunate in its geography and history. It was small, with a population of fewer than five million, which made it compact and easier to govern than a more heavily populated country would be. It was also more homogeneous than the other British territories in Africa. It did not have a large number of white settlers, so its politics were not complicated by the race issue, as in Kenya, for example. And it was relatively rich, with a lucrative cocoa trade and the world's largest supply of manganese. It also had a higher percentage of literacy and more educated leaders than the other British possessions in Africa.

But the changes which had come to the Gold Coast and the changes which were still to come would not have taken place at all or as quickly as they did without that most important factor—the personality of Kwame Nkrumah. Wherein, then, lay his power?

First, his goals were clear. He knew what he wanted, where he would like to lead the people of the Gold Coast.

He detested colonialism and imperialism in every form and was determined to eliminate foreign rule and foreign control in his country. He asserted:

Yes, we believe in peace and co-operation among all countries, but we also abhor colonialism and imperialism. We abhor man's inhumanity to man.

In place of foreign rule, he wanted freedom.

No people without a government of their own can be expected to be treated on the same level as peoples of independent, sovereign states. It is far better to be free to govern or misgovern yourself than to be governed by anybody else.

The elimination of colonialism and imperialism and the gaining of independence were not the chief goals. The end he sought was a better standard of living for all his people. As he phrased it:

. . . self-government is not an end in itself. It is a means to an end, to the building of the good life for the benefit of all, regardless of tribe, creed, color, or station in life. Our aim is to make this country a worthy place for all its citizens, a country that will be a shining light throughout the whole continent of Africa, giving inspiration far beyond its frontiers.

He was well aware that the people of the Gold Coast would have to learn much from other peoples, but he knew that they would eventually have to build their own type of society or a new African way of life. Speaking on this theme he said:

. . . most important of all, it must be recognized that an African way of doing things will certainly be evolved. Europeans, Americans, and Asians frequently approach the same problem by quite different routes, and just as frequently they adopt different methods of performing a single function. I suppose a single example here is to draw attention to the different ways in which Americans and Europeans use knives and forks, but the end result is the same. On a much wider scale—and here I am thinking more in political and social terms—we are bound to evolve our own way of doing things. . . .

But he added, with characteristic assurance, "I am confident that our mutual common sense will ensure that we produce a sensible and practical result."

His hopes and dreams, however, were not limited to the Gold Coast. He had a vision of a West African Federation and of Pan-Africanism—perhaps a United States of Africa someday.

Second, he drew strength from the fact that these goals were in tune with the times. The people of the Gold Coast had joined the world-wide revolt against colonialism and imperialism. Many of them were demanding freedom and independence. Most of them had joined the world-wide revolution of rising economic and social expectations. Many of them felt a bond of friendship with their fellow Africans, especially in West Africa, although the idea of a federation meant little to most of them.

Third, Nkrumah was able to make people proud of their past and hopeful of their future. Few people outside the colonial world can understand how much the restoration of confidence and pride means to the people of Africa and the rest of the colonial areas. For many years they had been ruled from abroad, by white people. They had been treated as inferiors and even told by many Europeans that they *were* inferior.

Nkrumah brought them new hope, new confidence, new dreams. He pointed to their past with pride and assured them that they could even surpass their past glories. Often he referred to the glorious Ghana Empire which had existed until almost A.D. 1100, when it was destroyed by the Moslems. He assured his people that they belonged to a group which had once been great and could be great again.

He also tried to build in the people a pride in their present, maintaining:

It is not an exaggeration to mention . . . that African music and dancing played no small part in influencing this revolution [of the modern arts], as you can see by observing some of the age-old tribal dances and even the present High Life dancing, which is really an old folk dance of the country under a modern name, which in turn gave birth to the calypso and other dances of this kind.

Fourth, Nkrumah was a clever strategist. He knew the methods which would bring the best results. His reading in the United States and England in philosophy, biography, political science, and history, and his years of study of political organizations in those parts of the world, had taught him many valuable lessons. Now he was ready to apply them to the Gold Coast with great success.

He had learned, for example, how important it is to involve everyone in a movement and to organize local units in as many places as possible. He knew that local organization was the strength of a movement.

He knew, too, that the people must be educated and that every means must be used to that end. He began to use the movies for that purpose and to send mobile units into rural areas. He organized schools and a college. He promoted adult literacy classes. He founded a newspaper and printed many booklets and leaflets. This, too, was important for a democratic nation and for a political party.

Then he was clear in his mind as to the strategy of winning independence. The first stage, he felt, was one of "positive action," when a movement uses non-violent methods to test its strength against an outside force, in this case the British. Following that was a period of "tactical action," a sort of contest of wits. Once political independence was won, there was a third period of providing economic gains for all the people.

In his efforts to achieve independence for the Gold Coast,

Nkrumah hoped that there would be no injection of the race issue. Over and over he affirmed his belief in the equality of all races. Typical of his thinking was the following statement:

> We believe in the freedom of the peoples of all races. We believe in co-operation. In fact, it has been one of my theses that in this struggle of ours, in this struggle to redeem Africa, we are fighting not against race and color and creed. We are fighting a system, a system which degrades and exploits; and wherever we find the system, that system must be abolished.

There were times when he attacked the British vigorously, even bitterly. But most of the time he recognized their part in the history of the Gold Coast and the need for continuing co-operation with them in the early period of independence. On one occasion he reminded his listeners that:

> The strands of history have brought our two countries together. We have provided much material benefit to the British people, and they in turn have taught us many good things. We want to continue to learn from them the best that they can give us, and we hope that they will find in us qualities worthy of emulation.

Finally, he knew that speed was important in all that he and his party were trying to do. He phrased it this way:

> What other countries have taken three hundred years or more to achieve, a once dependent territory must try to accomplish in a decade if it is to survive. Unless it is, as it were, "jet-propelled," it will lag behind and thus risk everything for which it has fought.

But more important than any of the four foregoing explanations of his power was the personality of Nkrumah himself.

In the past the people of this part of the world have looked to their tribal chiefs as their ideal. With the decline of chieftaincy as an institution, they are likely to look elsewhere for the man who personifies their ideal. They found such an ideal in Kwame Nkrumah, a handsome, charming man, an excellent listener, and a quiet, pleasing conversationalist as well. On the public platform he held a crowd in his hands as he talked with them, pleaded with them, issued orders to them. His rich, resonant voice was compelling, and people cheered, screamed, waved their handkerchiefs to urge him on, to accept his challenges, to agree to his commands.

In his frequent visits into the villages of Ghana, he was self-effacing and democratic. He ate with the people, played with them, slept in their houses, and enjoyed shared pleasures. To the masses he was "The Big Chief."

With all these qualities, it is little wonder that Nkrumah commanded tremendous support in the Gold Coast. He was not merely the leader of a party. He was the leader of a crusade for freedom.

In the 1954 and again in the 1956 election his Convention People's party won more than seventy of the one hundred four seats in the Assembly, with the other places divided among other smaller parties.

In a few years the Gold Coast moved rapidly toward independence, despite many problems and occasional deadlocks. An agreement was made with England whereby a special election would be held in 1956 and a motion for independence presented to the new legislators. If it passed by "a reasonable majority," then England would set a date for independence.

Those terms were met and the date was set for March 6, 1957.

On the evening of the fifth the Legislative Assembly met for the last time, and Nkrumah delivered one of the finest speeches of his career. One writer termed it "the testament of a new nation."

Early on the day of independence a huge crowd began

to gather at the Polo Grounds in Accra. They would gladly wait hours for the stroke of midnight—and independence. As the church bells finally struck twelve, a mighty roar went up from the crowd, followed by the chanting of the battle cry of the past years, FreeDOM, FreeDOM, FreeDOM. The people shouted, beat on their drums, shot off firecrackers.

When Nkrumah arrived at the Polo Grounds, another wave of chanting rose. This time it was FreeDOM, FreeDOM, NKRUMAH. He was carried through the crowds on the shoulders of his admirers. All over the city British flags were lowered and the red, green, and gold flags of the new nation of Ghana were raised.

Similar celebrations were being held in other parts of Accra, and elsewhere in Ghana. The talking drums had sent the message of independence into the most inaccessible parts of the country.

Throughout that day there were special events of many kinds. Parliament was opened by the Duchess of Kent, the representative of Queen Elizabeth II. There were receptions and dinners and parties. And during the day an arch was dedicated on the spot where former Gold Coast soldiers and other Africans had been killed in 1947.

Attending the celebrations on this memorable day were the representatives of more than fifty nations of the world, including Vice-President Richard Nixon, of the United States.

Now the big job of creating a new nation began. Ghana had made a good start under the British, but there were many problems she had to face.

As Nkrumah had pointed out during the week of independence celebrations: "We have fought and won the battle for freedom. We must now assail the ramparts of all the social and economic evils that have plagued our country all these years. . . ."

Roads needed to be built and more and better harbor

facilities provided. Unless a country has such facilities for export and import, there is no reason for a farmer to grow more crops or for a group of men to build a factory.

Ghana has long relied on her cocoa crop to support her. In fact, 70 per cent of her earnings in exports have come from this one product. But the way in which the cocoa was grown was unscientific and wasteful. Methods are being constantly improved. In addition, a disease known as the swollen-shoot disease had recently developed, threatening to ruin this highly important crop.

At the same time, Ghana needed to grow a wider variety of agricultural products, both for her own use and for sale abroad in order to earn dollars and sterling to buy the things she could not produce.

In addition, large tracts of valuable timber could be improved and used as an important part of her economy.

No country ought to have to import all her manufactured products from abroad. This makes the prices of such products too high and deprives local people of jobs which they would have if the goods were locally manufactured. But the policy of colonial powers in the past had been to discourage local industry. Instead, the raw materials of colonies had been sent to the homeland for processing and then sold to the colonies if they could afford to buy them. Now that Ghana was on its own, that practice must be abandoned. Ghana also needed to improve the mining of its rich resources of gold, diamonds, manganese, and bauxite.

The tribal barrier to unity exists in Ghana as in other African countries. For a very long time the area of what is now Ghana had been divided among various tribes, speaking their own languages and giving their allegiance to their own tribal chieftains. But a nation of five million persons cannot afford to have many languages. It cannot afford to have authority divided between the government and the chiefs.

It cannot afford to have intense tribal and regional loyalties at the expense of loyalty to the over-all government.

Another problem the new government faced was lack of schools. Only about 10 per cent of the entire population of the Gold Coast could read or write. Children needed to be given an education, adults needed to be taught to read and write, technical education needed to be enlarged, and textbooks and teachers developed. A herculean task confronted the new government.

Even more basic was the need for better health throughout Ghana, starting with clean water supplies, as most of the health problems of the country stemmed from poor water. Hospitals and health clinics were needed as well as doctors, nurses, and midwives. At the time of independence there were only about two hundred doctors in the entire nation, or one to every twenty-five thousand persons.

Then, too, Nkrumah and his colleagues faced the problems of foreign policy within Africa and with the rest of the world.

What a staggering list of problems for any government. And how much more difficult for a group of men who had to face them for the first time—and all at once. To add to their problems, many people in Ghana expected results from their new government immediately. They thought utopia would arrive with independence.

Fortunately, the British had left a small but efficient civil service in Ghana, and a good many of the British were invited to stay and help for a few months or years while the new government was getting under way. It is a credit to the Ghanaians that they asked the British to remain, and a credit to the British that many of them agreed to work under this new arrangement. In some of the other new nations this did not happen.

Within a year after independence, remarkable results had

been achieved in several of the areas mentioned above. A start had been made during the last months or years of the British administration, but much of the credit goes to the Nkrumah government.

In transportation and communication progress was obvious to all. The port at Takoradi had been improved, and a new port started at Tema, sixteen miles from the capital city. Roads had been built in several places and a new bridge constructed across the Volta River. In order to improve communication, radio-telephone links were established between Accra and Kumasi and between Kumasi and Tamale.

High on the list of agricultural improvements was the continuation of the ten-year campaign against the swollen-shoot disease. Every agency of society, from the schools to the radio and press, was enlisted in a nation-wide attempt to explain to the people the importance of destroying diseased trees. It was not easy to get old farmers to change their ways and destroy the source of their income, and it called for courage, but Nkrumah knew this was the only way. On the whole the campaign was successful. Some progress was made, too, in persuading people to diversify and raise crops they had never planted before.

As a part of its program of industrialization, the Black Star Shipping Line was established, with 60 per cent of its stock owned by Ghana and 40 per cent by Israel. A match factory, a biscuit factory, and several other smaller industries were started.

No solution was found to the language problem, but the national radio continued its broadcasts in five of the local languages plus the official language of English, and many publications of the government appeared in various languages, so that as many people as possible could have reading material in their own language.

Great progress was made, too, in education. The building

of the magnificent campus of the University College of Ghana near Accra continued, as well as further work on the new Kumasi College of Technology. Less noticeable, but perhaps more significant, were the scores of new school buildings in various parts of Ghana, built to accommodate the soaring school population, which had leaped from 80,000 children in elementary schools in 1948 to 500,000 in 1957.

In the area of health, several clinics were built and much use was made of the modern hospital erected in Kumasi.

The admission of Ghana to the United Nations as its eighty-second member was one of the important events in world affairs. Another was the holding of a Conference of African States in Accra in April 1958. This was a project dear to Nkrumah as he moved toward closer relations between the various political divisions of the continent, as a part of his lifelong dream of a Pan-African movement.

A great deal of effort was expended in those early months on trying to find funds to start an enormous Volta River project. In the long run, this would be the most significant economic undertaking in all of West Africa, for its plans called for the building of a dam which would provide electricity for homes, for small factories, and for a large-scale aluminum industry. The water which would be dammed would also be used for irrigation purposes in the southeastern part of Ghana. The government was not successful in its efforts until, in 1961, the World Bank, the United States, Great Britain, and other sources, including a consortium of private United States companies, loaned Ghana $133,000,000 to build the dam and an accompanying aluminum smelter, the first large industrial enterprise in Ghana. The Volta Dam brought Ghana into the industrial world. Its construction was one of Nkrumah's major accomplishments for his nation. Supplying the raw materials to keep industry working full-time there became another major problem to be met.

It was not easy for a man who had been an effective leader of an independence movement to become an efficient administrator, and Nkrumah made many mistakes in this first year of national freedom. But he did remarkably well in consolidating the gains of independence and in moving ahead on a vast array of projects.

His interest in Pan-Africanism continued, and in 1958 he called a conference of independent African states in Accra and later that year the first All-African Peoples' Conference.

In 1961 he attended the Commonwealth Prime Ministers' Conference in London and bitterly denounced the racial policy of the government of South Africa.

Of course there was opposition in Ghana itself to much that Nkrumah did. Sharper criticism grew as some disturbing evidences of a weaker side to his character began to show themselves. Critics said that he was inordinately conceited. They pointed to the larger-than-life statue of himself that he had permitted, even encouraged, to be erected in front of Parliament House in the capital city. (The statue was later severely damaged by dynamite explosions aimed at destroying it.) He wrote his life story and gave it the title *Ghana: The Autobiography of Kwame Nkrumah,* as if Ghana and Nkrumah were synonymous. He allowed his picture to appear on the stamps of the new nation. He named the university at Kumasi, Kwame Nkrumah University. Nor did he discourage the title *Osagyefo* (Redeemer) with which he was greeted by the worshipful crowds everywhere, who regarded him as their political savior, as indeed he was.

Although he publicly denounced corruption and ostentatious living among top leaders, he did nothing "positive" to stop it.

The auspicious beginnings of Ghana as an independent nation under this able and gifted man make the story of his downfall doubly tragic. An overweening desire for personal power, greed, vanity, all seem to have lured him into personal and government corruption, neglect of his country, and cruel vindictiveness toward any who opposed him or questioned his actions. Gradually he denied to the people of Ghana many of the privileges he had fought so long to obtain for them. Nkrumah had ceased to be a leader, but dictated arbitrarily. He seemed to have lost his vision of the new society he had long advocated for Ghana. In 1962, he had the National Assembly make him President for life. Free elections, a free press, and freedom of assembly were abolished. The Supreme Court was disbanded. All opposition was, in one way or another, liquidated. The jails were filled with political prisoners who had dared oppose the President. His one-time friend and political mentor, Dr. Danquah, had been imprisoned with Nkrumah by the British, but when Nkrumah came to power, he jailed his former friend again and let him die of neglect and abuse in a detention camp.

In 1964, he made Ghana a one-party socialist state. His government had become an oppressive dictatorship, more and more dependent upon the Communist bloc. He amassed a huge personal fortune.

Outside his own country Nkrumah was also coming into disrepute. He branded many of the new African governments "neo-colonialist" and meddled in their affairs. His neutralist policy in the conflict between East and West was understandable, but it brought him under fire from the West. He received $166.5 million in aid from the United States but called that country the "foremost" practitioner of "neo-colonialism" in Africa. In a book published in 1965 he wrote irresponsibly of American "colonialism," branding, for example, the Peace Corps as a tool of the Central Intelligence Agency, at the very time his own officials were asking for more Peace Corps workers to expand the work of the one hundred twenty-two members already in Ghana.

It was inevitable that Nkrumah should begin to live in fear of his life. He became a lonely figure, almost barricaded in Flagstaff House, his seventeenth-century castle home, behind a high wall, protected by police guards with tanks and a gunboat cruising offshore. His "home" estate included his office, an army camp, a military hospital, and a radio station.

Despite all precautions, several attempts were made on Nkrumah's life. They failed, but made him even more fearful.

In February 1966, Nkrumah left Ghana for a visit to Peking and thence went to Hanoi in North Vietnam. The plotters of the overthrow of his regime had been planning and waiting for this moment. Shortly before midnight on February 23, a military leader, Colonel Katoka, moved an army brigade into the capital city. At the airport, they were joined by a company of paratroopers and a second army brigade. At 2:30 on the morning of February 24, army units surrounded Flagstaff House. Other units surrounded the Post Office, the radio station, and the Ministry of Defense. By noon, the defenders of Flagstaff House had surrendered. Nkrumah's Egyptian wife and her three children were driven to the airport in an armored car, where they boarded a plane for Nkrumah's villa near Cairo. Communist aid officials likewise were driven to the airport for expulsion to Russia, East Germany, and China. Nkrumah became a refugee in Guinea.

Within a few days after the coup, the city of Accra had, on the surface at least, returned to normal. There had been little bloodshed. The military leaders stated that they were eager to turn over the powers of government to the civilians. "The myth surrounding Kwame Nkrumah has been broken," they declared.

More than eleven hundred political prisoners were released. These included many able and dedicated Ghanaians. Most of the released prisoners were found by the Red Cross to be in ill health, many partly blind or paralyzed, and most bearing marks of cruel beatings. Their friends and relatives, dressed in white, the symbol of victory in Ghana, pelted them joyously with white chalk powder as they emerged from the prisons.

Thus the able leader of the first independent black African state to obtain independence, the man who had inspired Africans throughout the continent to follow Ghana's example, who was the acknowledged leader in the Pan-African movement, the friend of all political refugees, had fallen. But when Ghana has found itself again, history must credit Nkrumah with having pointed the way and led his people to much that is good in their new nation.

SENGHOR
OF SENEGAL

From a gleaming new stadium, the pulsating rhythms of "Sophisticated Lady" echoed through the warm African night. Within the stadium, ten thousand people swayed to the beat of the music, and applauded thunderously at its close. The incomparable Duke Ellington and his orchestra had conquered another audience with their talents.

A mile away, in a strikingly appointed theater, the Alvin Ailey dancers whirled and stamped through their interpretations of the American "blues," to the delight of a sold-out house.

In a quieter mood, a thousand masterpieces of ancient and modern art, assembled from the museums of the world, held the attention of visitors to the Musée Dynamique. And nearby, the solemn arches of the Arabesque Cathedral rang with the revival hymns of Marian Williams and her gospel singers, so impressing a group of Russian talent scouts that they booked the troupe forthwith for Moscow. Even the French priests sitting in the front pews tapped their feet to the irresistible rhythms.

In a neighboring exhibit, Langston Hughes, the American Negro poet, had assembled over five hundred books by Negro-American and African authors and enthralled hundreds of interested listeners with readings from his own works depicting Negro pain and pride the world over.

Troupes from Mali, Zambia, Morocco, the Ivory Coast, and other African countries, dressed in appropriate costumes, gave superb performances of Africa's traditional dances. Comic Congolese dancers, painted white, were a big hit as they mimicked society ladies. Dancers from the Republic of Chad in Central Africa, dressed in costumes of blue, yellow, and red, the national colors of their country, fascinated their audiences with head-wagging, shoulder-shaking precision dances. Nigerian actors, whose bizarre costumes included handsomely feathered headdresses, performed the folk comedy *Danda*.

The time was April 1966. The place was Dakar, the beautiful capital of Senegal, the hot, flat, westernmost country of Africa. The event was the first World Festival of Negro Arts, organized under the sponsorship of the United Nations Educational, Scientific, and Cultural Organization, and the Society of African Culture. Forty-three countries from around the world had sent Negro musicians, poets, dancers, paintings, sculptures, and books, to charm, inspire, and inform over thirty thousand visitors to the Festival, many of them non-Africans. Over two hundred visitors were from the United States. All would readily agree with the Congolese poet Tchicaya U'tamsi: "The fruits of negritude should not be picked by black hands alone but also by the hands of men of good will throughout the world."

The mastermind behind this extraordinary exhibit of Negro genius and culture was the President of Senegal, Léopold Sédar Senghor, scholar, philosopher, poet, and statesman, who uses the word "negritude" to embrace all Negro cultural values. It is, as Langston Hughes pointed out, a term that describes "a way of revealing to the Negro people and the world the beauty within themselves." "Negritude" became the theme of the Dakar Festival.

How did such a scholarly, gifted man, whose primary interests as a youth seemed to be in learning and the arts, get into politics, particularly the difficult and often discouraging politics of a new nation?

This man of many interests and talents, who was to become

the first President of his country, was born in Joal, Senegal, on October 6, 1906. Joal is on the Atlantic coast of what was then French West Africa, and Joal grew up under French rule. His father was a well-to-do grower and exporter of peanuts, Senegal's most important product. The family was Roman Catholic in a country predominantly Moslem, so Léopold's respect for tolerance was nurtured from an early age. It was in the community of his childhood, located between the vast Atlantic Ocean and the dense African bush country, that the sensitive boy developed from his physical environment and in his home an appreciation of the beauty of Africa, its land, its legends, its poetry, and all the culture that later he was to describe in the term "negritude."

Léopold attended Catholic elementary and secondary schools. In fact, he had youthful dreams of becoming a priest, but gradually grew away from that ambition as other interests entered his life. He graduated with highest honors from the Catholic Liebermann Seminary in Dakar, in 1926.

Recognizing their student's superior ability and talents, his teachers at Liebermann Seminary were able to get Léopold a scholarship to the Lycée Louis-le-Grand in Paris.

One can only imagine what that city meant to a young man sensitive to beauty and avid for learning, as Léopold Senghor was. Suddenly he was in Paris. Paris, with its traditions of liberty, equality, fraternity. Here at his disposal were the Louvre, Notre Dame, the Tuileries gardens, the boulevards, the Opera House, the theaters, the Sorbonne. Fascinated, he plunged into this new world.

Paris also increased the young African's knowledge of the world of the Negro. Later, he was to say:

> If Paris is not the greatest museum of Negro-African art, nowhere else has Negro art been so well understood. . . . By revealing to me the values of my ancestral civilization, Paris forced me to adopt them and make them bear fruit.

In Paris, too, he met other creative Negroes and formed friendships that were to continue throughout his life. These friends included Louis T. Achille, who had taught at Howard University in Washington, D.C. and could talk to Léopold about the Negro's life in the United States, and Achille's cousin, Mlle. Paulette Nardal, whose salon was a meeting place for the literary-minded Negroes in Paris. Thus his knowledge of and interest in the Negro's place in the world was fostered. But he was interested in all literature. Avidly he read the French author Proust, the English Virginia Woolf, the German Rilke, and many other authors whose works were current at the time. He studied everything he could find that had been written about Africa. He was especially interested in poetry written by the American Negro. In the years to come, he was to translate and lecture on American Negro poetry.

In due time, Léopold passed the examinations for admission to the School of Philosophy of the Ecolé Normale Supérieure. While a student there, he wrote a thoughtful work on the French poet Baudelaire, who had attended Léopold's school Louis-le-Grand. Léopold was the first African Negro to win the diploma of *agrégé de l'Université*.

The next period in Senghor's life was spent as a teacher. He taught literature, first at the Lycée in Tours, the first African Negro to get such an appointment, then at the Lycée Marcellin Berthelot in Paris. His friends were the intellectuals, and among them he became the spokesman for his fellow Africans.

Then came World War II. Senghor was promptly drafted into an infantry battalion of French colonial troops. When France surrendered to Germany, he was interned by the Nazis. But Senghor did not succumb easily to a cruel misfortune. He saw an opportunity to serve France and mankind and he grasped it by organizing a resistance group in the camp. It was discovered by his captors, who immediately transferred the dangerous young rebel to a penal battalion.

His luck changed in a few months, however, and he was permitted to return to teaching at the Lycée Berthelot. Quietly, he coupled resistance work with his teaching. His activities on behalf of France, his second country, naturally fostered his growing interest in government and in people's struggles for freedom the world over.

At the end of the war, in 1945, General de Gaulle appointed Senghor to the Commission on Colonial Representation in the French Constituent Assembly. Coming from a French colony, Senghor was well fitted for the job and it interested him. One year later, he moved a step higher. Senegal elected him a deputy to the French National Assembly. He helped draft the 1946 constitution of France. At this time he was a member of the Socialist party, but in 1948 he founded a new party, the Bloc Démocratique Sénegalais.

With all his political activities both in Paris and in his native city, Dakar, Senghor remained a teacher for a number of years, part of the time at the École Nationale d'Administration, where he taught Negro-African languages. All the while he worked for the independence of Senegal. He joined the Group for Overseas Independence and was for several years its president. One might assume that such activity, aimed at the independence of one of its colonies, would mark Senghor as an enemy of France. Instead, and this is one measure of his character and the respect in which Senghor was held, in 1952 Premier Edgar Faure appointed him Secretary of State in the French cabinet.

As must always happen when people begin to think freely for themselves, division arose between the leaders of French West Africa. France at this time was interested in welding West Africa into a greater France. Senghor and Sekou Touré, another African leader, although pressing for independence, wanted French West Africa to remain within a federation of free African states. Another prominent West African, Felix Houphouet-Boigny of the Ivory Coast, believed each West African state should stand on its own, not as part of a united federal structure. A new constitution was drawn up, and all the territories of French West Africa, except Guinea, voted to join the French community. This was as Senghor wished it. Now Senegal had almost complete internal autonomy.

For a short time in 1959, Senegal joined with the former French Sudan to form the Mali Federation, named after the Mali empire that flourished in the region from the eleventh to the sixteenth century. In that period, the civilization of the Mali Empire had been one of which West Africans could be proud. Village craftsmen included skilled wood carvers, gold, silver, and copper smiths, weavers, and tanners. The fertile soil of land that had been cleared and carefully cultivated produced vegetables in variety. The Malis wore a fine-textured cloth which they wove from the cotton they grew. The meal from the baobab tree they made into tasty bread. Their homes were lighted with candles. Gold mines were the source of much of the Mali Empire prosperity. The gold was traded for salt and other goods brought across the Sahara Desert by Arab traders from the north.

Scholarship also flourished in the Mali Empire, and books and ideas were freely exchanged. A succession of weak rulers brought about the eclipse of the Empire by another about 1475, but the present generation of West Africans treasures the memory of a once great civilization that flourished in their land.

Senghor was elected President of the Mali Federal Assembly, which met at Dakar. The former Sudanese leader became Prime Minister. France granted full independence to the Mali Federation in June 1960. But the Federation dissolved in August of that same year when Senegal seceded and proclaimed itself a republic, with Senghor as President.

France formally recognized the new nation, and upon his election in September for a seven-year term, Senghor received a congratulatory message from General de Gaulle which described his election as "the best pledge of friendly and fruitful relations between Senegal and France within our community." Senegal became a member of the United Nations on September 28, 1960, and Senghor addressed the General Assembly when he paid his first visit to the United States in 1961. On that same brief visit he spoke at a Harvard luncheon in Cambridge, received an honorary Doctor of Laws degree from Fordham, and met with President Kennedy in Washington.

In 1961, on the first anniversary of Senegal's independence, Vice-President and Mrs. Lyndon Johnson visited the new nation, along with fifteen hundred other foreign dignitaries. The Senegalese people lined the streets to the presidential palace to see the Vice-President of the United States. As he passed, they shouted, *"Merci, merci!"*

The largest political party in Senegal is Senghor's party, the Progressive Senegalese Union. Two existing leftist parties were outlawed, but rivalry between Senghor and his Prime Minister, Dia, led Dia to attempt in 1962 to seize the government. He was unsuccessful. The uprising was quelled without bloodshed, and Dia was imprisoned for life. However, a new constitution resulted, replacing the parliamentary system of government with a presidential system. Of the one million who voted, 99.5 per cent approved the new constitution, which makes Senghor the strong man. All eighty seats of the National Assembly are held by the party of the President, who was re-elected to a four-year term in 1963. The party advocates a form of socialism based on traditional African communal institutions, but leaving a large place for private enterprise and foreign investment as well. It has particularly strong backing by the young Senegalese, although they sometimes criticize the President for keeping close ties with France. But Senghor wisely tries to keep the favor of the white French settlers whom independence displaced and of France, which in recent years had supplied through its aid one-half of the Senegalese budget.

What kind of country and people does Léopold Sédar Senghor lead? Senegal is the westernmost portion of Africa. A glance at a map of the world verifies its claim to be the crossroads of the world, a way-station between Europe and Latin America, the United States, and the Near and Far East, and between South Africa and the European and American continents.

The land is made up largely of rolling grasslands and low-growing vegetation. There are no high mountains. Four large navigable rivers flow in parallel lines from east to west. Over three million people live in this country of 76,000 square miles. French is the official language, but most of the people in everyday life speak Wolof, and a smaller number, Poular. Many in the cities can also speak English. The largest tribal group is the Wolofs, who include about half the population. There are numerous smaller tribes.

Senegal is one of the more highly developed countries of West Africa, and by African standards Dakar is a prosperous city. It is blessed with a fine harbor, whose docks are filled constantly with ships from every nation in the world. Dakar's modern airport is a stopping point for transcontinental aircraft, including the largest jets.

Many of the people of Dakar are modern and progressive, and they are of many origins—African, European, Asian. Although the young people are adopting European styles of dress, the traditional long flowing *Sabador* and *Grand Bonbou* are still common for formal occasions, and the less elaborate, loose-fitting robes of brilliant prints and colors for everyday. Pieces of carved gold jewelry are beautiful accessories to the costumes which help to preserve the picturesque charm of African life.

In the business center of Dakar are modern buildings up to fourteen stories high. The "Medina," in contrast, is a sprawling section of straw huts and small wooden or stucco houses, the homes of the poor of the city.

The modern, attractive suburbs of Dakar have been given names that reflect the interests of the residents, for example, Liberté I and Baobab (a popular tree of Senegal). The homes along the tree-lined streets are gaily painted and set off by small flower gardens.

Many of the Senegalese people are of Hamitic origin, that is, they are the descendants of people who emigrated from the Sudan area of the Nile River centuries ago. Legend says the Hamites of North Africa are descended from Ham, Noah's second son. In any case, these Senegalese are tall and graceful, with classic features and fairly light skin. About 80 per cent of them are Moslems. Smaller numbers are Christians and animists.

Several industrial establishments in Dakar and neighboring regions produce a variety of consumer products for export to other countries of West Africa. Fleets of tuna vessels sail in and out of Dakar and supply seven canning plants in Dakar. Most of the tuna is shipped frozen to various parts of the world. Fishing is common on the coast. The annual catch is about 50,000 tons.

Millet is the basic food crop, but rice is also a very popular grain food, and although Senegal produces some rice, many tons must be imported to meet the demand. The government is encouraging the farmers to grow more rice and so decrease the import figure, which weighs heavily on the country's economy. Twenty-five thousand acres of rice fields have been laid out in the area of the Senegal River, and a ten-year program will make 61,000 acres available for this important crop.

Because the climate is favorable, experiments are being carried on with sugar cane and other agricultural products. These include tomatoes, bananas, tobacco, and pineapples. Crop variation is a major objective of Senghor's government, which realizes that a one-crop economy, dependent upon the world market for one product only, can be disastrous when prices fall or crops fail.

Some years ago mining engineers discovered evidence of phosphate deposits in various places in Senegal. This led to systematic prospecting, which was successful. In 1966, about 600,000 tons of phosphate were mined, and the production is expected to increase yearly.

But the backbone of Senegal's economy is the peanut, which was brought to West Africa from Central America around 1920. It is produced in Senegal in tremendous quantities, over one million metric tons in a recent year, and shipped all over the world. Peanut plantations of thousands of acres were formerly small farms. Now they produce over 80 per cent of Senegal's total exports. Crop production, its processing into such by-products as peanut oil, and the marketing of this basic commodity is almost completely under government control. The government is trying to increase the yield per acre and is engaging in research to promote more extensive use of peanuts and peanut products around the world.

Despite its progress, Senegal's burden is the same as that of other new nations—poverty, ignorance, and resulting disease. Illiteracy is common. Most of the adults living in rural areas, where three-quarters of the population live, cannot read or write, and only about one-quarter of the children of school age go to school. Schools are being built, however, as rapidly as the means for doing so can be provided. The fast-growing University of Dakar, founded in 1957, has schools of medicine and pharmacy and departments of science, law, and the liberal arts.

Senegal has launched two Four-Year Plans of Social and Economic Development. One of the country's basic economic problems is that it must buy almost twice as much as it sells. The first Four-Year Plan reduced significantly the amounts of sugar, cotton, rice, and millet that had to be purchased, and improved railroads, roads, and air transport. The second Plan, now in operation, is concentrating on agricultural and industrial production, education, and health facilities.

President Senghor has drastically cut government expenses, including Civil Service bureaus. He emphasizes to the Senegalese people the necessity for sacrifice and hard work on their own part.

"It's no good calling on God for help before you have tilled your field," he tells them. "The Senegalese nation will be our own handiwork, or it will not exist at all."

To augment their own efforts, foreign investment is sought and encouraged by various means, including a generous Investment Code calling for high integrity in all things. President Senghor will not tolerate hiked contracts or graft of any type. He has been extraordinarily successful in keeping ethical standards high.

Economics, finance, politics—all seem foreign to the esthetic gifts with which Léopold Senghor was endowed. His literary works are considered classics in their field. He became famous in Paris literary circles when he published his first collection of African poems in 1945, *Chants d'Ombre*. His anthology of African Negro verse inspired Sartre's essay, *Orphée Noir*. This anthology, *Anthologie de la nouvelle poésie nègre et malgache de langue française*, was published in Paris in

1948 and was only one of the earliest of an impressive list of superior writings from the pen of this gifted man.

His *On African Socialism*, a book of essays, was widely acclaimed. Senegal, he states, must develop an "open, democratic, humanistic socialism," applicable to twentieth-century Negro-African realities. He frowns on using some foreign model, such as Communism, designed for other times and other people. "We can no longer accept Marx's vision of the future." He believed it to be to the country's advantage, however, to establish diplomatic relations with Communist China in 1964.

But no one should be deceived into thinking that his literary talent and artistic interests prevent Léopold Senghor from being a practical politician. He did not become President of Senegal because he wrote the country's national anthem, which he did. Philosopher and poet, he is also politically adroit, and ruthless when he deems it necessary, as when he imprisoned his Prime Minister and former friend, Dia, in 1962, and dissolved an opposition party. He has never lost an election.

Personally, President Senghor is quiet and unassuming. He is a small, soft-spoken man, who talks like the scholar he is. Some commentators have pointed out that he seems to have drawn his strongest support, not from the intellectuals, as might be expected, but from the peasants. His moderate approach does not always appeal to the intellectuals, especially the young, naturally impatient students, who relish drastic measures. His sincerity and sympathy do appeal strongly to the hard-working rural people, despite the fact that they are for the large part Moslems while their President is a Roman Catholic.

It is natural that President Senghor should be French in his outlook and manner, steeped as he is in French culture and learning. He married a French woman from

Normandy, whom he has described in characteristically poetic language as "the woman of my heart." With their three sons they live in the beautiful presidential palace in Dakar. He speaks French fluently, English fairly well, and the African Wolof dialect, about which he has written several scholarly works.

In recognition of his scholarship and achievements for his race and for the entire African continent, Senghor has received honorary degrees from Oxford and Fordham universities and the University of Paris. He believes in and refers often to the "civilization of the universal," for he is truly a citizen of the world. "The Negro will have contributed," he writes, "with other peoples, to reforging the unity of man and the world; linking the flesh to the spirit, man to fellow man, the pebble to God."

During President Senghor's visit to the United States in 1966, one of this country's authorities on Africa, speaking at an official luncheon given for the honored guest, proposed a toast to "a most noble man." Perhaps this expresses most accurately the success of Senghor's leadership. Through all the political skill, intelligence, patience, and scholarship, there shines the rare quality of nobility.

THE MIDDLE EAST AND
NORTH AFRICA

MOHAMMED V
OF MOROCCO

One of the most colorful pageants in all the world takes place every Friday in Rabat, the capital of Morocco, in the northwestern corner of Africa. Friday is a special day throughout the entire Moslem world, for it is then that the services are held in mosques for all devout male Moslems. But Friday is of special significance to the residents of Rabat and to visitors who have come from all over Morocco, and from other parts of the world as well, for it is on that day that anyone can see the King as he rides to the mosque in a procession with all the panoply of ancient monarchs.

Early in the morning people begin to wander toward the large open space between the palace and the mosque, anxious to get the best spots for viewing this parade. By noontime, thousands of people have gathered along the short route which the King will take.

A close look at the crowd reveals the variety of people in this country of more than thirteen million persons. In addition to Moroccans there are Frenchmen, Spaniards, Algerians, Italians, and Portuguese living in Morocco. Men, women, and children—sometimes alone, often in family groups, occasionally in delegations from the larger cities or the mud-brick villages of this kingdom—have come to the parade.

Many of the Moroccan women are dressed in long robes, or *djellabas*. Each *djellaba* is of a solid color, but there are many colors in such a large crowd as this one. Most of the women are also wearing colored kerchiefs or thin

veils over the lower part of their faces, but the eyes
of many of them can be seen—which is not the case in
many Moslem countries. Other women are there in Western
dresses and with no kerchiefs. A few are wearing the
djellaba and high heels, an interesting if strange combination.

Many of the men are also dressed in Western clothes,
although here and there are men in various colored *djellabas,*
either with a hood over their heads or with the hood tossed
back. Many of them are wearing yellow or white slippers
with pointed toes and no backs, or sandals.

Just before noon the King emerges from the palace in
an open gold chariot drawn by beautiful, sleek Arabian
horses and driven by a colorfully costumed driver.

The most colorful part of this procession is the palace
guard, made up of soldiers carrying lances and green pen-
nants, or rifles. In the summer they are dressed in white
and in the winter in red. Their striking costumes include
very full pantaloons with narrow pleats, white puttees, and
white blouses, topped with blue caps.

This is a great show, a splendid pageant. But it means
much more than that to the Moroccans. The King is their
spiritual leader, filling the role for them that the Pope does
for Catholics. For many years he was known as the Sultan
of Morocco, but some years ago his title was changed to
King. As such he is the political ruler as well as the
spiritual leader of the Moroccan people. For many years
the man of the hour on this sacred day was Mohammed V,
who was the Sultan, and later King, of Morocco from
1927 until his death in 1961. To Moroccans, Mohammed V
was the father of their nation.

Little is known about the childhood and youth of Mohammed V. This may seem strange in view of the fact that
he became the King of Morocco. But when he was a boy,

most people thought an older brother would be chosen to succeed his father as Sultan. Besides, the French were in control of Morocco and kept the Sultan's family well guarded. So almost all of his early life was lived apart from the people. He attended the Koranic school and learned the major tenets of Islam. He also obtained some French education, but he never studied in France as did many of today's leaders in Morocco, and he did not receive a college or university degree. Persons who knew him in those years say that he was especially interested in the history of Islam and of Morocco, and in biography.

His father, Moulay Youssef, was a strict Moslem, and Mohammed V was reared in the rigid observance of that faith, praying five times a day with his face turned toward Mecca, fasting each day until sunset during the entire month of Ramadan, and abstaining entirely from alcoholic beverages.

During those early years Mohammed learned to hunt and shoot, to play tennis, to swim, to drive fast cars. At the age of sixteen he was married to a girl selected by the family.

If Mohammed's life was largely uneventful in this early period, the life of the country he would rule someday was not.

Centuries ago this part of the world had been invaded by the Phoenicians, then by the Greeks, later by the Romans, and still later by the Vandals. But for nearly a thousand years it had been independent, under Berber or Arab rulers. One reason why it escaped the invasions that so many other countries experienced was that the Atlas Mountains, rising as high as 13,000 feet, form a barrier to the peoples to the east. Another reason was the warlike character of the original Berbers who inhabited what is now Morocco.

At the turn of this century, however, the leading powers of Europe surveyed the world for resources and markets.

They divided Asia, the Middle East, and Africa among themselves. Eventually, Morocco fell into their orbit. Several European countries were interested in Morocco, but by a series of agreements it was France which gained control of most of northwestern Africa. The only other country to win a part of the northwestern corner of Africa was Spain, which obtained a part of Morocco in the north and another section in the south.

France proclaimed a "protectorate" over her part of Morocco, and in the Treaty of Fez of 1912 pledged "constant support to His Shereefian Majesty against all dangers which might threaten his person or throne or endanger the tranquillity of his States." But it was soon apparent that this was more than a protectorate; in reality it was a colony.

French farmers were soon moving to Morocco by the hundreds. They were given special concessions in the purchase of land and in taxes, so that they soon owned large parts of the fertile plains in the northern part of Morocco. They did a great deal of good for Morocco, but unfortunately very little for the Moroccans.

Roads were built, irrigation systems installed, hospitals erected, and schools started, but most of these were for the French or for those who were willing to work "cooperatively" with them.

Many of the Moroccans never fully accepted the French, and it was years before the entire country was controlled by the newcomers. In 1912, there was a revolt in Fez, from 1919 to 1923 a war in the Middle Atlas Mountain area, and in 1925 and 1926 another uprising of the mountain tribes led by Abdel Krim. Not until 1934 were all the rebellious groups finally defeated by the French.

Many Moroccans would have liked to oust the French, but France was a world power and the Moroccans not strong enough to drive the French from their land.

And, of course, some Moroccans profited through jobs with the government, with the mining companies which had come to Morocco to exploit the mineral resources, or with the French *colons* or farmers.

Such was the situation in Morocco when an event took place which was drastically to change the life of Mohammed V. On November 17, 1927, his father died, and on the next day the *oulemas* of Fez gathered to select his successor. The *oulemas* were the leading religious men and Moslem authorities on law.

In most monarchies, the eldest son automatically becomes the ruler upon the death of a monarch. But this has not been the custom in Morocco, where any member of the royal family can be chosen King.

So the *oulemas* gathered to deliberate upon the choice of their new Sultan. Or at least that is what the people were told. Actually, the choice had already been made before they assembled. Mohammed V had been selected by the French. Nevertheless, the religious leaders went through with their deliberations, and curiously enough their choice was also Mohammed V!

There were two older brothers who might have been selected, but the French felt that a younger boy would be easier to handle.

Mohammed V was only seventeen at the time, and for a good many years he was the pliable puppet the French had hoped he would be. He had not had much education. Thus he had not been exposed to the revolutionary ideas that a student reads about in history or talks about in student circles in places like the Sorbonne in Paris. Neither had he traveled widely and learned about other lands and peoples from first-hand experience.

Yet the young Sultan had other qualities of which the

French were unaware or which they disregarded. One was his ability to listen, observe, and learn. This trait made it possible for him to develop as time went on, despite his meager background.

There was also a streak of obstinacy in him which came to light during World War II. When he was called upon to enforce the anti-Jewish measures of the pro-Vichy government of France, he refused to do so. He said that he was the King of *all* Moroccans, including the 250,000 Jews, and that he would not enforce acts which discriminated against any group of his people. This was his first act of defiance against the French. Later there were to be many others.

Throughout World War II he actively supported the Allied war effort. In September 1939, he issued a proclamation:

> From today and until such time as the efforts of France and her allies are crowned with victory, we must render every help without reserve. We will not stint any of our resources and will not hesitate before any sacrifice.

At the close of the war, de Gaulle gave the Sultan the Cross of Liberation for his help in the war effort.

A dramatic turning point in Mohammed's career came on January 22, 1943, when he dined with Franklin D. Roosevelt and Winston Churchill while they were in Morocco for the important Casablanca Conference. This was the first time that the Sultan had been permitted by the French to confer in private with high officials of other nations.

Presumably the French thought this would be merely a pleasant social occasion. But it turned out to be much more than that. President Roosevelt was impressed with the Sultan. He was apparently in an expansive mood and during the course of the conversation, he urged the Sultan not to permit foreigners to exploit Morocco's resources, but to encourage the Moroccans to develop them themselves.

According to Elliott Roosevelt's account of the dinner party, which he attended, Franklin Roosevelt also asked:

> Why does Morocco, inhabited by Moroccans, belong to France? Anything must be better than to live under French colonial rule. When we've won the war, I will work with all my might and main to see to it that the United States is not wheedled into the position of accepting any plan that will further France's imperialistic ambitions.

Later, Roosevelt wrote two letters to the Sultan of Morocco in which he apparently reiterated these points.

This was the kind of encouragement Mohammed V needed. Here was the President of the world's leading nation asking the same questions which many Moroccans had been asking. Undoubtedly this interview encouraged the Sultan in his future moves toward independence for his country.

Meanwhile, the movement for independence in Morocco was being strengthened by the formation of the Istiqlal (Independence) party. This group was composed largely of young men from the middle class who had been trained in French schools. They were doctors, lawyers, teachers, and businessmen who were well aware of the world-wide movement for independence and of the long history of nationalistic movements in France, in the United States, and, more recently, in India and other parts of Asia.

At first their program was quite moderate. They wanted a united Morocco. They also wanted independence, but were willing to gain it gradually over a period of years and through agreement with the French. They favored a democratic government with a constitutional monarchy.

At first the Sultan seemed wary of this group, either because he did not agree with them or because he was still under the domination of the French. But in Tangier in 1947 he spoke for the first time in public of his desire for eventual independence. The Istiqlal was overjoyed at this new stand taken by the Sultan.

The following year the Moroccans were allowed to select a few members of the new Council of government rather than having them all nominated by the French. As a result, eleven members of the Istiqlal party were included in the Council. This was merely an advisory body, but they felt that it was a step in the direction of self-government.

In 1950 the Sultan was invited to Paris. It apparently was the intention of the French government to dazzle him with banquets, official functions, and flattery in an effort to assure his continued co-operation. Instead, the French were confronted with two memoranda requesting the complete independence of Morocco. The French government evasively acknowledged the first request and did not deign to reply to the second.

Back in Morocco, the more conservative forces were beginning to be troubled by the Sultan's growing independence and his anti-French attitude. The chief opponent of the Sultan was Thami el Glaoui, a fabulously wealthy Berber leader who was known as "The Lion of the Atlas Mountains." He held great economic power, especially in the region around Marrakech, and was the most powerful of the Berber political leaders.

In 1950, El Glaoui went to the palace and warned the Sultan about the consequences of his actions, hoping to cow him into a more moderate position. But the Sultan did not take the warnings and ordered El Glaoui to leave the palace.

Friction continued to develop between the Sultan and the French, and in January 1951, the French Resident General, General Juin, ordered Mohammed V to dismiss the imperial cabinet in which there were Istiqlal members, to condemn the party as atheistic, and to exile its leaders.

Juin is reputed to have said, "Either do this or abdicate—and if you will not abdicate, I will depose you."

The Sultan was now caught in a dilemma. There was no doubt that the French were in control, and it seemed useless to oppose them. On the other hand, they had to be opposed or Morocco would not move toward eventual independence.

Eventually, Mohammed V made a statement praising the French for their positive contributions to Morocco, condemning Communist activities in the land, and censuring "certain parties" for dividing the people and obstructing progress. He also dismissed his cabinet. But he refused to condemn the Istiqlal party by name.

The French accepted this stand by the Sultan and took no action against him. But the final day of judgment had not been averted; it had only been postponed.

In the fall of 1951, Egypt requested that the Moroccan question be placed on the agenda of the United Nations as a violation of the charter and the Universal Declaration of Human Rights. Eventually this proposal was submitted to the General Assembly. It was defeated by a vote of 28 to 23, with seven nations abstaining. The move to involve the United Nations in the affairs of Morocco had failed, but it had served the purpose of focusing world attention on the troubles in that nation and, to a lesser extent, on all of North Africa.

The situation in Morocco had reached the boiling point. All that was needed for it to explode was an "incident." That incident occurred in December 1952, when a trade-union leader was killed in Tunis. Riots broke out in the larger cities of Morocco, and over one hundred leaders of the Istiqlal movement were exiled. Many more were imprisoned.

Egged on by the conservatives in France, the local French officials in Morocco, and the French *colons,* El Glaoui and his friends decided that the time had come to oust the Sultan and to gain more control themselves. So they met and proclaimed the deposition of Mohammed V. They said that the Istiqlal leaders were untrue to Islam and were collaborating with the Communists in impeding real progress in Morocco. They charged that the Sultan was a pawn in their game and that Prince Moulay Hassan (Mohammed V's son) was one of the most active collaborationists.

What they did not say was that their move was a part of the struggle of the rural *caids,* or chiefs, against the rising middle class of the towns and cities and an important part of a struggle for power between El Glaoui and the Sultan.

This time it was the French who were caught in a dilemma. It would not be easy to depose the Sultan, whom they were bound by the Treaty of Fez to support, and it would be a risky business to challenge the growing power of the Istiqlal movement. On the other hand, the French had long collaborated with the Berbers in Morocco and could not risk the loss of their support. Besides, the Sultan was growing more obnoxious to them with each passing year and he needed to be cut down somehow.

Mid-August 1953 arrived, and the Moroccans began their preparations for the great feast day of the year, Aid el Kebir (the Feast of the Sacrifice), held in commemoration of Abraham's proffered sacrifice of his son. It was essential that the Sultan personally sacrifice the first sheep on that holy day. But the people of Morocco wondered if there would be a Sultan to perform this rite, for Mohammed V's days seemed to be numbered.

At this point the hand of the French government in Paris was forced by events in Morocco, staged by a combination of French and Moroccan conservatives. General Guillaume, the Resident General of Morocco, had been in Paris in consultation with his superiors. He hurriedly flew back to Morocco to put the finishing touches on the scheme which had been worked out in his absence.

Surrounding the palace with his troops and disarming the palace guard, he demanded the Sultan's abdication. Mohammed V refused. The Resident General then signaled his security chief, who placed his hand on the Sultan's shoulder, indicating his arrest. At this point two French officers with revolvers in their hands entered the room and escorted the Sultan to an armored car, speeding him off to the military camp at Sousse. From there he was placed in a plane and whisked off to the island of Corsica.

Back in Marrakech, Moulay Arafa, the seventy-year-old uncle of the Sultan, was installed in the place of Mohammed V. He was a kindly, courteous, respected member of the royal family who, as Sultan, would be acceptable to El Glaoui and his friends and to the French.

Surprisingly enough, there was no outbreak among the people. Either they approved of the change or they were stunned by the removal of their Sultan.

Within a month it was clear they they had been shocked into temporary silence by the removal of the Sultan, considering this act a sacrilege to their religion as well as a political move. Most of the leaders of the Istiqlal movement were in prison or in exile, but new and younger leaders came to the fore, more disposed to violence than the original leaders had been. Armed attacks on the French and on their Moroccan friends were out of the question because of their superior power in weapons. So the people resorted to other methods. The crops of French farmers were burned, trains were derailed, French shops were blown up with homemade bombs, and French people were attacked by small bands of nationalists. The mosques were nearly empty on Fridays as another sign of protest against the removal of the spiritual head of their religion.

The French officials and the French settlers bore the brunt of these attacks, but their sympathizers were also attacked. The explanation given was that "before we can attack the French, we want to deprive them of their eyes and ears."

Then a nation-wide boycott of French goods, especially of tobacco, was launched as a quiet means of showing the French the power of the Istiqlal movement.

Meanwhile, the United Nations was again considering, over the protests of France, the Moroccan question. France claimed that this was an internal matter and outside the jurisdiction of the international organization. In 1952, a mild resolution urging France and Morocco to "settle their dispute in accordance with the spirit of the charter" was passed by a vote of 45 to 3, with 11 abstentions. France was not present for the vote and only Belgium, Luxembourg, and South Africa voted against the resolution.

In 1953, the Moroccan question again came before the United Nations. The nations of the Arab-Asian bloc pointed out that the fundamental rights of the Moroccans had been diminished rather than increased since the previous year. They urged that martial law be terminated, political prisoners released, and civil liberties restored, and that complete independence be established within five years in Morocco. This resolution was adopted in the Political Committee but failed to obtain the necessary two-thirds majority in the General Assembly.

Again in 1954, the Moroccan issue came before the United

Nations, but the negotiations between France and Tunisia at that time made it possible to pass only an innocuous resolution postponing any action for the time being, in view of the negotiations between France and Morocco which several delegations felt must inevitably follow.

By the time of the 1955 General Assembly meetings of the United Nations, events in Morocco had taken a sudden and dramatic turn.

For months there had been rioting and killing in Morocco on the part of both the Moroccans and the French. There had always been a small group of liberals among the French in Morocco who condemned the actions of their fellow countrymen. Now their numbers grew, and their demands in Paris for a solution to the impasse between Morocco and France became stronger. Changes occurred on the Moroccan side of the conflict, too. In the period between 1953 and 1955 many of the Berbers came to be among the staunchest and most bitter foes of the French and many of their leaders proclaimed themselves in favor of the return of Mohammed V.

Finally, in October 1955, El Glaoui himself issued a statement, read by his son:

> I identify myself with the wish of the Moroccan nation for a prompt restoration of Sidi Mohammed ben Youssef and for his return to the throne, a return that by itself can unify hearts and spirits in harmony.

In view of his previous stand, this was an incredible turnabout. But it reflected the shift of public opinion in Morocco, even among those previously opposed to the return of the former Sultan.

Earlier that month the ruling Sultan, Arafa, had been bundled onto a plane and flown to Tangier, where he was

to occupy a palace purchased for him by the French. For
a short time a Throne Council was to rule.

In the meantime, Mohammed V and his family had been
moved to the island of Madagascar, where they had spent
the last few months in exile in an old hotel. It had not
been a grueling experience like the exile or imprisonment
which many other future leaders of new nations endured,
but neither was it a pleasant one. And it proved to be
a big mistake on the part of France, for Mohammed V's
exile increased his popularity at home and provided a rallying point for opposition to the French.

Finally, the French yielded to the inevitable, and on
October 31, 1955, they flew Mohammed V and his family
and retinue to Nice. From there the former Sultan was
brought to Paris, where he was received with all the honors
accorded royalty.

There, too, he received El Glaoui, who crawled in on
his hands and knees, bowed his head to the floor, prostrated
himself four times, and kissed the Sultan's robe, declaring
that he was "a slave at the feet of Your Majesty." What a
humiliating experience for the man who, more than any
other, had been responsible for the exile of Mohammed V!

From Paris, Mohammed V sent a message to the people
of Morocco.

We hope to see tolerance and unity prevail in a new, free, and
independent Morocco, in order that all citizens, no matter what
their religion or nationality, will feel more security for themselves, their interests, and their liberty. May our return be the
occasion for contributing to the climate of confidence necessary
for the consolidation of friendship which should unite everyone,
Moroccans and French residents in Morocco.

On November 17, 1955, in Morocco, a crowd estimated
at 100,000 greeted the Sultan and his family, applauding

and shouting their greetings. Garlands of flowers were everywhere, and pictures of the Sultan jostled with signs saying "Now We Have Our Sultan; Next We Want Independence" or "Long Live Independent Morocco."

Now events transpired with great speed. On March 2, 1956, the independence of Morocco was declared, with Mohammed V the constitutional monarch. His title was soon changed from Sultan to King. On April 7, Spain ceded Spanish Morocco in the north to the new nation. On October 26, the Free City of Tangier was added. And in November, Morocco was welcomed to the United Nations as a member of the international family of nations. Also in November, Mohammed V appointed a Consultative Assembly composed of seventy-six members, representing the major parties and interest groups in the country.

In April 1958, Morocco and Spain signed an agreement by which Morocco regained sovereignty over the former Spanish protectorate in the southern zone, thus enlarging her territory considerably.

Let us take a look at the new nation over which Mohammed V was to preside, as its spiritual and political head

Its size: Approximately the same as California.

Its location: On the northwestern tip of Africa, with the Atlantic Ocean on the west and north, the Strait of Gibraltar and the Mediterranean Sea on the north, Algeria on the east and south, and Spanish Río de Oro on the south.

Its population: Slightly over ten million persons (it is now nearly thirteen million), of whom one-third were Arabs, one-third Berbers, and one-third of diverse backgrounds.

Its religions: Most Moroccans are Moslems, many thousands are Jews, a few are Christians.

Its major cities: Casablanca, its chief port, with a present population of nearly three million and 75 per cent of the nation's industry; Marrakech and Fez, in the foothills of the Atlas Mountains; and Rabat, the capital city.

Its major mountains: The Atlas and the Anti-Atlas mountains.

Its mineral resources: Phosphates are the major source of income; large deposits of manganese, iron ore, oil, coal, zinc, cobalt, and other metals.

Its major occupations: Farming. Some mining. A little industry.

Like all nations, and like other new nations in particular, Morocco had many problems.

One of the most difficult was that of providing food for its people. For many years it was able to grow enough for its own wants and for export. But the rapid growth of population in Morocco made it necessary to import rather than to export food.

During the leadership of Mohammed V, Morocco made tremendous progress in irrigating thousands of acres of formerly unproductive land. Efforts continued toward improvement of agriculture by introducing modern methods and modern tools and by speeding the development of irrigated lands. Attention was also given to a wider diversification of crops, with the growing of cotton, rice, tobacco, sugar cane, and beets encouraged by the government.

Since 85 per cent of the people still lived on the land, measures to improve the farming practices and output of the country certainly come high on any list of priorities.

Morocco is fortunate in having considerable mineral resources, and these, too, needed to be developed. Moroccans were trained as technicians, a railroad spur was built to the coal deposits in the northeastern part of the nation, and prospecting for oil was begun.

Under the King's leadership, a five-year plan (1960–64) was set up to increase production in agriculture and industry, improve transportation and health and educational facilities.

A three-year plan (1965–67) followed with much the same objectives, including a 3½ per cent yearly increase in gross production. Increased tourism is a major goal, for Morocco's beautiful beaches and warm coastal waters, mountain skiing, folklore festivals, museums, and ancient towns and cities have a strong appeal for potential visitors.

Until independence, Moroccan industry was neglected, chiefly because the French were interested in taking the raw materials to France for processing. After independence, however, several small industries sprang up, including canneries, textile mills, sugar refineries, and cement, paint, and iron works. There are also three steel foundries and a lead smelter.

Morocco was left with a better-than-average system of transportation when the French withdrew, but it was limited largely to major roads and railroads in the north. As a free nation, she extended the road system to the south and built better connecting roads to the main highways.

In all of these efforts, however, Morocco was still handicapped by lack of capital. Unsettled political conditions there and in Algeria scared away much of the foreign capital that Morocco expected to attract.

Like other countries, Morocco needed desperately to improve her educational system. In the past most of the government workers, from high officials to postmen and clerks, were Frenchmen. Since independence, Morocco has been training administrators, technicians, and professional people.

Some idea of the progress she has been able to make in education is given by the figures of school enrollment for 1956 and for 1964:

	1956	1964
Elem. school enrollment	547,068	1,150,000
Sec. school enrollment	20,000	160,000
Tech. school enrollment	9,447	9,596
Higher schools (inc. Mohammed V Univ.)		6,979
Students abroad		2,500

In addition to these gains, approximately ten thousand volunteer teachers were enlisted to combat adult illiteracy, especially in the rural villages.

As a result of all these efforts, illiteracy fell from around 92 per cent in 1956 to approximately 85 per cent in 1965, but Morocco still has a long way to go before she achieves even a minimum education for most of her people.

Mohammed V was intensely interested in all of the problems just mentioned, but especially in the development of education. Long before independence he had used his own private funds to start schools and had urged the local *caids* to start schools too, insisting that:

> If these feudal notables spent on education half of the money they waste on feasting, Morocco would turn into a garden blossoming with the achievements of science, and our youth would acquire a culture that would enable them to contribute to the well-being of their fellow citizens.

He saw to it that his own children, boys and girls alike, received a Koranic education in their early childhood and a Western education as they grew older. He also encouraged his first son to obtain his law degree in Paris as part of his preparation for making a contribution to Moroccan life.

Asked by an American reporter what kind of education the children of Morocco needed in preparation for the next fifty years, he responded:

Spiritual values are the key to any proper education at any time and in any place, but especially now when materialism is stressed so much in some parts of the world. Youth in our country as well as around the world need to have this spiritual base. Then, with that, they need to learn to live in peace with all kinds of people or life will not be worth living. And they need to have scientific orientation, too. In fact, what they need is like a building with a spiritual base, a scientific superstructure, and with arms reaching out in many directions to the people of their own and other nations.

In health and housing, the rapidly increasing population of Morocco taxed the existing facilities and made it imperative that the nation use some of its resources and manpower to attack these problems. The problem of housing is heightened by the fact that many Moroccans are moving to the cities, living under slum conditions that have to be seen and smelled to appreciate how awful they are. Acre upon acre of shanties built of oil cans, pieces of wood, cardboard, and old rags testifies to this vast increase of population on the outskirts of the city and is in terrible contrast to the ultra-modern skyscraper apartments being built in Casablanca. The government has built thousands of small new houses for its people, but it has barely touched the problem.

Despite these enormous difficulties there were many unifying factors in Morocco on which Mohammed V could start to build a new nation. One was that almost all of the people are Moslems. A second was their pride in their past and their spirit of independence. A third was the nationalistic struggle through which they passed, with an outside enemy, France, to unite them. There are several thousand Berbers who speak only their own language, but for the most part Morocco is not plagued by the problem of many languages, as some new nations are. The improved highway system and the increased ease of transportation are also aids to building nationalism. And finally, the state radio is a promising development in reaching a large percentage of the people of this new nation.

Mohammed V himself was the personal symbol of the new Morocco and a popular figure with most people in the nation.

He was not a great orator or even a polished speaker, but his words usually carried weight because of his position and his sacrifices for the formation of Morocco.

Of Mohammed V as a politician, here is what Rom Landau, a prolific writer on Morocco, has said.

> Not conspicuously intellectual, not exceptionally well educated, Sidi Mohammed yet possesses a remarkable flair for affairs of state. His years of religious training, observation, and contemplation have given his mind both range and depth; a more thorough modern education might easily have blunted some of his perceptions.

If one had to find one word to describe King Mohammed V, that word would probably be "balancer." In many respects he was a product of the Middle East and Moslem world. He read the Koran, faithfully observing the religious practices of Islam. He spoke Arabic, and his education and life were largely limited to Morocco. He also dressed in the *djellaba* of his people. In some ways he could be criticized for being too conservative for the fast-moving events in his country, in North Africa, and in the world.

Yet he also became Western in many ways. He had a gym and swimming pool in his villa, liked to drive automobiles, and often wore Western garb. He spoke French well, having taught himself over the years. He ran his farm with modern scientific methods and constantly tried to discover the new ways opened up by science and technology with a view to introducing them in Morocco.

When asked at one time about his dreams for the future of Morocco, Mohammed V revealed this basic philosophy of balancing the old and the new by saying:

> Ours is a country with a glorious history. We intend to keep the best of our traditions—those which everyone agrees are best. But we are living in modern times and we want to learn from other countries and profit from their experiences. We want especially to learn from those nations which are spiritually and materially advanced, for they are the ones from which we can learn most. In the next fifteen to twenty years we want to synthesize the best from the past with the best from the present to develop a modern state.

It was Mohammed's dream to grant to Morocco a constitution to "allow all members of the nation to take part . . . in the conduct of their country's affairs." The first elections ever held in Morocco took place in May 1960. Between 70 and 75 per cent of the electorate cast their ballots for their representatives in local governments.

In 1961, King Mohammed V died after minor surgery. His eldest son, Hassan II, became King and Premier of Morocco. The young man had been, since 1960, Vice-Premier. One of the young King's most gratifying accomplishments was the drafting of a new constitution, such as the one his father had dreamed of, which he personally wrote. It was overwhelmingly approved in a national referendum on December 7, 1962.

BOURGUIBA
OF TUNISIA

In the middle of Tunisia's fight for independence in the early 1950s, a prominent French official said to a group of Tunisians, "Why not forget all about Bourguiba? After all, he will not be remembered in a few years."

Perhaps these words were said half in jest. Possibly they were uttered merely to discredit the leader of the independence movement. At any rate, they were fighting words to the Tunisians. How foolish could the French be? they asked.

Did they not know that Habib Bourguiba was the father of the revolution, the founder of their powerful Neo-Destour (New Constitution) party, a man who had spent a good part of his life in hiding, in prison, or in exile because of his activities on behalf of freedom for their country? Asking them to forget Bourguiba was like asking Americans to forget George Washington. And they did not forget him. They hid him when he needed to escape. They slipped food to him when he was in prison. They carried out his suggestions and commands when they were sent to them secretly by loyal followers. They even laid down their arms when he asked them to, though many of them did not believe that the French would really yield, as Bourguiba thought they would.

Then on June 1, 1955, when he returned from exile, they gave him the greatest welcome that had ever been accorded to anyone in the centuries of Tunisia's history.

Who is this man who has meant so much to Tunisia and who became one of the most prominent politicians

and statesmen in the world? How did he become so beloved by his people?

His story starts on August 3, 1903, in the small fishing
village of Monastir on the eastern coast of Tunisia, on the
Mediterranean Sea. That was the day Habib was born.
He was the youngest of seven children—two of them girls,
five of them boys.

Habib's mother died when he was very young, and at
the age of five he was sent to live with his oldest brother,
Mohammed, in the city of Tunis. There he spent his school
years. During the summer and other vacation periods, however, he returned to Monastir, an ancient walled city of
picturesque white houses with blue shutters and old Roman
baths carved out of the rocks.

Habib was not a strong boy, and in the middle of his secondary school work he became quite ill. The doctors feared
that he had tuberculosis and sent him off to the hill country to recuperate. After a few months he was able to return
to the French *lycée* to continue his studies.

His school studies were not easy for him, but Habib
was a hard worker and made a respectable record. He
completed elementary school at the age of twelve, which he
says was "too young." He liked geography and history best.
Then he moved into secondary school, where his favorite
subjects were poetry and literature, both Arabic and French.
He recalls an especially good teacher of literature, who gave
the students a free choice of passages to memorize. Often
the boys dramatized brief passages, working in groups of
three or four.

There wasn't much time for sports in a French boarding
school, but Habib did enjoy soccer, which he fitted into some
of his precious free time.

Meanwhile, he was imbibing ideas of revolution from his
family and friends. At home he learned that his grand-

father and uncle had been jailed for opposing the Bey, or ruler, of Tunisia (before the French took over control of the country in 1881) and of his father's protests against the unjust taxes his people had to pay the French.

Sometimes, as he wandered among the ruins of the monastery of Ribbat in Monastir, Habib wondered why his home town, which had once been a great center of culture, now had little but its past to talk about.

Then in 1922 he took his first action as a young revolutionary. An Arabian newspaper had printed the story of the abdication of the Bey and had consequently been suspended by French officials. Everyone knew that the story the newspaper had printed was true, but few people did anything about it. Young Habib, however, telegraphed to the French Resident General his protest over the suspension of the paper. He was only a schoolboy and no action was taken against him. Little did the French know how many more serious protests that schoolboy would make in the years ahead—and with what success.

In 1924 Habib completed secondary school and was ready to go to Paris to continue his studies. At this time the idea of helping his people was firmly in his mind. IIe did not know how, he did not know where, he did not know when this would be. But somehow, sometime, somewhere, he would help to recover the past glory of Tunisia. In some way he would help to build a better tomorrow for his people.

In Paris he studied law and political science. Often he sat in the cafés and discussed local, national, and international politics. Somehow these discussions always seemed to come around to the theme of colonialism and what to do to promote nationalism and eventual independence for Tunisia.

During those months in Paris, Bourguiba read widely

among the writings of the French philosophers of the eight-
eenth century—Voltaire, Rousseau, Diderot—and the great
figures of French literature—Molière, Hugo, Racine, Corneille.
He committed many favorite passages to memory.

Occasionally he would scrape together enough francs to
go to the theater. But the small sum of money which his
oldest brother sent him as an allowance did not go very
far, and sometimes he had to supplement it by writing for
some of the French newspapers.

In 1927 he returned to Tunis with his certificate to practice
law and his degree in political science. His wife and their
young son, Habib Jr., went with him. His wife was French,
and they had much in common, especially in their love
of literature, for she had been a teacher of literature in a
French school. Their first-born son was to become, after
Tunisia's independence, the new nation's first foreign ambassador when he went to Paris in that capacity.

Bourguiba had developed into a bright and handsome
young man, but he was not too promising as a breadwinner
for the family, for he had already developed revolutionary
ideas which might well get him into trouble later.

His wife probably had little idea when she married Habib
Bourguiba what the years ahead would bring. But she has
been a wonderful help to him throughout his turbulent
career. When he went to prison, she tried to live as near
the prison as possible. When this did not work out, she
contrived to send things to him.

Meanwhile she had to run the house on a very small
allowance from the Neo-Destour party, in which her husband was a leader. And in addition to their son, there were
always several nieces and nephews to care for, bringing
the household often to a total of twelve or fourteen persons.
But she was a skillful cook of both Arabic and French
dishes and a clever manager and hard worker. To make

matters doubly difficult, she was often snubbed by her fellow countrymen, who considered her a traitor. Was she not the wife of the leading Tunisian revolutionary?

Cut off from her own community, she developed her own circle of friends, and these women eventually became "the brain trust" of Tunisia's women, aiding much in the fight for freedom and independence.

Upon his return to Tunisia from Paris, Bourguiba took up the practice of law as a profession. He had to earn a living for himself and his family, and this was the work for which he was prepared. But his real passion was for politics. So in his spare time he wrote for the magazine *Libéral*, the organ of the Destour party, and took some part in local politics.

Soon he realized that he did not know his country well enough to function properly as a political leader. He had known something about Tunisia as a boy, but there had been many changes since he went abroad.

So he got into his seven-horsepower Peugeot and covered the entire land to rediscover his country. Tunisia is about the size of New York State, and Bourguiba traveled east and south and west and north, meeting people in the villages, on the farms, in the small towns. He learned at first hand about their problems, made his own observations, and began to shape his plans for the future.

Everywhere he went he saw the ruins of the past—relics and reminders of two thousand years of successive invasions by the Romans, the Vandals, the Byzantine Empire, the Spanish, and the Turks of the Ottoman Empire.

In the north and in the east he saw fields of wheat and barley and plots of vegetables, as well as many fine vineyards and groves of olives. But all too often he learned that these were owned by the French or others from abroad. Here was wealth, but too much of it in foreign hands.

He saw, too, deposits of phosphate used in fertilizer and in munitions—about a third of the world's supply—and some deposits of iron ore, though not of a high grade.

As he crossed central and southern Tunisia he was appalled by the poor, parched land and by the erosion which had taken place over the centuries. He began to realize that lack of water was probably the most pressing problem of Tunisia. If only wells could be dug and irrigation systems started, some of this land might be restored.

He observed on these trips also that most of the educated people lived in Tunis and other towns of the north and east. Schools must be built and teachers trained in order to raise the level of living of the more than four million inhabitants of Tunisia.

He was shocked by the status of the women of his country. Most of them were still kept indoors a large part of the time and required to wear veils when they went outside. Polygamy was still being practiced in many places. And it was the men, not the women, who profited by the laws regarding divorce. That, too, would have to be changed someday.

Even in the capital city of Tunis he noted the vast difference between conditions in the French section and those in the areas where the Tunisians lived. Moreover, almost all the government jobs were held by Frenchmen, even the small jobs, such as those of clerks and postmen.

Certainly there was much to be done to improve the lot of Tunisians in their own land. But how to do it? That was the big question.

One way was to get people thinking and talking about their problems. That could best be done through speeches and newspaper articles. He had already written some for *Libéral*. But the men who ran that journal were too conservative, too cautious. So Bourguiba and his friends started a paper known as the *Voix du Tunisien*. It ran for a few months and then had to be discontinued. So they started another journal, known as *L'Action Tunisienne*.

Perhaps the difference between these two titles indicates the way in which Bourguiba's mind was turning. He was less and less interested in airing opinions, more and more interested in action.

A second way to tackle the problems of Tunisia was to organize the people. At first Bourguiba worked with members of the Destour party, but soon he became dissatisfied. As he became more and more aware of their strategy, he realized that "they limited their action to protest—solemn protest—solemn articles on paper—solemn telegrams—but without doing anything serious to impress the French."

So he and some of his friends cut their ties with this conservative group and established the Neo-Destour party, a party which would press for action, fight for the freedom of Tunisia, push for the independence of the country.

From that time on Bourguiba was a marked man. In the eyes of the French he was the leader of a dangerous movement, and the best place for such a person was in prison. So for the next twenty years he spent most of his time in prison, in hiding, or in exile. The measure of the man is found in the indomitable courage and spirit with which he faced that terrible period in his life.

In September 1933, *L'Action Tunisienne* was suppressed, and Bourguiba and his colleagues were sent to a camp, called Borj-LeBoeuf, on the edge of the Sahara. There they lived, unprotected from the summer's heat and the winter's cold. They had to carry their own water, feed themselves on the few francs that were allotted for food, and cook their own meals. But in their spare time they could discuss their plans for the future and conduct classes to keep their minds occupied.

Among the group interned in the camp were some of Bourguiba's closest friends. His brother Mohammed was there —until he signed a paper promising not to engage in politics again and was freed. His old friend of Paris days, Dr. Materi, was there, and this was a great boon to Bourguiba, for he had always looked upon the doctor as a kind of father and wise counselor. Also in the camp was Salah ben Youssef, an active revolutionist—smart, courageous, and realistic, but also ambitious, jealous, and desirous of having money, power, and pleasure—a man about whom we will hear more later.

Eventually this group of agitators was moved to another camp and then in 1936 they were freed by a new Resident General.

The next two years were busy ones for Bourguiba and his friends. The people of Tunisia needed to be aroused from centuries of slumber. They needed to be organized. Little could be accomplished by a small group of leaders. To be effective there must be a mass movement.

So Bourguiba toured Tunisia again, talking to the people about their ancient history and their present problems. He painted a picture of life as it could be if they were masters of their own land.

Everywhere he went he organized local cells of the Neo-Destour party. Soon the party was no longer based on the efforts of one man or a group of men. It became a democratic organization with a membership of around 100,000, well organized and well disciplined, with units in every part of the nation. Here was the strength needed to conduct mass demonstrations and to carry on strikes. Here was power— power from the people.

This strong party organization had not come any too soon, for in 1938 Bourguiba was arrested again. Back he went to prison to spend the next five years in confinement or in exile. While he was away, he kept in touch with the leaders as best he could. But he was confident that the movement would go on without him under the able leadership of his lieutenants.

Being separated from his co-workers at this time was a great trial to him, for these were important years in the Neo-Destour party's history and in the history of the independence movement for Tunisia. But he kept up his courage and optimism. At one point, in 1942, he wrote a letter which he thought might possibly be his last political will and testament to the party leaders.

Twice during this period he narrowly escaped death. Once it was rumored that there had been found on an Italian courier a letter in which Bourguiba called for an open revolution against the French. A few days later his wife and son were told to report to the prison gates to claim his body. But when they arrived, they discovered to their great joy that the French Governor had decided that he had enough evidence of Bourguiba's guilt to have an open trial and expose him to the general public. At the trial, Bourguiba proved that the letter was a forgery.

On some occasions, Bourguiba seems to have had a charmed life. For example, in 1942, during World War II, he was lined up against the wall for execution by the French. Just at that moment German staff cars entered the prison grounds, as the Nazis took over this section of France from the Vichy government.

The Germans and Italians thought that they could make Bourguiba a collaborator by promoting Tunisian independence after the war. They took him to Italy and treated him as if he were royalty or the head of an independent state. But their efforts were fruitless. All through the war he had maintained that the Allies should win and would win, and had urged his followers to support them. He was not willing now to support Germany and Italy, even if they promised him the one thing which he wanted most in the world— Tunisian independence. At the close of World War II, Tunisia was returned to France.

Back in Tunisia, Bourguiba tried to carry on discussions concerning independence with the French authorities, but became discouraged over the possibilities. It was during this period that his friend, Farhat Hached, established in Tunisia the powerful labor union called the Union Générale des Travailleurs Tunisiens, or General Union of Tunisian Workers. From the time of its formation, it has been one of the most powerful allies of the Neo-Destour party.

By this time Bourguiba had become convinced that he needed the support of other nations if he were to succeed in gaining more freedom for Tunisia. Why not turn to the Moslem countries of the Middle East?

And so in 1945 he set out for that part of the world. The French would certainly not permit such a visit if they knew about it, so he arranged with a fisherman to take him by boat to Libya. From there he crossed the wide expanse of that country, largely on foot. It was a grueling and hazardous journey of thirty days, but he finally arrived in Egypt. For a while it looked as if he were in for further trouble, for he was picked up by the police without a passport to identify himself. He was able to establish his identity, however, and was freed.

During the next few months he tried to win support for his movement but found little knowledge of or interest in Tunisia in the Middle East. He made a trip to Mecca, the holy place of the Moslem world, spent a short time in Europe and another brief period in the United States, where his aim was to contact various delegations to the newly formed United Nations.

But these were largely months of waiting, waiting, waiting.

Finally, in 1949, he returned to Tunisia and was accorded a tremendous reception as he visited many parts of the country and talked to party leaders and with the people. He was pleased to find that the party had continued to grow, even as an underground movement, and to find that the labor union formed by his friend Hached had become a potent influence in Tunisia.

After five months of such activities, Bourguiba went to Paris and tried to gain further concessions there. He met with some success and in July 1949 a new cabinet, sponsored by the Neo-Destour party, was formed in Tunis.

Meanwhile several nations had received their freedom, and Bourguiba felt that he should try to win further support throughout the world for an independent Tunisia. In 1951 he toured the world, visiting Pakistan, Turkey, India, England, and the United States.

But by December of that year, he hit another snag. The French government rejected further proposals for local autonomy and said it intended to keep Tunisia under French rule indefinitely.

What next? Where should Tunisia turn now? Perhaps the United Nations would be the best place to present its claims against France. On January 14, 1952, the Tunisian government made an appeal to the UN. For weeks her case was debated, and finally a weak resolution was adopted urging France to examine carefully her relations with Tunisia.

The French were unhappy over this turn of events. In retaliation, they arrested the leaders of the Neo-Destour party and clamped down on the population of Tunisia. Bourguiba was the chief troublemaker in their eyes and so he was shipped off to La Galite, an island north of Tunisia, where he was placed in solitary confinement. Thinking that even that spot might be too close to his homeland, they transferred him to Groix, an island off the coast of France.

These were probably the most difficult months in Bourguiba's life. The physical conditions were the worst that he had had to endure, and he felt that recent events had set the freedom movement back considerably. Yet most of the time he was his own confident, optimistic self.

Events soon proved that the efforts of the past years had not been in vain. The people of Tunisia kept up their resistance despite great odds, and public opinion around the world began to turn against France. Even within France there were many people who felt that her policy had to be changed.

During the summer of 1954 Pierre Mendès-France became Prime Minister in France, and he decided that the French must yield on the Tunisian question. On July 31 he flew to Tunis and issued what was known as the Declaration of Carthage, granting Tunisia the right to rule herself internally.

There were those who said that that was not enough, but Bourguiba urged them to accept this offer and to work for full independence later. His views won, and on June 1, 1955, he returned to his homeland to be enthusiastically received by half a million people in the capital city.

Early in 1956 new negotiations were begun in Paris, and on March 20 an agreement was signed by France and Tunisia, establishing full independence for that former territory.

The people of Tunisia then voted in their first general election for a Constituent Assembly, and Bourguiba was elected President of it by acclamation. On April 16, 1956, he formed the first government of independent Tunisia. The new nation became a member of the United Nations in November 1956.

One might think that one who had fought the French so

many years and had been imprisoned by them so long would be bitter against them. But that was not the case with Bourguiba, for bitterness has never been a part of his make-up.

All through these years of struggle he has maintained his regard for the French and his love of French culture, even though he has deplored the actions of French politicians. Why? Probably because he was educated in French schools in Tunisia and in France and has always had regard for French writers and thinkers. He also developed a belief that the best way to achieve his goals was through co-operation and negotiation rather than through military force and bitterness. An understanding of that philosophy helps one to understand Bourguiba's actions and attitudes.

In his message to the people of Tunisia upon his return in 1955, for example, he declared:

> Now that I am returning to my country after a struggle of so many years for our national ideal, and after all the painfully tragic events which have so profoundly disturbed our national life, I should like in my first words to you, my Tunisian brothers, and to you, my French and European friends destined to live together with us on our traditionally hospitable soil, to call upon you to establish harmony, to appease your spirits, and to forget the conflicts and quarrels of yesterday.

A near parallel is found in the words of Abraham Lincoln in his second inaugural address, when he pleaded for a spirit of "malice toward none, with charity for all."

There was a practical side to Bourguiba's plea, too, for he knew that without French money, French technicians, some French government officials, many French teachers, and at least some of the French farmers, the country could not move forward rapidly.

Some of the French left the country at the time of independence, but most of them stayed. The same was true of other Europeans—the Italian wine-growers, the Maltese shop-keepers and craftsmen, the Greek sponge fishers, and the Jewish tradesmen.

To all of them, Bourguiba said:

We are all Tunisians now, whether we are French or Arab, Christian or Moslem or Jew. We are all children of one coun-try, and all of us must work together for the good of all.

In the same vein he enlarged the circle to include people in other parts of the world, saying:

We must respect everyone who lives on this earth, be he French or foreigner. We must treat him as a brother so long as he re-spects our freedom, our personality, and our dignity.

These were not mere words. They are basic beliefs of this man Bourguiba.

Another of his firm beliefs is the importance of youth. As he has pointed out:

Educated young men furnish the most active recruits to the nationalist cause, and it is from their ranks that we must draw the governing class of tomorrow. These young men must lead and educate the masses, develop their feelings of patriotism and civic responsibility, and endow them with moral principles to such an extent that the interests of the nation as a whole seem more important than class struggles.

In politics he early turned away from Communism as the method of bringing change. As far back as his student days in Paris, he rejected the wooing of the Communists and the theories of Marx, Engels, and Lenin. He has said: Com-munism may be good for some countries, but it is not a regime fit for us."

Upon several occasions he has warned the Western powers

that if he did not receive more help from them he would have to turn to the Communist countries, but he has been extremely patient in many instances in waiting for help from his friends.

He has been well aware, however, that being anti-Communist was not enough. As he has phrased it:

> To keep free of Communism, Arab nationalism must not content itself solely with an assertion of its rights. It must remake the economic and social structure of the Arab countries. . . .

One well-known journalist has said that Bourguiba has two great qualities in abundance—patience and logic. Another writer has come to almost the same conclusion, saying:

> In the history of the Arab national movement, it has always been difficult to find a mean between the well-heeled conservative politicians like the Egyptians Wafd—men of democratic speeches and large motor cars—and the frustrated, explosive, and often murderously revolutionary lower-middle-class radicals, whose nationalism is near nihilistic. Bourguiba seems to be this missing middle term. In a political milieu which is everywhere else destructive and fanatical, he is a reformist, and conciliatory.

But how does a man develop such a philosophy of government and of life? When Bourguiba was asked to explain where his ideas came from, he mentioned first of all his father and his oldest brother. Of them he said that they were "proud, honest, responsible, and very original." They instilled in him the idea of doing his duty without talking much about it. To them he also has said that he owed his idea of sensitivity to injustice—looking out for every man, woman, and child to whom wrong has been done.

Then, too, he has said that he was much influenced by his reading of literature and philosophy, especially the writings of Rousseau. From this reading his own ideals of courage, perseverance, and stoicism were further nurtured.

Referring to other sources of his ideas, he has said:

> Yes, I have learned much from history. I have been especially interested in people who have changed their countries—like Caesar, Napoleon, and Garibaldi. As a boy I was much impressed with the story of Kemal Ataturk, and I often wondered how he had managed to change Turkey so greatly. There was a country which had been great and had fallen into decay, but Ataturk was able to rebuild it. Only later did I learn that some of his methods were not good. Still, he was a great reformer in the Moslem world.

And of course that last fact appealed to Bourguiba, for he, too, is a member of the extensive Moslem world.

Bourguiba says that he has studied the work of other leaders and learned something from each of them. He has admired Bolivar and his work for freedom in South America, but Bolivar's methods were those of a military leader fighting against a military power far away. He respected Gandhi, but his methods were primarily religious and the man was a saint, which made his tactics immensely difficult for ordinary men to imitate. He felt that Nehru was closer to being a practical model of leadership, but Bourguiba's part of the world has a very different history and geography from India's, so he could not emulate Nehru.

The result has been that Bourguiba has developed a philosophy and a methodology which are his own. Perhaps they can be summarized best in the phrase "moderate revolutionary." His political philosophy is known as Bourguibism.

However, it is the man much more than the methods which has appealed to the people of Tunisia.

Bourguiba's first name, Habib, means "the loved one," and that is how he has been viewed by a large number of his people. What is there in this man that appeals to them?

Of course different characteristics appeal to different people, but here are a few of them:

Some like his looks. He is short and stocky and quite handsome. He has piercing eyes, and he knows how to use his hands eloquently to drive home his points.

Some like his sense of the dramatic. At a press conference at the time of independence, he entered the room and sat down at his desk. Everyone expected him to begin speaking immediately. But not Bourguiba. There was a long pause and absolute quiet. He twirled his glasses. Then he began at one corner of the room and eyed each reporter, as if to size up the situation. Then he started to speak. That is the drama in the man. Or at public meetings he seems to sense the exact moment to arrive—and to leave—for the greatest effect.

Some like his simplicity. For even though he was a poor boy and might well have longed for the "good things of life," he has always lived simply. So simply, in fact, that some of his admirers like to compare him with Gandhi in his disregard for possessions.

Some like his friendliness and his generosity. Everywhere he goes he seeks out people. Sometimes they are important personages, more often they are simple, ordinary folk. He may have only a moment to chat with them, but they feel that he is their friend. And often he does share what he has with all manner of people. It may be an old friend of the family who comes to see him, a student who pays him a visit, or a fellow fighter in the resistance movement. If he finds they need clothes, he will remember that he has an old suit or some shirts they could use. If he decides that they need money, he will always have some in his pocket which he urges them to take. If it is a farmer who has suffered from a drought on his farm, he will pen a note to someone to see that he gets assistance.

Some like his speaking ability. There he is a master. He

speaks over the radio to the people of Tunisia and makes many other talks during a year. He rarely writes out a speech or even makes notes. Instead, he sits for a long time, going over what he will say in his mind, waiting for the spontaneity of the moment and his speaking ability to carry the message across.

These and other characteristics have made him a hero to the Tunisians. They have already turned his birthplace into a national shrine and have named an avenue or street in nearly every village and town after him. Crowds assemble twice daily at the presidential palace to see him enter and depart, and when he goes to the mosque there is a crowd there, too, to see him.

As one commentator has written: "He teases them and they tease him. He cultivates a relationship of camaraderie. He lifts the veil of an Arab woman and jokingly tells her she should reveal 'that lovely face.' He picks up children, slaps their bottoms, throws his arm around the shoulders of a delighted Arab worker or farmer, listens attentively to problems and complaints and fears."

He is warm, human, genuine. The people sense that and love him. In crowds they shout, "Yah, yah, Bour-gui-BA. Yah, yah, Bour-gui-BA." And in private they talk about him affectionately.

He needs to be adept in convincing people, for the Tunisians are a difficult people to convince. Centuries of rule by foreigners have made them wary, cautious, and at times defeatist in their philosophy. Bourguiba has restored their confidence in themselves. He has rebuilt their national pride and national feeling. He has recovered for them their dreams for the future. Above all, he is the man "who has never let us down."

Behind him is this powerful personal support of loyal individuals. But behind him there is also the strong support of organizations. One of these is the well-knit Neo-Destour party. Another is the UGTT Labor Federation. A third is the Union Générale des Étudiants Tunisiens (The General Union of Tunisian Students). A fourth group consists of the former resistance fighters, many of whom are members of some of these other organizations.

Of course not everyone is fond of Bourguiba, and even his best friends know that he has faults. He is an impatient and intense man who sizes up situations quickly and expects others to react as quickly as he does. Even some of those who work closest to him admit that he is not a good administrator and does not know how to delegate responsibility.

Some critics go farther. They say that he is a demagogue, playing on the emotions of the people, and that he is interested more in himself than in the nation.

Others say that he is too changeable, blowing hot and then cold. They point out that he has made statements one day which are pro-French and a few days later statements which are strongly anti-French. They claim that they do not know where the man stands on many issues.

The most virulent criticism of his entire career was based on his relation to the so-called rebels in Algeria, who were fighting for Algeria's independence from France. Many Tunisians felt that he did not take a firm enough stand on aiding them and that he thus played into the hands of the French.

On the whole, however, Bourguiba is one of the most popular rulers in the world today. In 1964 he was re-elected President for a five-year term by over 96 per cent of the voters. He needs all this support; for a man is likely to lose some of his friends when the going gets rough.

And problems there are—galore.

Although Tunisia is much more advanced politically than most of the new nations and somewhat more advanced economically and socially than these other new countries, she has a long way to go to establish herself on a sound footing.

When Bourguiba took over the reins of government an army had to be organized, local and regional governments established, a court system reorganized. In addition, a federal government had to be set up. Each of these has been done with considerable speed and efficiency. In the organization of the courts the centuries-old religious courts were abolished, which was a blow to conservative religious leaders, but met with little opposition elsewhere.

At the insistence of Bourguiba, polygamy was abolished and divorce was made easier for women. These were revolutionary measures, for Turkey is the only other Moslem country which has abolished polygamy, and in the other nations of the Moslem world the divorce laws are still much more favorable to men than to women.

These radical changes were possible in Tunisia only because its Moslems are not as orthodox as those in other countries, because the church officials are not so powerful, and because Bourguiba and other nominal Moslems with a Western education have pressed for such reforms for a long time.

France left Tunisia with many miles of good roads, several good harbors, and a fairly good railroad system. In these resources she had a good start, and there has been progress since independence, especially in the building of new roads and in the improvement of older ones as a vital aid to the transport of goods and of people.

Tunisia's biggest problem is unquestionably how to increase agricultural production, for she is primarily an agricultural country. Her land is still concentrated in the hands of the French and a few rich Tunisian landowners, and her laws regarding land ownership need revision. She needs more land for the landless and better land for all. Above all, this program requires more wells and more irrigation, especially in the arid regions of central and southern Tunisia.

In this large area of economics, the new government has made considerable progress. It has continued a vast plan for the development of the Medjerda Valley in the north, which was started before the French left. This large undertaking has already brought new land under cultivation by the reclamation of salt marshes, drained many more acres which were formerly lost to agriculture, irrigated thousands of acres of land which was too dry to farm, and added much new land through soil conservation.

In addition, some changes have been made in the land laws, and new land in other parts of the country has been given to the landless, with preference to families of former resistance fighters.

Some attention has likewise been given to the distribution of better seeds, to the construction of grain storage facilities, and to the introduction of tractor pools in which farmers join together to purchase equipment which they could not afford individually.

In 1965, Tunisia embarked on a ten-year development plan. The International Bank for Reconstruction and Development promised credits of $100,000,000 toward the support of the plan.

In 1966, an Italian-owned company discovered large petroleum deposits in the southwest, on the Algerian border. This was an important "find" for Tunisia. The oil should bring in millions of dollars to the country, for it will not only supply Tunisia's domestic needs but leave plenty of surplus for export.

Tunisia's Atomic Energy Commission is planning to establish a pilot plant for the extraction of uranium from two recently discovered sources. One source is a phosphate deposit, which yields one hundred grams of uranium per ton, a second is a mineral deposit which contains over five hundred grams per ton.

Another favorable financial prospect for Tunisia lies in the tourist trade, in which Bourguiba is very much interested, for he sees its possibilities. Tunisia's tourist attractions include many miles of magnificent, unspoiled sandy beaches, the fascinating Roman ruins to be found in this country, which was once one of the richest areas of the Roman Empire, and its ancient, walled towns with their narrow, winding streets. Bourguiba's government has invested several million dollars in hotel construction, road improvement, airport enlargement, and extension of electrical supply lines—all to make travel easy and pleasant for visitors. These efforts have paid off. In a recent year, about 150,000 tourists spent over fourteen million dollars in Tunisia.

Bourguiba is working toward associate membership for Tunisia in the European Common Market, to which he feels his country has much to contribute and from which it has much to gain.

In this connection it is revealing to note some of the Tunisian exports which have increased in quantity in recent years. They include livestock, sponges, fresh vegetables, fruits (of which the increase has been very large), olive oil, canned fish and shell fish, macaroni, jams and fruit juices, and cement.

In education the problems have been to increase the number of school buildings, to find enough teachers for the rapidly growing school population, and to persuade girls as well as boys to attend school, especially secondary schools. This is the field in which the government has probably made the greatest gains, as the people are eager for more education if the facilities can be provided. Figures on the number of children attending school are only one index of the changes under way, but they are an important indication of progress.

In 1883 there were only 3000 children in school in all of Tunisia. By 1911 the total had jumped to 40,000. By 1936 it had grown to 92,000. By 1957 it had leaped to 265,000, and in 1963 there were over 575,000 children in school, by far the largest number being in the primary grades. One can imagine the problems of providing buildings and teachers for increases like that. In the first year of the new government, five hundred new schools were opened and five hundred new teachers trained as part of the effort to keep up with the demands of the people for more schooling.

Bourguiba has had to make wise and courageous decisions in foreign policy as well. During the war between France and Algeria, Tunisia was in a tight spot. Tunisia's next-door neighbor is Algeria, and the Algerians are their friends. Moreover, they were fighting a battle against the French which was similar to the one Tunisia had to fight before winning her independence. In most ways the fight of the Algerians was harder, for France was much more reluctant to yield in Algeria than she was in Tunisia.

As in so many other cases throughout his life, Bourguiba was the man in the middle. On the one hand he was definitely pro-Algerian. On many occasions he proclaimed his sympathies for her: "We give the insurgents what help we can, short of war. . . . We are not neutral. . . ."

But at the same time he tried to prevail upon the Algerians to accept limited autonomy or partial independence as a first step toward complete independence. What he feared was that the Algerians would turn in desperation to Nasser or to the Communists. Bourguiba was opposed, of course, to the Nasserites and to the Communists. He knew that either group would smash his dream of Maghreb, a North African Federation of Morocco, Algeria, Tunisia, and Libya.

His support of the Algerians cost Bourguiba a great deal.

France withdrew much of her financial aid to Tunisia, and he had to turn elsewhere for help. He received considerable aid from the United States, but not enough.

In 1961, France ended its exhausting war in Algeria and withdrew from the country. Thus one of Bourguiba's problems was solved.

Pressures inside the country and pressures from outside caused Tunisia to join the Arab League in the fall of 1958. But within two weeks Tunisia had walked out of the sessions of that body and had cut off diplomatic relations with Egypt, charging her with providing asylum for the exiled Tunisian leader, Ben Youssef, and with plotting the assassination of Bourguiba. At the time of this rupture, Bourguiba spoke out against the Communists, warning that "once the Iron Curtain drops, there is no escape from Communism." He thereby implied strongly that Nasser and the Egyptians were already in the grip of the Communists.

Bourguiba continues to be opposed to the Arab League for reasons which he frankly states. In a long memorandum sent to the heads of state attending the third Arab summit meeting in Casablanca in 1965, he wrote:

> The Arab League itself is considered by Egypt as a provisional body to be used when it is felt necessary to bring the Arab states together. But Egypt does not regard the League as capable by itself of ensuring the fulfillment of the Egyptian revolution. . . . Only Egypt has the right to take initiatives and to lay down a policy to be followed . . . without confidence there can be no Arab League, no sincere brotherhood, and no fruitful co-operation. We think that if there is lack of confidence it mainly springs from the Egyptian ideas about Arab unity. . . . The movement of history is a race we must win and the leaders have an important part to play in winning this race. Through their wisdom, patience, and imagination, they can direct the course of events and speed up the pace of evolution.

Tunisia and Egypt broke off diplomatic relations in the spring of 1965.

With so many problems to face and such an intense interest in all of them, it is no wonder that Bourguiba is eager to get home in the evening and enjoy the beautiful house and gardens in the suburb of Sayda, where he lives. It is a restful spot, with a long lane flanked by giant geraniums, a yard filled with orange trees, cypress trees, and bushy African pines, and flowers everywhere. His home is a large, comfortable, attractive house with whitewashed walls and blue shutters, much like the house in which he lived as a boy. In front it looks out on the Mediterranean Sea, and from the porch one can see the ruins of ancient Carthage, the center of an empire in the days of Tunisia's former greatness.

It is a relaxing atmosphere, where Bourguiba entertains his friends, sees an occasional film, goes horseback riding, or walks around the garden, along the sea, or through the ruins of ancient Carthage. Here he gathers strength for solving the problems that face him daily as he continues to build a better Tunisia.

NASSER
OF THE
UNITED ARAB REPUBLIC

The Middle East has for some time been a giant bowling alley, with governments falling or tottering like tenpins. The title of champion political bowler in that strategic area unquestionably belongs to Gamal Abdel Nasser of the United Arab Republic, which was formerly known as Egypt.

Like that of any successful champion, Nasser's success has come from a combination of skill and practice, plus an unusual amount of good luck. Whether he will continue to hold his title or be replaced by a new champion is uncertain. But regardless of what the future may bring to him or his country, Nasser's record to date has been a remarkable one.

In 1952, Nasser and his teammates took over control of Egypt, ousting the corrupt playboy, King Farouk. Four years later, they seized the Suez Canal and nationalized it. For this they were attacked by the combined forces of France, Great Britain, and Israel, and were saved from defeat by the intervention of the United Nations, with both the United States and Russia supporting Egypt.

In 1958, Nasser and his team made even greater headway. In February they accepted Syria's plea to unite with that country and formed the new nation known as the United Arab Republic. In March, the little country of Yemen joined the U.A.R. in a federation called the United Arab States. And in March of that year King Saud of Saudi Arabia turned over much of his power to Crown Prince Faisal, a man much more sympathetic to Nasser than King Saud had been.

In May of 1958, anti-government forces in Lebanon, which were also pro-Nasser, started a civil war and eventually ended President Chamoun's attempt to change the constitution so that he could be re-elected for a second term. In July of that year pro-Nasser forces seized power in Iraq and not only toppled the government of that country, but terminated the newly formed anti-Nasser merger of Iraq and Jordan known as the Arab Federation.

Meanwhile, there were repercussions of these Nasser victories in many other places, including Aden, Jordan, Kuwait, Libya, the Sudan, and as far west in Africa as Algeria, where the rebel forces were receiving considerable aid from the Nasser government in their fight against the French.

Anyone who can pile up a string of victories like that must be an unusual human being, and Nasser is just that. How he came to acquire such power is quite a story.

He was born on January 15, 1918, in the ancient city of Alexandria, Egypt, while World War I was still raging. His family background was not unusual. His father was a minor civil servant in the Egyptian postal system, and his mother was the daughter of an Alexandrian contractor. They were members of the lower middle class and had to work hard to survive, as did so many million Egyptians. Writing later about his people, Nasser said, "We all formed one family and the lords of the earth treated us as slaves."

The part of Egypt in which they lived was rich from the alluvial deposits of the Nile River, but it was crowded, too. Parts of the delta area had as many as thirteen thousand persons to the square mile. No wonder there was little wealth except for a few landlords and the royal family.

Gamal entered school at the age of eight, first in Alexandria and then in Cairo, where he completed his secondary school work.

As he looks back on his childhood, he remembers very little about school. That did not loom large on his horizon. But he remembers vividly the political atmosphere of those days, recalling how he would look at the planes in the sky and shout at them, "Almighty, may a calamity betake the English!"

The Egyptians were smarting then under the rule of the British, their latest conquerors in a long list of invaders, which included Persians, Greeks, Romans, Arabs, Turks, Mamelukes, French, and British over a period of nearly twenty-five hundred years. So it was natural that a small boy would absorb some of the political discontent and hurl such curses at the British aviators who represented the oppressors.

On December 2 of each year he went on strike with his fellow students as a protest against the Balfour Declaration of 1917 which promised the Jews a national home in Palestine. He also took part in other demonstrations and street fights. The first real tussle came when he was fourteen years old, and he still carries a scar from that early fight.

As a university student he took part in student demonstrations and on one occasion was tossed into jail. He was there only a day, but it left an indelible impression upon his mind and increased his hatred of the monarchy which would permit such events.

His work as a political leader lay far in the future, but he was already being prepared by such indoctrination against colonialism.

Meanwhile, his education continued. His father wanted him to become a government official; his mother wanted him to become a lawyer. Nasser adored his mother and it was her more ambitious plan which won, at least for a time. He wrote her regularly of his successes and failures, until one day his father sent word that she was too busy to write. He wondered about this strange turn of events but did not learn the real reason until he returned home at the end of the year—to discover that she had died.

His father had not wanted him to stop his studies and so had concocted this strange excuse for the absence of letters from her.

When Nasser had first applied to the police and military academies, he had been turned down and had studied law instead. Later he was able to wangle entrance to the military academy, from which he graduated in 1938.

During this training period he became bitterly disillusioned by conditions in the new army which the British had allowed the Egyptians to organize as a result of a treaty in 1936. Most of its officers were still British, augmented by some Egyptians, largely from the landowning aristocracy. Their military strategy was archaic and their weapons outmoded, and Nasser and many of his friends were disgusted with the training. But they stuck it out, and Nasser rose to the rank of quartermaster sergeant in 1937.

Upon completion of his training, he was sent south to the Sudan to do garrison duty. While there he led a revolt against the senior officers—the first of a long series of intrigues in which he was to take part.

The next ten years were uneventful ones—at least on the surface. During the day he was an instructor in the staff college, lecturing and drilling. But his real work went on in the evenings. Then he would gather a small group of young officers around him, talking with them about the future of Egypt, about the idea of revolution, and about the strategy of change. Or he would produce and distribute tracts on Egypt and its future.

The idea of revolution was still stirring in his mind and he was looking for others who combined an intense spirit of patriotism with intelligence and courage. He would toss a provocative question at a group of young officers and sit back and watch their reactions. When he spotted a young man who met his requirements, he would cultivate his friendship and eventually invite him to join the group of future revolutionaries.

In those early years Nasser and his friends maintained contact with any group that was interested in freedom for Egypt, including the right-wing Moslem Brotherhood and the left-wing Communists. But when the Communists approached him to join their party, he refused, saying he "could not take orders out of the unknown."

At the age of twenty-six Nasser married the daughter of a merchant whose family came originally from Iran. His wife is retiring and quite content to keep in the background, maintaining a pleasant home for their two sons and three daughters. Theirs is a close-knit family group. They live in an old, unpretentious house in the suburbs of Cairo, rather than in one of the ancient royal palaces reserved for him as President of the United Arab Republic.

The big turning point in Nasser's life came with the granting of independence to Israel in 1948. This was the event that the Arabs had dreaded ever since the Balfour Declaration had been announced. To them this was a direct attack on the Arab people, depriving them of the land which they had owned for hundreds of years. Here was an alien group in their midst, established not merely as settlers, but as a full-fledged nation.

In 1948, Nasser found himself involved in a large-scale attack on this new state of Israel, and discovered that the Israeli soldiers were far better trained and equipped than the Arabs. Thus the Israelis were able to repel the invaders in almost every part of their new country.

Nasser's unit was surrounded at Faluja, a few miles from Gaza, and was probably saved only by the truce arranged by the United Nations. While in the trenches there, he thought about the reasons for their defeat—the lack of ammunition, inferior arms, and many ill-trained officers. He said to himself: "Here we are in these underground holes, besieged. We were cheated into a war unprepared and our destinies have been the playthings of passions, plots, and greed. Here we lie under fire, unarmed."

Then, he says, his mind would jump back to Egypt and he would think: "There is our mother country, a far, far bigger Faluja. What is happening in Palestine is but a miniature picture of what is happening in Egypt. Our mother country has likewise been besieged by difficulties as well as ravaged by an enemy. She was cheated and pushed to fight unprepared. Greed, intrigue, and passion have toyed with her and left her under fire, unarmed."

He began to see what the real battle was in Egypt. He saw that his homeland had to be saved from itself before it could defeat others. The men who had supplied inferior and even defective weapons in order to make profits out of the Palestinian war must be driven out. The grafters in public office must be dismissed. The problems of food and people, of land ownership, of health and education, must be tackled. Demonstrations and assassinations might be necessary, but they were not enough. More positive action had to be taken.

All this led to the formation in 1950 of the Free Officers Committee, a group of men in their thirties and early forties, most of them under the rank of major. These men planned and plotted to overthrow the corrupt regime which was then in control of Egypt and discussed what to do once they had achieved power.

The palace soon learned of their existence and laid plans to capture them. But the Free Officers moved first. During the night of July 22 and 23, 1952, special squads seized the approaches to Cairo, rounded up the top generals and colonels of the army, and gained control of the palace itself.

This was a bloodless revolution, and within a short time King Farouk was ousted, the constitution suspended, and a republic established. Farouk, the Queen, and their seven-month-old son went into exile, taking over two hundred trunks of their possessions with them, but leaving behind stacks of comic books, hundreds of suits, and one of the largest collections of pornographic pictures and literature in the world.

The revolution had overturned the inefficient and corrupt government, but it had proved a disappointment to Nasser and his friends. They had expected a groundswell of support from the Egyptian masses. In Nasser's words, here is what actually happened:

> We needed discipline, but found chaos behind our lines. We needed unity, but found dissension. We needed action, but found nothing but surrender and idleness.

It is not surprising, therefore, that Nasser chose as the slogan of the Revolution the three key words "Unity, Discipline, and Labor," dramatizing them by three interlocking rings. These were the three things which were needed desperately if Egypt was to pole-vault into the twentieth century.

At this stage in his career Nasser was still content to stay in the background and to let others perform the public work and receive the public acclaim. At the head of the new government the Free Officers Committee placed Major General Mohammed Naguib, a quiet, hard-working, self-effacing older man of action, who was popular with the masses.

This combination of Naguib and Nasser made an excellent team. Each man complemented the other. Nasser was strong in theories and in organizational ability, and Naguib was strong as an administrator and as a popular figure with the people.

By 1954, however, Naguib had lost favor with the ruling clique. He was ousted and placed under house arrest for ten years. Just why this happened is not yet fully known and may never be. Some people believe it was the pressure of the army for more drastic action than he was willing to take. Some say that it was the disagreement between Naguib and Nasser over the speed with which parliamentary government should be restored, with Naguib calling for more speedy action than Nasser. Others say it was largely due to differences in temperament and jealousy between the two top men in Egypt.

Nasser's own terse comment on Naguib was that "he was a good man, though a simple one. He was really ignorant. Power spoiled him." That is one explanation, but hardly a sufficient one.

Now in full control of the Egyptian government, Nasser needed to turn his attention to the economic and social revolution which must accompany every political revolution if permanent changes are to be accomplished. The Naguib-Nasser-Free Officers group had already made a start in the fall of 1952; now they needed to accelerate the rate of change.

The conditions which confronted them were staggering.

Egypt (now called the United Arab Republic) is about the size of California, Arizona, and New Mexico combined, but 95 per cent of it is a vast desert. Consequently, the nearly thirty million inhabitants are crowded into a very small part of the country. Millions of them are concentrated in the rich delta area in the north of Egypt, and other millions jostle one another in the twelve- to fifteen-mile strip of green land on either side of the Nile River which looks like a narrow green carpet running through a brown countryside. The population density of the country as a whole is more than two thousand people per square mile.

Thirty million people, increasing about one million per year, are too many for a land like that. It meant that most of them lived a grim existence, eating two thousand calories a day when they should have had three thousand or more, living an average of forty years when they ought to have lived to seventy, and earning about one hundred dollars a year per person instead of much, much more.

Two-thirds of the people in Egypt live in villages, most of which consist of a few mud huts that look from the air like gray or brown crusted wasp nests. The water which the people drank before the Revolution in 1952 was almost always polluted, with the result that about 60 per cent of them were victims of bilharziasis, a water-borne disease. Flies and filth were common and accounted for the high incidence of trachoma, an eye disease especially prevalent in Egypt.

Before the Revolution, men, women, and children were slaves to the soil, to the wealthy landowners, and to un-scrupulous moncylenders. Approximately half of the peas-ants did not own any land but spent their lives scratching the soil with sticks or driving their water buffalo through the mire with old-fashioned plows like those used by their ancestors thousands of years ago. Too many of them still farm in this fashion, but gradually they are learning new methods. Nearly two million farmers owned one acre of land each and about a half million, plots of from one to five acres. On these tiny "farms" a family had to grow enough corn and beans and fruit and vegetables to feed the family and enough fodder to feed the water buffalo—their most prized possession. If there was enough land left, they could try to grow cotton, Egypt's most important money crop.

Everyone in the family worked. The girls gathered twigs, mud, and manure for the fires and carried water in jugs for the home. The boys, even from a very early age, drove the water buffalo or helped to irrigate the fields.

The days were long and the work was hard and there was no time for school or few schools to attend. Illiteracy was estimated at as high as 90 per cent.

No wonder the mass of Egyptians had been too apathetic to support Naguib, Nasser, and their friends. Just to keep alive took all their energy and interest.

In contrast to such a hard way of life was the plush existence of the rich landowners and the few industrialists, most of whom lived in the modern sections of cities like Cairo and Alexandria or in pretentious houses in the villages of the delta or along the Nile.

But as the years rolled along and changes began to appear in their country, the underprivileged began to take hope. Their personal affection for Naguib was great, but gradually they developed a feeling of adulation for Nasser, partly as a result of his economic and social reforms but much more by political events. Nasser has been able to accomplish some amazing things in the years following the Revolution.

First of all came the efforts of land reform, started within a few weeks after the seizure of power in July of 1952. In an effort to obtain more land for the *fellaheen*, or peasants, the government took about 600,000 acres of arable land from the big landowners. They also acquired some other plots of ground from other sources. Some of the land was used for governmental purposes and some given to the graduates of the Egyptian agricultural colleges, but a total of about 525,000 acres was made available to the poor people of Egypt. No one individual in the country was permitted to own over 200 *feddans* (a *feddan* is slightly more than one acre), unless he irrigated and made productive desert land that he already owned. In 1961 this was reduced to 100 *feddans*.

By 1958 about 90,000 families have profited from small parcels of ground turned over to them, and a total of about 330,000 acres had been distributed. Realizing that this was merely a start, the government set out to reclaim other land, concentrating on two projects, one of them southwest of Cairo and another in the delta of Alexandria. By the end of 1965, about 725,000 *feddans* had been reclaimed, and the acreage increases annually.

Still another approach was made in adding new land by irrigation, with the biggest project consisting of 10,000 acres in the western desert. The ultimate objective, however, was 100,000 acres of new land—if or when the High Dam at Aswan was constructed.

At the same time, attention was being paid to the improvement of the lucrative cotton crop, to the elimination of insect pests, to the development of cattle-raising, and to the establishment of co-operatives and farm credit banks. Cotton accounts for 60 per cent of Egypt's exports and provides 20 per cent of the world's supply. But this one-crop economy is giving way to diversification, and the farmers are being encouraged to plant wheat and vegetables.

The results of all these efforts were not as spectacular as many people had hoped, but they did give the people a feeling that something was being done and a new confidence in their government.

Egypt could not hope to achieve a better standard of living for its people merely by improving agriculture. Some industrial development was also necessary. There were too many people trying to make a living from the small plots of fertile land. Many of these small farmers would be better off in industry. So the government turned its attention to the fostering of new factories. A first and ambitious five-year plan was set up in 1960, calling for an expenditure of over $700,000,000 and an annual increase of 10 per cent in industrial production.

As a part of that plan a large steel mill was built near Cairo, refineries and a huge fertilizer plant were started, a new oil pipeline laid between the Suez and Cairo, and new factories built for batteries, tires, china, ceramics, electrical appliances, jute, medicine, and other products. Thousands of jobs were thus created, and there was money with which to purchase not only domestic products but desirable goods from abroad as well. Enough oil is now produced to make it possible to export crude petroleum.

Securing capital for these new plants was not easy, but much of the needed money came from Europe and the United States and some of it from the Soviet Union.

In public health, similar progress was made. Egypt's basic problem was to provide decent water for its people, and it was at this level that the government made the most progress. It renovated and expanded forty existing aqueducts and built forty new ones, so that by 1966, the entire rural population of seventeen million had access to clean water, an increase from two million at the time of the Revolution. This was an amazing accomplishment, but many villagers still prefer to use the "life-giving" waters of the Nile. It will take time and education to wean them from ancient beliefs and practices.

Since tuberculosis is one of the most dreaded diseases in Egypt, thirty new TB infirmaries were established in the five-year period after the new government took over and the incidence of the disease has been much reduced. A pathetic sight in Egypt a few years ago was the countless children with eye diseases, but the government, through regular clinical examinations and treatment, available without cost, has greatly reduced the number of children so afflicted.

In 1951 there were 5200 doctors in Egypt, or one for every 4000 inhabitants. In 1964, there were 13,000 or one for every 2000 inhabitants. In addition, general hospitals, mental hospitals, infant welfare centers, chest-disease hospitals, and rural health clinics have been built. Free midday meals for all schoolchildren are building health and resistance to disease.

Even more spectacular was the increase in educational opportunities. When Nasser's government took over, the total school population was less than two million. Soon the government was opening new schools at the rate of two every three days. In 1966, the number of children and young people in school was about four million. A new university was opened, and the old Islamic University was greatly expanded by the addition of colleges of science, medicine, and engineering. The Ministry of Education's budget increased from 40.2 million Egyptian pounds in 1951 to 96.5 million Egyptian pounds in 1964. Primary and high school education is free, and for children from six to twelve it is compulsory. Nasser's government is working hard to have all children in school, but the law is often unenforceable because the farmers need their children during the cotton-growing season. Once again, as in all new countries, economic and social problems must be solved together.

As part of its world-wide attack on illiteracy, the United Nations Educational, Scientific, and Cultural Organization established a training center at Sirs-el-Layyan in Egypt where teachers for the entire Arab world could be trained in what has come to be known as fundamental or basic education. Although a UN project, it is being carried on with the co-operation of the Egyptian government. Its purpose is to develop teams of men and women who can help to improve conditions in small communities in health, agriculture, recreation, and the arts and crafts, as well as teach the basic skills of reading, writing, and arithmetic.

In order to carry out these and other programs the new regime abolished all parties except the Liberation Front. This included the Communist party, which was outlawed and its members made liable to fifteen years' imprisonment. While it is true that Nasser has gained considerable support from the Soviet Union, he has not permitted the Communists within Egypt to gain new power. This is a fact which Nasser and his friends stress when they are accused of being Communists or Communist sympathizers.

At the same time Nasser attacked the reactionary right-wing group known as the Moslem Brotherhood, and reduced its power measurably.

Nasser's great dream for improving conditions in Egypt, however, was the Aswan Dam project. This was a plan for the construction of the world's biggest dam, four hundred miles south of Cairo, with a reservoir three hundred fifty miles long. This daring project called for the irrigation of two million acres of land and an increase of electrical output in Egypt of five times what it had been previously. It would take ten years to build and would cost approximately $1,300,000,000.

The plan was not a new one with Nasser, but it had lain dormant for several years. To him and to the Egyptian people it was not only a vast economic and engineering project; it was also a symbol of political power and independence. It was to be a dramatic symbol of the progress Egypt was making.

Approaches were made to the governments of the United States and Great Britain and to the World Bank for help, for Egypt could not afford to do this alone. Progress in reaching agreements was slow, and the Egyptians began to talk about the possibility of Russia's helping them. This turned the trick, and the United States agreed to aid considerably, lest Russia gain a foothold in Egypt by helping on the Aswan Dam.

Soon, however, it was learned that the statements of Russia's interest in the dam had been fabricated, and on July 19, 1956, Secretary of State Dulles announced in sudden and peremptory fashion that the deal was off and that the United States would not help.

This was a body blow to Nasser and his friends. They had built up a tremendous amount of propaganda about the dam in Egypt and they could not afford to swallow their words now. They were infuriated and bitter. Nasser denounced the whole deal upon numerous occasions with expressions like those he had used as a boy against the British. "Americans, may you choke on your fury," he declared. In an important speech in Cairo he added:

> Our answer to them is that we will not permit any imperialists nor oppressors to rule us militarily, politically, or economically; we will not submit to the dollar or to force.

At this time, Nasser could have reviewed his plans for the project and have undertaken a less ambitious program. To do so might have been economically more feasible than the High Dam. But it would also have been political suicide, for he had promised his people the dam and he had to make good his promise.

He had been driven into a corner and, like a desperate man, he took desperate action. In a dramatic gesture of defiance, he seized the Suez Canal, one of the world's "super-highways" of trade. The profits from it would now be used to finance the dam, he asserted, pointing out that the net profit of around $30,000,000 a year would provide a large part of the cost of the dam if it were

used in that way for ten years. As a matter of fact, the
U.A.R. today derives more than $160 million a year from
tariffs charged to ships that pass through the Canal.

That the seizure of the Canal was a psychological as
well as an economic move was admitted by Nasser later
in an interview with a *Look* magazine reporter. Questioned
about his motives, he replied:

> When you said you would not build the High Dam, we had to
> show you that you cannot insult a small country and get away
> with it. If we had accepted the slap in the face, you would
> have slapped us again. Also, we needed to raise money to
> build the dam ourselves. The Canal tolls were a logical source
> of income.

After the seizure of the Canal, a series of conferences was
held in London from July to October 1956. But little progress
was made in those meetings.

That fall England, France, and Israel took drastic action
themselves. They were motivated by different considerations,
but each of them wanted to cut Nasser down. England and
France could not survive long economically without the oil
of the Middle East, and they were desperate. Some authorities feel that they feared Nasser's growing control in
that part of the world and wanted to get rid of him
before he gained any more power. Israel was prompted by
other considerations, as outlined in the chapter of this book
on Ben-Gurion.

On October 29, 1956, Israel launched an all-out attack
on Egypt, in retaliation for alleged border raids by the
Egyptian *fellaheen.* On October 30, Britain and France
warned Egypt and Israel to cease hostilities, and demanded
the right to occupy the Suez in order to protect the Canal.
That demand Egypt rejected.

Obviously this situation could involve other countries and
flare into another world war, so the question was taken up

NASSER OF THE UNITED ARAB REPUBLIC 173

in the Security Council of the United Nations. A resolution calling on Israel to withdraw and on all member nations to refrain from force was vetoed by England and France.

The following day the British and the French began to bomb Egypt, and on November 5 an invasion was begun by British and French forces.

Most of the world was alarmed by this aggression by two world powers, and the United Nations called for a cease-fire and a United Nations police force to supervise the cessation of hostilities. In an almost unprecedented show of agreement, the United States and Russia united in this appeal to Britain, France, and Israel.

This short-lived war came to a sudden end. The Israelis had beaten the Egyptians badly, and the British and French had done considerable damage in their short attack on that country. On the surface it might seem as if Nasser had been defeated. Though after a few months of negotiation Nasser still held the Canal, ships of the Black Star line of Ghana (40 per cent Israeli-owned) were passing through the giant waterway. Futhermore, Israel was using the Gulf of Aqaba, which it had not done before October of 1956, and a United Nations police force was stationed in the Gaza strip which had previously been held by Egypt.

But to the Egyptians, Nasser and his colleagues had won a victory. The Israelis, British, and French were no longer in their territory or attacking them from the skies. All British and French property in Egypt had been sequestered, and British influence was gone forever. Egypt had lost a battle but won the war. The booming Suez Canal business now belonged to Egypt. Nasser had made all this possible and become a great hero. He had saved the Egyptians from the Israelis and from the Western "imperialists."

And it was not the Egyptians alone who considered that they had gained a victory. Throughout the Arab world, with its seventy million persons, Nasser's prestige was greatly enhanced. He had been the only Arab in their memory who had defied the great powers of the world and had won against them.

Proof of his popularity in other parts of the Middle East was not long in coming. Conditions in Syria had been moving from bad to worse economically and politically. A combination of leaders of the army and the Ba'ath party had won control there and had obtained arms from Russia and a $200,000,000 long-term loan. They seemed to feel for a time that they could obtain this much-needed aid without becoming a Russian satellite. But within a few months it became apparent to many of the Syrian leaders that this was not the case. The army and the Ba'ath party reassessed their situation and decided that there was no way of salvaging their country from the inside. They decided to ask for union with Egypt.

Nasser, they argued, was a strong man and had been able to obtain help from Russia without being absorbed into the Russian orbit. He had even outlawed the Communists in Egypt. Why not join with him in a union of Arab states? Why not end the eleven years of Syrian independence with its six military coups, its twenty-one different cabinets, and its four constitutions? Then others could be urged to follow suit and a union or federation of all Arabs would become a reality rather than an age-old dream.

After a short period of negotiations the two countries were joined, and on February 1, 1958, the United Arab Republic came into being, with Gamal Abdel Nasser as its President and Syria's former President, Shukri al-Kuwatly, as Vice-President. From now on there would be one army, one parliament, and one flag—of black, white, and red stripes with two green stars in the center. And Cairo would be the new federation's capital.

From a geographical and historical point of view a union with Jordan and Iraq would have seemed more logical, but they were still ruled by kings and pro-Western in their orientation, so that was out of the question.

To Egypt's twenty-nine million persons now were added the four million inhabitants of Syria. Like the Egyptians, they are largely Moslems and speak Arabic, so they had these two points in common. Most of them are farmers or desert people, raising cotton and wheat, vegetables, and fruits. Oil had been discovered, but this resource has not been developed and there are no other known mineral deposits. Their one asset in that respect is the fact that oil pipelines from Saudi Arabia and Iraq run through their country, making it a strategically located country.

This action of Egypt and Syria was a threat to the existence of the kings of Jordan and Iraq. Within two weeks they countered with the formation of a rival union known as the Arab Union, with King Faisal of Iraq at its head and King Hussein of Jordon his deputy. This union did not last long. Faisal was killed in the uprising in Iraq during the summer of 1958 and the union was dissolved.

Few people know to what extent Nasser was involved in the overthrow of the government in Iraq or in the civil war in the summer of 1958, but it is certain that pro-Nasser forces were at work in both of these situations, even if Nasser and his friends did not have a direct hand in them. It is also certain that the radio broadcasts from Radio Cairo to the Arab world had been whipping up sentiment for Nasser and Arab unity.

After the landing of American troops in Lebanon and British troops in Jordan, Nasser unleashed a torrent of invective against the Western "imperialists," vowing that:

> The flags of victory will fly over every Arab city and also in
> Algeria. Then there will remain no imperialist agents in the

Arab world, no matter how they try to disguise themselves. The Arab people will destroy them.

He also hinted strongly that King Hussein of Jordan would meet the same fate as his cousin King Faisal, thus encouraging assassins to attack Hussein.

When the Lebanon-Jordan situation was taken to the United Nations, Nasser joined in a rare show of Arab solidarity. The ten nations of that part of the world met and hammered out a resolution to bring peace there, empowering the Secretary-General of the UN, Dag Hammarskjöld, to try his skill at mediating the difficulties. This led to the withdrawal of American and British troops.

In 1961, Syria withdrew from the United Arab Republic, but Egypt retained the name. In 1963, Egypt, Syria, and Iraq failed in an attempt to form a United Arab Republic.

After the Suez crisis, Soviet aid and the purchase of Egyptian cotton by the Eastern bloc of nations saved Egypt from economic collapse and enabled Nasser to continue his reform program. The aid of Western nations had been cut off. In 1964, Premier Khrushchev of the Soviet Union visited Egypt and promised a 100-million-pound loan.

The Aswan Dam probably will be completed in 1967–68 with heavy Soviet aid. It will triple Egypt's hydroelectric output and thus supply cheap power to Egyptian industry. This, in turn, will provide more jobs and more money for the Egyptian workers. The dam will reclaim over 1.3 million acres of crop-producing land.

But Egypt's large and fast-increasing population demands more food each year. There are 2.7 per cent more mouths to feed annually, a tremendously high rate of increase, which is due largely to the reduced infant mortality rate and to the longer life span of Egyptians since the health reforms of the government. President Nasser calls the population problem "the most dangerous obstacle that faces the Egyptian people in their drive toward raising the standard of production in their country." In 1965 a Supreme Council for Family Planning was set up.

Nasser has other problems, both domestic and foreign. He has had threatened revolts by the army and by a dissident group known as the Moslem Brotherhood. High prices cause grumbling and discontent. The economy is not all that was hoped for when the second five-year plan was initiated. And agricultural production is still, for most of the peasants, on a subsistence level only. In foreign affairs, Nasser has become increasingly isolated from the rest of the Arab world. Jordan, Saudi Arabia, and Syria are unfriendly. He sent troops into Yemen in 1962 to fight on the side of the newly created republic. Many thousands of Egyptian soldiers were killed and the cost to Egypt ran into the millions. After four years, Nasser stopped the war. But Egyptian troops remain in Yemen. Many observers believe Nasser's interference in Yemen affairs is a part of a power struggle between Nasser and Saudi Arabia for the rich oil lands of the entire Arab peninsula.

King Faisal of Saudi Arabia is Nasser's political rival in the Middle East, Jordan's King Hussein is resented, Syria is an enemy, and Israel is despised and feared. Tunisia is openly disapproving of Nasser and his government.

Nevertheless, Gamal Abdel Nasser is the potent force in the Arab world. He is considered by knowledgeable people as the pace-setter for economic and social reform, not only in the Arab world, but in Africa.

Several years ago Nasser wrote in a little book entitled *The Philosophy of the Revolution* that:

> The annals of history are full of heroes who carved for themselves great and heroic roles and played them on momentous occasions. It seems to me that in the Arab world there is a role wandering in search of a hero.

Whether at that time he thought of himself as that potential hero, no one will probably ever know. But the spin of the wheel of fortune and his own qualities have made him such a hero to a large part of the Arab world today.

What qualities does this man have which have made him the modern Saladin, the twentieth-century counterpart of the twelfth-century Sultan of Egypt and Syria who defeated the Crusaders?

One factor in his favor is his personal appearance. He is a handsome, well-built man more than six feet tall, with wiry black hair which is beginning to turn gray, dark, soft eyes, a long, high-bridged nose, and a warm, quick smile. He is an imposing and attractive figure.

He has an uncanny knack of sizing up people, gained probably from years of observation of men when he was probing their thoughts and character as an army officer before the days of the 1952 Revolution.

For several years he was able to play a cat-and-mouse game with the Western world and the Soviet Union, courting the favor of each and winning concessions from both without becoming committed to either side in the cold war.

Another quality on which even his enemies will agree is his personal incorruptibility, a quality which is of high importance in a country such as Egypt which had long been noted for its graft and corruption in government circles. There is corruption and waste in his government, but Nasser, personally, has apparently not been involved in it and does not condone it.

The fact that he came from a lower-middle-class family and has fought his way to the top is still another element in the President's favor. The people can identify with him as a man who was once like themselves.

He has been a clever propagandist, too, making full use of the radio as the best means of reaching his own people and the peoples of other lands, since most of them cannot be reached through the written word. In his early years he did very little speaking and was not a good orator, but in recent years he has perfected this art.

But more important to his success is the fact that he appeared when he did, for the Arab world had been waiting for a long time for a man who could unite it and build for it a place in the councils of the international community. Millions of Arabs picked Nasser as their hero because they needed a hero and he was the most likely candidate available.

In 1964, Nasser introduced a provisional constitution in Egypt which provided for parliamentary government. The Parliament has three hundred sixty members, three hundred fifty of whom are elected and ten appointed by the President, who also holds veto power. The Prime Minister, who is also the Vice-President, is the leader of Parliament. In 1965, Nasser was elected President for six years.

In June 1967, war broke out between Israel and the Arab states. In six days the Israelis broke the blockade Egypt had imposed on their only outlet to the sea, the Gulf of Aqaba, knocked out the Egyptian air force, and defeated the army.

President Nasser took full responsibility for the defeat and resigned. He reconsidered, however, when the assembly gave him a vote of confidence and in the light of "popular demand." But whether, in the face of such an overwhelming defeat, Nasser can retain his position of leadership in Egypt and the Arab world is questionable.

BEN-GURION
OF ISRAEL

At the age of fourteen young David Green and two of his friends decided they would start a club in Plonsk, a small town in Poland, about forty miles from Warsaw. This was to be no ordinary club organized to play games or to earn money for good times together. This was to be a club to teach young Jewish boys the Hebrew language, to learn about the life of the great Zionist leader Theodor Herzl, and to raise money for the Zionist cause.

They chose the name Ezra for their club because Ezra had renewed the Torah and built the Second Temple in Jerusalem centuries ago. Now, as Zionists, they were going to help renew the Hebrew language and rebuild the ancient land of Palestine.

This was an ambitious undertaking for teen-agers, but all three of the club's founders worked hard and within a year they had thirty members from among their friends and classmates in Plonsk. Their club was the talk of the town. Clubs were not common in Poland in 1900, especially those with such a serious purpose.

When duties were assigned, David Green was chosen as spokesman, or public speaker, for the group. This turned out to be an excellent choice. He was a good student and a forceful speaker. He had enough knowledge of the Bible to talk intelligently with the rabbis, and enough understanding of Zionism to hold his own in arguments, even with adults.

And arguments there were. The turn of the century was an exciting time for the Jews of Europe, especially of Eastern

Europe. Since their exile from Palestine hundreds of years ago, many Jews had been wandering over the face of the earth, staying in one place until a new pogrom, or persecution, forced them to move on. In many places they had been isolated and compelled to live in ghettos. They had been forced off the land and into the towns and cities for mutual protection. They had been driven into work that others did not want, largely as petty shopkeepers and tradesmen.

But recently there had been a wave of hope for a brighter future. Theodor Herzl, a Jewish journalist living in Vienna, had been disturbed by a new wave of anti-Semitism in Europe and had concluded that the best solution for Jews was to return to their own homeland. This was not a new idea, but he revived it with vigor, clarity, and tremendous emotional appeal in a booklet entitled "The Jewish State," written in 1896.

Many people were ready for this stirring statement and for his prophetic personality. Now Zionism, or the promotion of a Jewish state in Palestine, became a potent force among Jewish groups, especially in Eastern Europe.

There were other ways of meeting opposition and improving the lot of Jews, however, and Zionism was as fiercely attacked as it was enthusiastically supported. One group maintained that it was important for Jews to stay where they were and fight corrupt and oppressive governments, such as that of Czarist Russia. Another group said that the best solution to their plight was to emigrate, preferably to the United States. Still another segment of the Jewish community feared Zionism as an attack upon its religious faith, pointing out that many of its leaders were socialists who encouraged the use of Hebrew, which most of the rabbis and orthodox Jews felt was too sacred to be used as an everyday language. A few were willing to accept the offer of the British for settlement in East Africa.

It was a difficult but an exciting time in which to live, and David and his friends became deeply involved in the arguments and debates of their day.

Considering his family background, it is not surprising that David Green had become a Zionist. His grandfather was an outstanding citizen of Plonsk who had learned Russian and had drawn inspiration from Tolstoy and his rebellion against the Russian society of his day. David's grandfather had gone so far as to challenge the tight grip which the local rabbis held on their people in Plonsk.

David's father had gone even further. He had become a leading Zionist, subscribing to the periodicals of that movement, contributing to the cause, and opening his home as a center for Zionist discussion and organization. He had even persuaded one of the best-known local rabbis to join the Zionist movement. So intense was the feeling in Plonsk in those days that this rabbi was dragged from his prayers into the street and given a public beating by those who disagreed with him.

Into this home and in this tense period of history David Green was born on October 16, 1886. He was the sixth child of Avigdor and Sheindal Green, or Grin. He attended the local Jewish school and took private lessons from tutors. At home he listened to discussions of politics and religion.

His mother died when David was eleven years old, a crushing blow to him and one from which he never completely recovered.

Later he moved to Warsaw to continue his studies. But he was more interested in politics than in education, and he became active in Poale Zion, a movement which combined Zionism with the goal of a socialist society. He began making speeches and taking part in demonstrations.

Soon he was picked up by the police and thrown into jail.

His father came to intercede for him and finally got him out of prison. He chided David for his activities, but David knew very well that his father was proud of him and so did not take his reproofs to heart.

Back in Plonsk, David and the other founders of the Ezra Society decided that they ought to go to Palestine to take part in the colonization by Jews of that ancient land. One of them set off alone, but eventually turned up in the United States rather than in Palestine. Another reached Palestine and stayed a few months before returning for a brief visit to Plonsk. David stayed at home and took part in organizing the workers in his home town and in speaking there and in nearby cities. Already he had become well known as a dynamic and forceful speaker in the Zionist cause.

When his friend returned from Palestine, David was thrilled by his stories, even though they included many accounts of hardship and suffering. He decided that he would go with his friend when he returned to Palestine. The two boys, with an old rabbi friend of the family and his daughter, set out in the fall of 1906, made their way to Odessa on the Black Sea, and from there traveled on an old Russian cargo boat to the port of Jaffa in Palestine.

Later David wrote of his arrival at Jaffa in these words: "My heart overflowed with happiness as if I had entered the realm of my legend. The work was hard, the wages low, the food poor, the accommodations primitive, the dangers of disease great and ever present. Pioneering certainly was not easy."

He spent a year working at Petah Tikva as a farm laborer. Then he moved to Rishon le Zion, where he worked in the famous wine presses and helped organize the laborers to improve their general working conditions. From there he went north to Sejera in Galilee.

In this last settlement, the young immigrant learned that

the farmland of the Jewish settlers was guarded by Arabs hired for that purpose. He objected strenuously. If this was to be a Jewish enterprise, he said, it should be all-Jewish. Certainly this sensitive job of protection should be in the hands of their own people. Countering this argument, some of the settlers warned that a change in policy would bring trouble from the Arabs. David Green won, but considerable trouble did follow from the Arabs who had lost their jobs.

Not long after this event, David was invited to go to Jerusalem to edit the journal called *Achdut,* (Unity). He was hardly the same youth now that he had been upon his arrival in Palestine. He was bronzed, physically tougher, and had streaks of gray in his hair. He was clearer in his goals, more outspoken in his public comments, and much better informed on the country and its problems. He had made many friends, taken an active part in Jewish politics, and added Arabic to the growing list of languages which he could speak.

On the masthead of the journal he had begun to edit was the name "David Ben-Gurion," for he had also changed his name in keeping with the movement in Palestine to use only Biblical titles. He retained his boyhood name of David and added to it Ben-Gurion. (Ben means "son of" and Gurion "lion cub.")

Soon it became evident that the Jews in Palestine would need the most talented legal counsel that they could find for themselves and their young labor movement. They could not find lawyers among their own ranks, so a group of younger men was selected to go to Constantinople to study law. This decision was made because Palestine was then a part of the Ottoman Turkish Empire and subject to its laws. That group included Ben-Gurion, the future Prime Minister, and Ben-Zvi, the future President of the Republic of Israel. In 1913 they set out for Constantinople, but within a year they had to return, because World War I had broken out.

Turkish reverses early in that war resulted in the persecution of all those in sympathy with the Allies. Ben-Gurion was on the list of the supposed sympathizers and was banished from Palestine in 1915. Some months later he came to the United States.

In the next few months he and his friend Ben-Zvi and other young leaders from Palestine wrote and spoke and tried to promote the cause of Poale Zion among the Jews of the United States.

During those months Ben-Gurion was also forced to change his attitude toward the Allies. He had previously favored siding with the Turks, believing that they would be more favorable to the aspirations of the Jews in Palestine. Furthermore, he had not been able to bring himself to support a cause in which the Russians were leading members. Two events occurred, however, which made him change his mind and come out in favor of the Allies. One was the overthrow of the Czarist regime in Russia. The other was the proclamation by the British of the Balfour Declaration.

In that famous document the British government viewed "with favor the establishment in Palestine of a National Home for the Jewish People. . . ." The wording of that statement was vague, and for years people would argue as to whether it meant that a part of Palestine or all of it was to be turned over to the Jews. But it was the most important statement that had ever been issued on this subject, and it gave fresh hope to the Zionists.

Most of the credit for this Balfour Declaration is given to Chaim Weizmann, a Russian-born Jew who had settled in England and had been teaching chemistry at the University of Manchester. At a critical moment in the war, when England desperately needed acetone to made TNT, he discovered a process for obtaining it from horse chestnuts, which were readily available in England. The only reward he asked was that England help Zionism in Palestine, a movement in which he had been an influential leader. This is generally believed to have been an important factor in the decision by the British government to issue the Balfour Declaration.

Meanwhile, Ben-Gurion had married a young woman in New York, Paula Munweis, who had started on a medical career, but because of family circumstances had been forced to cut short her training and become a nurse.

Ben-Gurion enlisted in the British Army and was soon promoted to the rank of corporal. At the insistence of Jewish leaders, a Jewish Legion was formed as a separate unit, rather than having all the Jewish soldiers scattered throughout the British Army. This enabled them to plan and work together and to dramatize their contribution to the war effort.

At the close of World War I, the possessions of Turkey in the Middle East were handed over to the League of Nations and entrusted to France and England as mandates which they would govern. One area under such British control was Palestine and another Transjordan.

The Jews were allowed to migrate to Palestine, but they were barred from Transjordan, a state consisting of only 320,000 persons, half of whom were nomads known as Bedouins.

At the end of the war Ben-Gurion threw himself vigorously into the organization of labor in Palestine. A new group was formed, known officially as the General Federation of Jewish Labor, better known popularly as Histadruth. From 1921 until 1935 he was its Secretary-General.

His work was chiefly with laborers, many of whom had come to Palestine in the 1920s without money and without skills, drawn there by their belief in Zionism or because of the severe restrictions placed upon immigration to the United States in that period.

Histadruth had only about eight thousand members then, but it was well organized and became a powerful force in Palestine. It developed its own bank, its own schools, and its own theater. It started its own collective farms and semi-collective villages. It launched a transportation co-operative and a health insurance plan. It was a strong, tightly knit, influential force, the main organization through which the governing British allowed the Jews to act collectively.

Meanwhile, a bitter fight was going on in Jewish circles throughout the world. One faction strongly supported the idea of a Jewish state in Palestine. Another said that the solution to anti-Semitism was for Jews to become effective citizens in their own lands. This latter group pointed out that there were sixteen million Jews in the world and that tiny Palestine could not possibly hold even a small proportion of that number.

Even among those who supported Zionism, there were often sharp differences of opinion. Ben-Gurion was one of the militant faction, determined to build a Jewish national home, eager to move ahead rapidly, and outspoken in his criticism of those who urged moderation and delay. Chaim Weizmann of England was one of the chief protagonists of a more cautious policy. He pointed out that even if the Jews could someday establish a separate nation in Palestine they would have to live on friendly terms with the Arabs of that section of the world, and that negotiation and conciliation would pay rich dividends in the future.

Ben-Gurion was drawn by all these counterforces into more and more political activity. To protect the rights of Jewish labor and to reach the goals he had set for his people, he had to devote more and more time to politics. So he decided to form a strong labor party by uniting the various splinter groups which had existed in the 1920s. By 1930 the Mapai party had been organized, with Ben-Gurion as its leader.

In 1933 he was elected a member of the Executive Committee of the Jewish Agency for Palestine, a world-wide Jewish organization for the promotion of Jewish welfare and aid to the immigrants of Palestine. In 1935 he was made its chairman, a post which he held until the establishment of Israel in 1948.

The improvement of working conditions in Palestine, the tightening of immigration to the United States, the growth of the Zionist movement, and the rise of Hitler in Germany combined to increase the number of people emigrating to Palestine. Between 1920 and 1923, 30,000 went there; and from 1933 to 1936, 164,000. In the first wave of immigration nearly half the group came from Poland and another fifth from Russia. By 1936 the largest group were from Poland, the next largest from Germany, and the rest of the settlers from many parts of the world.

The Arabs of this region were not well organized and at first were not particularly disturbed. But gradually they began to see what was happening. In 1922 eleven persons in every one hundred in Palestine were Jews; by 1931, sixteen in every one hundred. By 1937 the figure had risen to thirty out of every one hundred.

With funds from Jews in the United States and other parts of the globe, farmland was being purchased and villages established. Naturally the Arabs became alarmed at this steady "infiltration" into what they considered their home. Storm clouds were beginning to appear on the Middle Eastern horizon.

More was involved than immigration and land ownership, however. Here were two groups of people with quite different ways of life, living within a small and economically under-

developed area. The conflict between them was summarized
by the Peel Commission, a group appointed by the British
government. In their 1937 report they wrote:

> An irrepressible conflict has arisen between the two national
> communities within the narrow bounds of one small country.
> About 1,000,000 Arabs are in strife, open or latent, with some
> 400,000 Jews. There is no common ground between them. The
> Arab community is predominantly Asian in character, the Jew-
> ish community predominantly European. They differ in reli-
> gion and in language. Their cultural and social life, their ways
> of thought and conduct, are as incompatible as their national
> aspirations. These last are the greatest bar to peace. Arabs and
> Jews might possibly learn to live and work together in Palestine
> if they would make a genuine effort to reconcile and combine
> their national ideals and so build up in time a joint or dual
> nationality. But this they cannot do.

From this emerged the suggestion of a partition of Palestine. Ben-Gurion was enthusiastic about this move. "I regard the government's declaration in favor of a Jewish state
as one of the greatest acts in history," he said. "This is the beginning of redemption for which we have waited two thousand years. We have established a great new political fact
in that our rulers have spoken to us of independence."

But others did not share the views of the Commission or of
Ben-Gurion. Another commission was dispatched to Palestine,
and it reversed the recommendations of the earlier group. It
looked as if an impasse had been reached. In 1939, shortly
after the outbreak of World War II, the British government
issued a White Paper, or policy statement, which severely
restricted Jewish immigration and the purchase of land by
Jews in Palestine.

These measures were blows to the Zionists, but there was
no doubt where their sympathies lay in the global conflict
which had started. Had not Hitler already killed thousands

of their people? Were not the governments of Germany and Italy fascist dictatorships?

At this point Ben-Gurion declared:

> The Jews of Palestine happen to be the only community in the Middle East whose very survival is bound up with the defeat of Hitler. We shall fight the war as if there were no White Paper, and the White Paper as if there were no war.

Eventually a Jewish Brigade was formed as a part of the British Armed Forces.

The war years rolled along, and Ben-Gurion kept at his job of persuading the British and others that a separate state of Israel would be essential at the end of the war. His days and nights were spent in following the events of the war, in aiding the Jews who escaped to Palestine, in the interminable politics of world Jewry, in fund-raising and organizational problems, and toward the end of the war in gathering surplus war material and stockpiling it secretly in Palestine. He worked doggedly, persistently, relentlessly, sometimes ruthlessly. He won some people as friends, alienated others.

The mass murder of nearly six million Jews in Europe shocked the world and changed the political picture. England, the Netherlands, Canada, the United States, and other countries welcomed thousands of Jews who had escaped the "human furnaces" built by the Nazis. But these countries said that there was a limit to the number of refugees they would take.

The dangerous old "washtubs" onto which hundreds of refugees crowded in the hope of reaching Palestine, even without legal permission, dramatized the plight of the Jewish refugees and the determination of the British to prevent them from landing in Palestine, lest they add further fuel to that inflammable situation.

What, then, was to become of these homeless people? At

the close of the war the British tossed the whole question of Palestine into the lap of the newly formed United Nations. Discussion on it started in April 1947. All through that spring, summer, and early fall the discussions continued. Ben-Gurion was summoned. The Arab leaders were called.

Finally, a majority report was submitted to the United Nations. It proposed the partitioning of Palestine. A minority report was also submitted. It suggested the establishment of a federal state.

On November 29, 1947, the General Assembly of the United Nations voted in favor of the majority report by a vote of 33 to 13. In that vote the United States and Russia voted on the same side—in favor of the partition of Palestine.

At midnight on May 14, 1948, the British were to terminate their rule of Palestine. That moment would have been in the Jewish Sabbath, so at four o'clock that afternoon Ben-Gurion read to a small group of people the Proclamation of Independence. Then thirty-six representatives of various political parties filed past a table and signed the document. Overhead was the portrait of Theodor Herzl, whose dream of a Jewish homeland had inspired so many of these people over so long a period.

Before night had fallen over the new nation, it was at war. Incensed by the establishment of Israel, embittered over the loss of the land they had held for hundreds of years, fearful of Jewish territorial ambitions, the Arabs in the neighboring states were determined to snuff out this tiny state before it began to grow. The Egyptians moved from the south, the Transjordanians and Iraqis from the east, and the Syrians from the northeast.

Their attacks, however, were not well co-ordinated except in the Jerusalem area, a territory sacred to Christians, Jews, and Moslems. The forces of the new state, recruited largely from Haganah, the Jewish defense organization, were able to hold their own almost everywhere against the combined troops of nations representing about thirty million persons.

Aware that this fighting might lead to another world war and that their decision to create Israel had prompted this outbreak, the United Nations met in special session, appointed a truce commission, and authorized the appointment of a mediator. Despite appeals to both sides by the UN, the fighting continued. Finally a thirty-day truce was declared on June 11 and a second cease-fire on July 18.

Count Bernadotte, a Swedish diplomat appointed by the UN as mediator, was murdered in Israel by Jewish extremists who feared that he would compromise the Jewish position in his desire to bring peace to the Middle East. After weeks of negotiation, his successor, Dr. Ralph Bunche, an American serving in the Secretariat, succeeded in getting agreement on the boundaries and an armistice. By this action the city of Jerusalem was divided; the old city was included in Transjordan and the new city in Israel, with a narrow strip of no man's land between them.

This armistice is still in effect. Not one of the Arab nations has recognized Israel as a state, and they have isolated her as much as possible by strangling her trade and refusing entrance to their nations if a person's passport shows that he has been in Israel. Open fighting has stopped, but forays have taken place into both Arab and Jewish territory. For years there has been an uneasy peace which is merely a cessation of open warfare. Hostility meanwhile continues.

But Ben-Gurion and his fellow Israelis could not devote all their time to external relations, important as they were and are. They had to build a nation, reclaim and develop a desert land, mold a culture, form a government, and solve many other problems.

Ben-Gurion was elected Prime Minister of the new nation of Israel. His was a gigantic undertaking. There had been nothing like it before in history. As Ben-Gurion pointed out, "Unlike other nations, we have not centuries at our disposal. Israel must accomplish in a few years what has taken others generations."

The most obvious task before them was to aid the thousands of immigrants who were pouring into Israel. Altogether there were well over a million more people in Israel at the end of its first ten years than there had been at the outset. There were 900,000 immigrants, and 300,000 more by natural increase.

These people were from seventy-nine countries of the world. They were all Jews, but they had little in common. Many of them did not even speak Yiddish, the everyday language of many Jews. Very few of them knew Hebrew, the official language of their new homeland.

Furthermore, they had learned over the centuries the ways of life of the countries from which they came, and wanted different kinds of food, different kinds of clothing, and different kinds of shelter.

Most of those who came had lived in cities and preferred to live in large centers of population in Israel. But what Israel needed was fewer city dwellers and more farmers.

Some of them came with high enthusiasm for the new land, but many of them were tired, beaten, depressed by years of isolation and persecution or by recent troubles in their former homelands.

The immigrants from Western or Central Europe came with a good education, but most of those from Asia, the Middle East, North Africa, and Eastern Europe had little or no formal education.

In health, too, many of them were deficient. They needed

medical care and good food before they could be of much use to this struggling state.

The problems which confronted Israel, however, were not all concerned with these new settlers. Israel needed to survey its new territory and to discover its resources—the minerals and the land that could be irrigated or developed in other ways to make it productive. It needed roads and ports and hundreds of miles of pipelines to carry water to irrigate the desert.

Then, too, Israel was torn asunder by the differences among religious factions and political parties. Among the extremists were a few who did not even recognize the new government, for they believed that Israel should be a religious community rather than a political state. Then there was a large group who frowned upon modern practices like mixed swimming and dancing and looked upon Ben-Gurion and other leaders as far too liberal.

These and other differences led to the organization of twenty-one different political parties that entered candidates in the first general elections in 1949.

Added to all this was the problem of finance. The new settlers brought little if any money with them and could not start earning anything for at least a few weeks or months. And the government was desperately in need of capital for all the developments it felt were necessary.

With such unsettled conditions and changes in ways of living, there were bound to be people who felt insecure and who took out their frustrations on others. So, like other nations, Israel was confronted with the problems of juvenile delinquency and adult dislocation.

In the face of such obstacles, it would take strong men and women and young people to launch a new nation. It would also take plenty of idealism, good organization, top-notch leadership, sacrifice, and adjustment.

Despite the differences among the people, they did have a sense of belonging together. As Ben-Gurion has pointed out:

> There is a national unity of the Jews of the world—a unity based upon a common destiny, a great common historical heritage, and common aspirations for the future.

Coupled with this was their determination to make a success of their new country. This is apparent in all new nations, but it is especially noticeable in Israel. And where there is a will, people are likely to find ways of implementing their desires.

Israel was also blessed from the beginning with the financial and moral support of Jewish communities all over the world and especially in the United States. Jews everywhere urged their educated leaders to go to Israel, even if for short periods, to help in the building of the new state. And money was forthcoming in large amounts once the organizing genius of the Jewish people tackled this task.

Then, too, there were more highly skilled people in Israel than in any of the other new nations, and more than in most older nations. This was especially true of doctors, for there are now more doctors per thousand persons in Israel than in any other country of the world.

Given these and other assets, this tiny nation could go far and fast. No one who has visited Israel since its independence can fail to be impressed with its phenomenal development in industry, agriculture, education, and health services.

There are other signs of vitality which cannot be stated quite so simply. One of those is that the percentage of people living in the cities has fallen. Some of the people have moved to the suburbs, but Israel has used almost every device possible to relocate the immigrants on the land and to encourage city dwellers to become farmers. This is essential for her life as a nation. The country needs people on the land to produce food, to settle the newly irrigated desert areas, and for military security.

In the early days many immigrants to Palestine lived in *kibbutzim,* or collective settlements, where the land is jointly owned and farmed and the people eat together in common dining rooms. More recently another type of settlement has come into being—the *moshavim,* or co-operatives. In these villages the land and property are commonly owned by individuals who work together and share in the output of their labors. Although there is vigorous community life, the individual families eat and sleep as family units. It is a less radical form of community living and has appealed in recent years to more people than have the *kibbutzim.*

Especially dear to the heart of Ben-Gurion was the development of the Negev. This is a mountain and desert section in the south of Israel. No one lived there when the nation was established, but extensive surveys indicated deposits of copper, manganese, iron, clay, potash, and potassium. In some parts of this area oil has been discovered. Pipelines have been laid to carry oil from tankers. The town of Beersheba has grown from a hamlet to a small city. And in the southern tip of Israel, at Eilat, a port has been built.

It was one of Ben-Gurion's dreams that Eilat would be a great harbor permitting Israel to trade with Asia. To dramatize the need for the settlement of this area, he spent months in the *kibbutz* at Sde Boker in the Negev desert, where a group of young pioneers had settled. There he helped with the shearing of sheep as his contribution to the colony, living with his wife in a three-room frame building, eating in the common dining room, and spending many evenings with the group talking, singing, and listening to the radio.

Another of the dramatic changes brought about in Israel in recent years has been the revival of the Hebrew language. Today it is the official language of the country and more and more the everyday language of the people. As Ben-Gurion has pointed out, the learning of a new language by an entire nation is "unique, unparalleled in history."

A modern group of buildings has been built for the Hebrew University on the outskirts of Jerusalem, and research and technical institutions, such as the Weizmann Institute in Tel Aviv and the Technion in Haifa, have been established.

There have been psychological benefits from all this creativity. Ben-Gurion believes that the creation of Israel has freed the Jewish people of two complexes from which some Jews abroad have suffered—"a complex of superiority and . . . a complex of inferiority." Again he has stressed that "the State of Israel straightened the back of every Jew, wherever he lived."

Much of the progress in Israel was the result of careful research and planning; much of it the result of the hard work of thousands of people. But it could not have been done without capital, too. These funds have come from several sources. From the United Jewish Appeal around the world there came over $667,000,000 in the first ten years. From the Israel Bond campaigns in the United States came another $321,000,000 and in that same period from German reparations for damage to Jewish property and the destruction of Jewish lives, $337,000,000. Loans and grants from the United States government amounted to $328,000,000. Since then, millions of dollars have been given to the new nation by the Jewish people everywhere.

Life was exciting and difficult during those first ten years. Often there were quick decisions to make and criticism to face. One of the strangest episodes occurred in 1957 when the army of Israel, under the leadership of the one-eyed General Moshe Dayan, swept across the one hundred twenty miles of the Sinai desert in four days and threw back the Egyptian Army which Israel feared was poised to attack, for Egypt has been an enemy of Israel since its founding.

In July 1956, Nasser seized the Suez Canal for Egypt. He did so in answer to a rebuff from the United States, followed by France and Great Britain, in the form of a refusal to finance the Aswan Dam after they had promised to do so. Their refusal was based on serious doubts as to the practical efficacy of the dam. After nationalizing the Canal, Nasser announced that the tolls collected from the Canal would be used by his country to build the Aswan Dam. Because both Britain and France were so dependent upon the Canal as vital trade routes to Asia, they were alarmed by Nasser's move and prepared to resist it. To make the situation in the Near East more dangerous, in October, Israeli armies marched across the Sinai peninsula to the Canal and routed the Egyptian forces, with the aid of Britain and France. Under pressure from the United States and the United Nations, Britain and France withdrew their forces, but Israel resisted for some weeks, then finally also withdrew.

The world was aghast at Israel's action against Egypt, and many in Israel itself criticized Ben-Gurion and his government harshly. His answer was that the Sinai campaign had brought gains, even though Israel eventually had to withdraw from the territory it had overrun. The action had removed the instant menace of attack by Egypt, prevented the infiltration of the Gaza strip, restored Israel's faith in her own strength, and opened the very important harbor at Eilat.

It was a bold stroke by a bold man. But boldness is only one characteristic of Ben-Gurion. One biographer has summarized her impressions of him in these words:

> The dominating idea, the core of the man, is a sense of history—history pulsing forward through the time spans of human lives as well as history tugging backward at the past.

Coupled with this is a singleness of purpose which dominated his thinking and actions from the time he was a boy in Plonsk through his service in the government of Israel as Prime Minister or Minister of Defense, or both at once. That purpose was to promote the "in-gathering" of the Jewish people and the building of a national homeland for them.

His ability to analyze and to make quick decisions, gathering all the evidence he can, weighing the pros and cons of a proposed action and then acting, usually without the advice of others, has led some people to call him dogmatic, pugnacious, domineering. The quality has lost him good friends at various times in his life—Chaim Weizmann, Dr. Judah Magnes, Rabbi Abba Hillel Silver. Perhaps this was necessary. But perhaps a more moderate approach would have cost him less among his own people and among the nations of the Middle East.

Certainly he is an original thinker, with an enormous capacity to comprehend many aspects of living. Much of this comes from a keen mind and a curiosity about life. His reading reflects this. As a young man he was entranced by the great Russian and Hebrew writers—Tolstoy, Turgenev, Dostoyevsky, Bialik, Herzen, and Bielinsky. Later he became an avid reader of Jewish history and the Bible, believing that "nothing can surpass the Bible in lighting up the manifold problems of our life and their recondite cause . . . (and that) there can be no worth-while political or military education about Israel without profound knowledge of the Bible."

Then he became engrossed in the writings of the Greek philosophers, especially of Plato, which he learned to read in Greek, then those of the Chinese and Indian philosophers. Thucydides' *History of the Peloponnesian War*, and Plato's *Republic* are his all-time favorites. In more recent years he has plunged into a study of world developments in science and of the role of health on the mind.

Ben-Gurion retired as Prime Minister of Israel in 1963. Centuries ago it was Moses who led the Children of Israel out of bondage and into a new freedom. In many ways David Ben-Gurion resembles that courageous and dedicated prophet of olden times, even though he has been a political rather than a religious leader. Perhaps Ben-Gurion might be called a twentieth-century Moses.

HUSSEIN
OF JORDAN

Before they are twenty-five few people have completed their education and advanced to the top in their profession.

At the age of twenty-three, King Hussein of Jordan had done just that, and much more. He had undergone more important, exciting, and harrowing experiences in that brief span of years than most people face in a lifetime.

By the time he was twenty-three Hussein had witnessed his grandfather's assassination. He had observed his father's brief rule and abdication as King. He had fought off a revolution led by one of his best friends. He had married and had a child. He had steered his country through its federation with another nation, a federation which had proved to be short-lived.

Hussein was born on November 14, 1935, in Amman, in what was then Transjordan, a tiny state in the Middle East. He was the first child and was given a name which would indicate just who he was. The name Hussein Ibn Talal el Hashem means that he was the son of Talal and a member of the Hashemite family, or dynasty. In fact, he was the forty-first generation of that dynasty, tracing his ancestry back to the prophet Mohammed.

At five he entered an Arab kindergarten and the next year was transferred to an English school. In the fourth grade he enrolled in the Bishop's School in Amman, completing his education in that city in the Islamic College, which would be called a high school in the United States.

It might seem strange for the son of the ruler of an

Arab country to get his early education almost entirely in English schools, but Transjordan was then a British mandate and most of its schools were run by the British.

When it came time for him to go to a college or university, however, he was sent to Victoria College in Alexandria, Egypt, the leading center of Arabic learning, so that he might imbibe more of the learning of his own people, the Arabs.

Throughout these early years Hussein led as normal a life as a boy of his background could. His companions were carefully chosen by the family, and were usually his classmates at school. They went through the usual round of boys' games, starting with mock battles, moving on to marbles and tops, and graduating to bicycle riding and soccer. At an early age Hussein learned to ride horseback over the stony, hilly countryside around Amman, as boys had done in that part of the world for centuries. Very early, too, he learned to shoot. A favorite sport was hunting gazelles.

His was an easy and enjoyable life, but not an extravagant one. The royal family was not wealthy, and grandfather Abdullah was a bit tightfisted with the family funds and saw that they were not squandered.

The family home was a modest five-room house with one bathroom. One day young Hussein received a bicycle from his wealthy cousin, Prince Faisal of Iraq. He was as happy as any ten-year-old boy would be with such a wonderful gift and as grieved when, later, his mother had to sell the bicycle for fourteen dollars to make ends meet.

Eventually Hussein reached the stage where he enjoyed tinkering with and driving automobiles, "souping them up" as boys like to do wherever they can afford automobiles of their own and driving them as fast as possible over the hills and around the sharp bends of the few good roads.

Such driving was dangerous, and he was often admonished by his parents, but he persisted. Maybe it was his way of compensating for the fact that he was small and slight in build, or of showing the other boys and girls that he was a "regular fellow," even though a prince.

During his boyhood a number of events took place which were important to his tiny country, though Hussein was not aware of their significance at the time.

At the beginning of World War II the Arab Legion of Transjordan fought valiantly in Iraq and later in Syria and Lebanon against Axis forces.

Then in March of 1946, Transjordan became a nominally independent state, with Hussein's grandfather Abdullah as King. This was a momentous occasion in the long history of that part of the world, but the ten-year-old Hussien of course took little notice of it except to enjoy the celebrations and festivities.

In 1948 came the establishment of Israel and the united Arab attack on that new country. By now Hussein was aware of the importance of the fighting and eagerly followed the exploits of the famed Arab Legion, the best-trained and best-equipped fighting force in the Middle East. He knew its commander, Glubb Pasha, a British soldier, and many of the legionnaires. When they were defeated by the Israelis he was sad, and when they were successful in defending their own land he was jubilant.

With the signing of the armistice agreement, drastic changes came in the status of Transjordan. Up to that time it had been a tiny state of fewer than 500,000 people on the east bank of the Jordan River. To it was now added a large section on the west bank of the Jordan, with another 500,000 citizens. Plans were under way to change the name of the country from Transjordan to the Hashemite Kingdom of

Jordan, and the formal act of union was to take place on April 24, 1950.

But this was not all that was happening. From what had been formerly Palestine a torrent of refugees was pouring into Jordan, many of them bringing nothing or next to nothing with them. Altogether nearly 500,000 of them, destitute and bitter over their fate, fled into the territory ruled by King Abdullah. That number is the equivalent of fifty-five million refugees in the United States—a staggering number of newcomers to care for.

These refugees, crowded into tent villages maintained by the United Nations, had no work and nothing to do but dwell upon the experiences of the past few weeks and plan for their return home someday. They constantly discussed their vague plans to drive the Jews into the Mediterranean Sea and recapture their former homeland.

King Abdullah's acceptance of the partition of Palestine between the Jews and the Arabs, which incidentally added the west bank to his territory, incensed many of the refugees. To them it meant that he had accepted the permanent existence of Israel as a nation and that their cause was lost. This, they said, was unforgivable. Something had to be done about it. Some of them plotted to avenge Abdullah's action.

During these exciting times Hussein spent many hours with his grandfather King Abdullah. The older man enjoyed the boy's company and frequently told him, "My boy, I want you to come always to me and try to learn what you can from what you see at the palace. Who knows? The time may come when you will replace me on the throne."

Hussein liked being with his grandfather. He admired him greatly, and he enjoyed hunting, riding, inspecting the troops, and visiting many of the villages with him. He also sensed that this man had a sharp political intelligence which made him one of the most important people in the entire Arab world.

On July 20, 1950, Hussein and his grandfather were together for the last time. On the previous day they had witnessed a parade of the Arab Legion Air Force in Jerusalem. There was little to do on the morning of the twentieth, so the King decided to drive to the town of Nablus. There he sipped coffee with the mayor and talked an hour or so with the local people.

As it was nearing noontime, the people begged him to stay for the service in the mosque, but he declined. He had promised to worship in the Dome of the Rock Mosque in Jerusalem and must keep his promise.

When he arrived at the great mosque, its blue, yellow, and white mosaics resplendent in the sunshine, several hundred people were already in the vast courtyard, jostling each other to get a better view of their monarch or trying to find their way in to the service.

The King stopped to talk with them at various points and chided his escort for trying to hold back the crowd, saying, *"La tasasni, ya Habis"* ("Don't imprison me, O Habis").

Thus, unprotected, he stepped into the mosque alone, where he was met by the *shaikh,* or chief Moslem judge, who came forward to kiss the King's hand. At that moment a man stepped from behind the huge door, cocked his pistol, and fired at the King. The King fell to the floor, killed by a fanatic, an Arab extremist who was convinced that Abdullah had given in to the Israelis.

The young grandson had witnessed all this. More than that, one of the assassin's bullets had ripped a medal off his chest. But the boy thought little of what had happened to him. His grandfather was dead, shot in the mosque on his way to the place of prayer.

Such a shocking experience could encourage a boy to be timid, cautious, fearful. Or it could teach him to be courageous, brave, unafraid. Time would tell which lesson Hussein would learn from the tragedy.

To fill the void left by the murder of the King, Abdullah's eldest son, Talal, was recalled from Switzerland where he had been combating a serious illness. For a few months he tried to carry on his duties as King, but he was not capable of doing so. Frequently recurring periods of despondency and mental disturbance made it necessary for him to return to Europe in the summer following his accession to the throne. After a few weeks he returned to Jordan. But it was obvious that he was unfit to continue the reign. A secret session of Parliament was held, and Hussein was selected to succeed his father.

Hussein was not quite seventeen. Since he was still too young to rule, a regency was appointed, and he was sent back to continue his studies. He completed his work at Harrow, a prominent English private school. Then he was sent to Sandhurst, the British West Point, for eight months of military training.

He worked hard to complete his studies satisfactorily, but at the same time he enjoyed weekends in London attending court functions, dances, and private parties.

Hussein was a good-looking young man with dark eyes, a trim figure, and wavy black hair. His smart clothes and charming manners made him a favorite in London court circles. He also got along well with his classmates, although they joked about his daring exploits and his love of uniforms and medals, nicknaming him "Brazen Hussy."

In April 1953, Hussein returned to Jordan, and on May 3 he was crowned King.

The job he took over was not one which many people

would want, for Jordan is one of the least stable countries in the world.

In shape it resembles a large hatchet, with a short handle pointed in the direction of Iraq. In area it is 37,900 square miles, about the size of the state of Indiana.

Its location is also a handicap, for it is almost landlocked. A tiny port at Aqaba, in the southwest, is its one outlet to the Red Sea. To the north is Syria, to the east are Iraq and Saudi Arabia, to the south Saudi Arabia, and to the west Israel, blocking Jordan's passage to the Mediterranean.

To add to its woes, the soil is not fertile except for small strips along the Jordan River and on the eastern shores of the Dead Sea. The rest of the country is dry and barren, with sand dunes and rocky cliffs occupying much of its surface.

The climate is hot and dry in the summer and mild in the winter, making it possible to raise some wheat and barley as well as some citrus fruits and vegetables.

Nor is Jordan rich in minerals. There are some valuable mineral deposits in the Dead Sea and some phosphate in the area between Amman and the Gulf of Aqaba, but these deposits are not large and have not been well exploited as yet. However, natural gas has been found, and engineers feel certain that there is oil as yet undiscovered.

Although economically extremely poor, historically and culturally Jordan is a veritable museum. It is the ancient land of Ammon, Edom, Gilead, and Moab of the Old Testament, and of Samaria and Judea of the New. The area that had been added to Transjordan to form Jordan included the Old City of Jerusalem, with its markets similar to those that thrived in the time of the Old Testament prophets and of Jesus. Here, too, is the Via Dolorosa along which Jesus is said to have carried the Cross, and, nearby, Calvary and Golgotha.

In the capital of Amman, an old Roman amphitheater stands almost in the center of the city, and to the south is the celebrated rose red city of Petra, hewn out of the sandstone cliffs. In Jerash one can see the triumphal arch of the Roman Emperor Hadrian, built about A.D. 129, and the well-preserved ruins of the Temple of Zeus.

There have been many reminders of Jewish history in Jordan, including the outer wall of the mosque in Hebron, said to have been built over the cave in which Abraham and Sarah were buried, the Wailing Wall in Jerusalem, and the Dome of the Rock Mosque, built on the site of Solomon's Temple.

Jordan is an archeological treasure house. In 1966, a team of searchers uncovered an urban block of houses built in 900 B.C. The mound excavated covered twenty-five acres and rose one hundred thirty-eight feet. It contained seven layers of habitations of earlier civilizations: Roman, Hellenistic, Persian, and four "floors" of the Second Iron Age. There is evidence that more centuries of ancient civilizations remain to be uncovered.

Another discovery was a palace of the Persian period, 532–520 B.C.

There is natural beauty in Jordan, too. In the spring the almond and peach trees bloom and the eighteen- to twenty-inch purple, white, and red anemones vie with each other for attention, brilliant against the dull green setting of the olive trees and the gray and buff cliffs of the countryside.

But the tragedy of Jordan is that it has never been a nation and its people have no feeling of a common past, a common present, or a common future. It is in many ways a divided land. For four hundred years this entire area was a province of the Ottoman, or Turkish, Empire, and before that a district of Syria ruled successively by the Greeks, Romans, and Arabs. But it has never been a country.

Furthermore, many of its people do not want it to be a country now. Some would like to belong to Syria and some to Iraq. Many would like to re-establish their own land of Palestine, others to join Nasser's United Arab Republic.

Among the present population are the three groups already mentioned—the original native people of the Hashemite Kingdom, the former Transjordanians, and the Palestinian refugees.

The people are also divided socially and economically. The largest group are urban dwellers, with some education and some experience in government of the Western European type. About 200,000 are Bedouin camel breeders and sheep and goat herders with little education and a close feeling of loyalty to their tribes. About 900,000 are farmers who live in villages and are often suspicious of the other two groups.

To make matters worse for the young King, Jordan could not support itself financially at the beginning of his reign. At best it could provide about one-quarter of its annual expenses. For the rest of its money it had to rely on other nations. When it was a mandate, Britain had supplied the necessary additional funds. But with the withdrawal of Britain after World War II, Jordan had to look elsewhere for help. It tried to obtain financial aid from other Arab countries, especially oil-rich Saudi Arabia. But finally it fell back largely on the United States for a major share of its support. The United States was willing to help because of its interest in maintaining Jordan as a separate state, friendly to the Western nations.

Fortunately almost all of the people of Jordan were Moslems by religion and Arabs by culture, speaking the Arabic language. At least they had that much in common.

Such was the country which Hussein was supposed to rule and mold into a modern, united nation. It would have been a terrific job for an older, wiser, more experienced man. For a young, inexperienced boy it looked like an impossible assignment. Many people predicted that Jordan would not last long as a country, certainly that Hussein would not last long as King.

During his first five years in power, the country was engaged in a constant tug of war politically. On one side were the pro-Nasser forces, eager for some kind of alliance or union with Egypt and for more power for the people as opposed to the King. With them was often aligned the small but powerful pro-Soviet group. On the other end of the rope were the pro-Western forces, represented largely by the army and the former Transjordanians.

Between them stood King Hussein, trying to balance himself like a tightrope walker.

To complicate matters, people kept pulling the rope from either end. The weight in numbers, in education, in experience, in parliamentary representation, and in popular appeal seemed to be on the side of the anti-West faction.

In 1954, Iraq suggested unification with Jordan, but Hussein and the Jordanians rejected this proposal, largely because it would alienate them from the other Arab states.

In 1955, strong pressures was brought to bear on Jordan to enter the Baghdad Pact with Iran, Iraq, Pakistan, Turkey, and Great Britain, thus providing a ring of defense against the U.S.S.R. in the Middle East. There was violent opposition to such a move. Riots, which the army eventually quelled, broke out all over Jordan. In the end, however, the government decided not to enter into the pact. In that same year, Jordan joined the United Nations.

On March 1, 1956, Glubb Pasha, the Chief of Staff of the Arab Legion, was summoned by the Prime Minister and the Minister of Defense and told that the King had decided that Glubb needed a "rest." In other words, he was being fired, and he was told to leave the country in a matter of hours.

This was apparently a shock to Glubb, as it was to the world. He had been in Transjordan and Jordan for twenty-six years and had built the Arab Legion into a powerful fighting force. Just what the reasons were for his dismissal no one knows, although it looked like an attempt on Hussein's part to bolster his popularity after the riots of 1955 and to ingratiate himself with the anti-West forces in his country.

Then came the nationalization of the Suez Canal by Nasser, the attack on Egypt by Israel, and the support of Israel by France and Great Britain. King Hussein is reported to have volunteered at this time to lead the Arab Legion Air Force himself in an attack on the city of Tel Aviv in Israel, an offer which was vetoed by Nasser and others.

Now Jordan's bitterness against Israel was fully released. Nasser's stock as hero of the Arab world soared. The pro-Nasser forces were winning the struggle in Jordan and were able to form a new government with Suleiman Nabulsi as Prime Minister. Nabulsi was an enemy of the King and violently anti-West.

Throughout all these internal struggles, it was the army which had been most loyal to the King. This was due largely to the fact that it was composed chiefly of men from the Bedouin tribes of old Transjordan. But with the dismissal of Glubb Pasha, things began to change in the army. In Pasha's place King Hussein appointed a close personal friend by the name of Nuwar. At least Hussein thought he was a close personal friend, until he discovered that Nuwar was plotting against him, apparently in league with Nabulsi.

On a trip to Syria, Nuwar had arranged with the Russians to supply the Jordanians with modern arms in return for recognition by Hussein. He and Nabulsi then told Hussein of their plan and urged him to recognize Russia, as his part of the deal. This Hussein refused to do. Moreover, he made Nabulsi promise that he would not press for such recognition in the cabinet. Nabulsi promised the King that he would forget the whole affair, but shortly after that the cabinet voted for the recognition of Russia.

The young King's troubles were mounting. He realized that he must take a firm stand or abdicate. He decided to stand firm, and on April 10, 1957, he dismissed the entire cabinet, abolished all political parties, and declared a state of emergency. His advisers urged him to get rid of Nuwar, too, but Hussein could not yet believe that Nuwar was plotting against him.

Soon he was to realize that Nuwar was indeed his sworn enemy. Events came to a head on April 13, 1957, when Nuwar ordered the First Armored Regiment to surround the castle. The men knew what this meant, and they mutinied. Word was then sent to the infantry that the artillery was in revolt against the King. Believing this lie, the infantry attacked the artillery and several men were killed in the melee.

Word of the mutiny was telephoned to Nuwar at the palace and was overheard by King Hussein, who said that he would go to the army camp himself. He asked Nuwar to go with him, and in the dark of night the two men set out in the King's own car. Before they reached the camp they were stopped by some of the army men, who told them of Nuwar's plot and the mutiny, apparently not realizing that the two men they were talking about were both in the car. The King then stepped out and told the men to return to camp.

Then he got back in the car and started on. At this point Nuwar begged that he be dropped—and Hussein sent him back to Amman, going on alone to the army camp at Zerqa.

Arriving at the camp, he walked through the fighting lines in a dramatic show of courage and spent four hours bringing order out of chaos, each moment risking an assassin's bullet. With order restored, he returned to the palace.

The armored cars and their men, who were supposed to have surrounded the castle and taken the King prisoner, were there. And Nuwar was there, too. He had ordered the men to return to the army camp at Zerqa, since the "incident" was over, but they had called him a traitor and refused to go.

Now they told their story to the King. Nuwar tried at first to place the blame elsewhere and then offered his resignation. Once this was accepted, the King appointed a new Chief of State, only to discover he, too, had also been implicated in the plot.

Having settled on the resignation of both men, the King received a group of political leaders who had not yet learned about the sudden change of events and who were trying to force Hussein's hand in the appointment of a new cabinet. The King listened to their suggestions, which verged on threats, and dismissed them with harsh words.

All night he consulted with his counselors and finally called on Said el-Mufti, one of the elder statesmen of Jordan, to form a new cabinet. Meanwhile, Nuwar was gathering his family together for a sudden exit to Syria.

The next day there were riots in the streets again, but the army was behind the King and the rioters were soon quelled.

This was the closest brush with death Hussein had had since the assassin's bullet had ripped a medal off his chest when his grandfather was murdered. Again Hussein had escaped. Although that rope he had been walking had been pulled violently in both directions, he had hung on. His ability had been tested in the most trying circumstances, and he had proved his skill and his courage. This raised his standing with his people.

In the spring of 1957, Egypt, Syria, and Saudi Arabia agreed to support the Jordanian government financially and to aid it militarily if necessary. At the same time the Sixth Fleet of the United States moved toward Jordan. Jordan quieted down again, with King Hussein still on the throne.

Egypt and Syria's promises of financial help were not kept, but King Saud did pay his share. This aid was unusual, for Saud had long been an opponent of the Hashemite dynasty. However, he seemed to feel that it was important now for the kings of the Middle East to stick together, as the downfall of one might hasten the downfall of others. Moreover, he was not happy over the growing power of Nasser in the Middle East, and any support he could give to Jordan would probably help to strengthen Jordan's opposition to this strong man of Egypt.

Even though Hussein has by necessity been primarily concerned with political events, he has had a hand, too, in economic and social development in Jordan. No long-term progress can be made until more jobs are provided and drastic changes made in the economy of the country. Despite all the political disturbances, there has been considerable progress in industry, agriculture, health, and education.

In 1952 a Development Board was established to encourage the extension of irrigation, foster the development of co-operatives, improve communication and transportation facilities, exploit the potash and phosphate industries, and oversee the construction of a port at Aqaba.

In 1948 there were practically no factories in the country. Today there are cement, soap, cigarette, clothing, furniture, fruit- and vegetable-processing factories, and olive-oil-refining plants. A cold storage plant has been installed at Aqaba with help from the Food and Agriculture Organization of the United Nations, and a refrigerated transport system set up between Amman and Aqaba. A sugar refinery, a textile mill, and a distillery have also been built.

In agriculture, most attention has been paid to increasing the food supply through irrigation, better seeds, insect control, and other measures. These efforts have yielded results. The output of wheat and barley has increased manyfold.

One of Jordan's most valuable products is phosphate. This has been extensively developed and the output increased from 40,000 tons in 1953 to 614,000 tons in 1963.

With help from the United Nations, the United States, and other sources, the numbers of hospitals, clinics, doctors, and maternity and welfare centers have increased spectacularly.

Special programs to combat malaria and trachoma have been very successful, even though neither of these diseases has been conquered in Jordan yet.

In education there have been similar gains. The rapid increase in the total number of students in public and private schools and those studying abroad is revealed by this chart:

	1949-50	1962-63
Number of students	31,845	325,527
Number of teachers	739	9,205

Education still is not compulsory in Jordan, but it is free to those who do choose to attend school. The greatest gain has been in the rising enrollment of girls, something new for Jordan, as for many other parts of the world.

Whether Jordan can ever make herself economically independent is open to serious question. Her land is not fertile and she lacks mineral resources in sufficient quantity to support herself. Perhaps she could become an industrial country, but that would take enormous capital.

Her greatest hope seems to be in federation or union with some other country. This was one of the factors in the mind of King Hussein when he and his first cousin, King Faisal of Iraq, agreed in February 1958 to form the Arab Union, consisting of Iraq and Jordan.

Economically this federation held out high hopes for Jordan. Iraq is a larger country than California, but with a population of only 6,500,000 persons. It has a tremendous amount of oil and considerable industrialization, plus good farming land.

It looked as if the new federation, which was proclaimed on February 14, 1958, might help to ease the problems of Jordan, helping the Jordanians with their normal expenses, providing jobs for some of the men who were willing to go to Iraq, encouraging resettlement of many of the refugees in Iraq, and lowering prices on oil, gasoline, kerosene, and other products.

This new federation, however, was established for political even more than for economic reasons. At the beginning of February 1958, Egypt and Syria had joined to form the United Arab Republic, under Nasser's leadership. Eventually either Jordan would have to join this new group or unite with some other country to consolidate its position in the Middle East. King Hussein did not want to join forces with Nasser, and the only logical alternative was a union with Iraq.

Thus a hastily contrived federation was formed, with King Faisal of Iraq as King of the two countries, but with each nation retaining its own sovereignty.

At this point the future looked brighter for Jordan than it had since it had been established as a country. Then on July 14, King Faisal and Iraqi Prime Minister Nuri as-Said were killed by Iraqi nationalists, and a group of pro-Nasser army officers took over the government. Hussein was proclaimed head of the Arab Union and prepared to march into Iraq with his troops to fight the rebels.

But he was prevented from doing so in large part by the British and the Americans, who feared that a world war might break out in the Middle East.

Afraid that a similar attempt to overthrow the monarchy might be made in Jordan by pro-Nasser forces, King Hussein called for British troops, and they were flown in. Meanwhile American troops were being dispatched to Lebanon at the request of that government, which was also facing an internal rebellion.

Sparks were flying from the Middle Eastern tinderbox, and the chances of war were great. This was obviously an issue for the United Nations Security Council, and it was taken up there as a threat to the peace of the world. In a surprising show of solidarity, the Arab nations agreed upon a resolution empowering the Secretary-General of the UN to try to work out arrangements for the withdrawal of troops from Jordan and Lebanon. The efforts were successful and the British troops were withdrawn.

Relations between Jordan and the United Arab Republic worsened when Jordan opposed Nasser's Arab Higher Committee for Palestine, which had been created to "liberate" Palestine from Jewish control. Immediately the Cairo radio began a propaganda campaign against King Hussein. When the King visited the United Nations in 1960, his speech to the General Assembly attacked both the Soviet Union and the United Arab Republic, accusing them of fomenting trouble in the Middle East. The following year, in a conciliatory mood, Hussein offered to meet Nasser in Cairo and discuss their problems. The meeting did not take place, but tension was notably relaxed for a few months, until Syria pulled

out of the United Arab Republic and was recognized by
Jordan, which of course displeased Nasser. In 1964, Hussein
did meet with Nasser and other Arab leaders in Cairo,
where they made plans for mutual defense against Israel.

In 1962, Jordan and Saudi Arabia joined military forces.
This move was directed against Nasser, who was publicly
denouncing the monarchical regimes of the Arab world such
as King Hussein's and King Faisal's. Nasser's radio advocated
the overthrow of "the last of the Hashemites."

King Hussein experienced a domestic crisis in 1963, for
he has problems at home, too. A revolution in Syria brought
to power leaders interested in Arab unity and thus in the
United Arab Republic, from which they had formerly pulled
out. This move on Syria's part gave the enemies of Hussein
in his own country an opportunity to make trouble. Hussein
acted quickly, dismissed the leftist Prime Minister and put
in his place an elder statesman whom he trusted. But anti-
government demonstrations broke out, and the King again
replaced the Prime Minister, this time with his uncle. An
election in July was so rigged that only the King's supporters
were returned to office.

King Hussein was caught in a squeeze between Nasser
and his rivals among the Arab states. Those thus involved
were chiefly Syria, Iraq, Saudi Arabia, Yemen, and Egypt.
About the only thing they have in common is their bitter
animosity toward Israel. Jordan felt particularly vulnerable,
for she had over 350 miles of joint frontier with Israel. This
long border was guarded by patrols, alerted to act in an
emergency. In June 1967, war broke out between Israel and
the Arab states. The Israeli forces quickly occupied all of
Jordan's territory west of the Jordan River, including the Old
City of Jerusalem. The Jordanian air force was knocked out
and thousands of men in its small army were killed. After the
ensuing truce Hussein flew to New York City to state his

country's case before the United Nations, although nothing definite was settled concerning the future of the Middle East at that time.

Up to this point, King Hussein has been a lucky young man, who wants to have fun despite his heavy responsibilities, and does so with such a diversity of activities that he might be said to live *several* lives. He is a go-cart racer on the Amman airport race course, a skin diver with an air tank on his back, an aviator in the air force, a parachute jumper, a tank driver, and a hiker across the Jordanian hills. He has never outgrown his boyhood interest in engines and likes to tinker with them and read magazines devoted to mechanics. He is a good dancer and likes jazz and Latin American music.

The young King dresses smartly and always to the occasion. Ordinarily he wears a Western-style suit, often a light gabardine, suitable for the warm climate of Jordan. If he is on his way to one of the villages, he may have a red and white checkered kerchief, called a *kaffieh*, on his head. On top of the kerchief will be a loose, four-sided headpiece which looks like two black coils. This *ukal* holds the headpiece in place. Such a colorful headdress has been worn for centuries by the Bedouins as a protection against the sun and the desert sands. At military functions, Hussein's neat uniform is decorated with his own special medals.

King Hussein enjoys the advantages of his kingly status. But he is at the same time a humble, simple, natural person, standing on little formality or protocol. One of his friends says of him, "He shares his happinesses and keeps his troubles to himself." He is very democratic. He does not live in a royal palace but in a small villa about ten miles from Amman. His home is no more elaborate than those of neighboring wealthy merchants. It is a buff-colored limestone house, situated on a hill overlooking the capital city. His oak-paneled office is in his palace home. Next door is an office building, guarded by men dressed in long black robes, with red scarves around their necks, black leather boots, black sheepskin hats, and carrying swords. On either side of their robes are six silver hand grenades, attached to the robes like pockets. Sharing guard duty are soldiers in natty blue uniforms with gold buttons, and blue caps with narrow red trim. Such color and pageantry reflect the cultural history of Jordan.

King Hussein's English-born wife, Princess Muna, daughter of a British army officer who was based in Jordan, is an athletic young woman who shares her husband's interests and often cooks his breakfast, if the King does not cook the eggs and sausages himself, as he likes to do. There are three children in the family, two sons and a daughter.

The young King is sometimes referred to as a "soft touch," because he is always ready to help friends and acquaintances who find themselves in financial straits.

Hussein's outstanding trait is personal courage, which he has demonstrated over and over again. He lives and reigns in a dangerous, constantly teetering situation. "Danger is just a part of life," he says. It is fortunate for Jordan that her King has that kind of courage. But whether, in the face of his recent military defeat, King Hussein can long remain in power is questionable.

ASIA

JINNAH
OF PAKISTAN

"Enter to Learn: Go Forth to Serve." Those were the words carved over the stone entrance to the Sind Madrasah School in Karachi, a small town in India in the late nineteenth century. Those were the words that young Mohammed Ali Jinnah read many times during the four years he spent in that school from the time when he was eleven until he was fifteen.

Mohammed Ali was a bit baffled by those words, as hundreds of thousands of other boys and girls have been in the hundreds of schools around the world where this famous phrase has been placed before them by well-meaning adults.

He had entered to learn and had studied harder than most of his classmates. Everyone told him that he had a good mind and he had used it well. But "to serve"—what did that mean? Had the object of that verb been omitted? What was one supposed to serve? Why didn't they tell you that? Why all the mystery?

Sixty years later, a tall slender Moslem with the bearing of an aristocrat stood before a throng of people in the same town where he had studied as a boy. This time he was being installed as the Governor General of a new nation of eighty million people, the sixth most populous country in the world. Many people had helped to form this nation but the man who addressed the people today had been its chief architect, and on this day, August 14, 1947, his dream of an independent Pakistan was coming true. Allah be praised!

It had taken some time for Mohammed Ali Jinnah to

learn what that phrase over the entrance to his high school meant. But eventually he had learned what it means "to serve," and he had served his people and his cause exceedingly well.

His life is possibly the most curious of all the lives of the leaders of new nations, for midway in its course it took a sudden and abrupt change. But in order to understand its development, one must follow his life from its beginning to its climax in the founding of Pakistan.

Mohammed Ali was born in Karachi on Christmas Day, 1876, the first of seven children. His father was a hide merchant of moderate means. When Mohammed Ali was six he started to school in Karachi, and when he was ten he was sent to Bombay for a year, where he attended the Gokul Das Tej Primary School. After that period away from home, he returned to Karachi and entered the Sind Madrasah High School, later spending a year in the Christian Missionary Society High School.

He was an unusually bright and quick student, and friends of the family urged his father to send him to England to study. His father was reluctant, but finally decided that the boy could go. So in 1892 young Jinnah headed for London. He set a scholastic record there, completing his work for entrance to the bar within two years, to become the youngest Indian student ever to be admitted to the bar.

As a boy he had been known as the lad with the long yellow coat. This he abandoned in England. Instead, he bought English clothes and a monocle, which he wore as a distinguishing feature the rest of his life. In England he also perfected his use of the English language, becoming more proficient in it than in the Urdu language spoken by many of his own people in what is now West Pakistan.

During his years in England, Jinnah had the good fortune to meet or see many of the leading political figures of that day—the venerable William Gladstone, Joseph Chamberlain, and Lord Morley. He was thrilled to hear or even see these English statesmen.

We know little of his everyday life in England, but the few stories that have been recorded make us wish there were more. For example, he toured England with a Shakespeare company, and on one occasion at least he was arrested for taking part in the pranks of college boys on the night of the famous Oxford-Cambridge boat race.

In the fall of 1896 he returned to India to practice law. In those days a young lawyer either joined the British government, which ruled the entire subcontinent of India, or moved to a large city where there was enough work for private lawyers. Jinnah decided to take the second course. He moved to Bombay.

In Bombay he trudged to an office each day for nearly three years before he got his first "break." This came when the Acting Advocate General invited him to work in his office. Very soon Jinnah became known as a brilliant pleader in court, collecting facts with care, assembling them with astuteness and logic, and presenting them in a slow, cold manner, with rapier-like thrusts.

Even then people were beginning to tell stories about the times he challenged the judges. On one occasion the judge chided him, saying, "Mr. Jinnah, you should respect me at least for my gray hair." To which Jinnah retorted, "I am not going to respect those gray hairs unless there is wisdom beneath them."

For such retorts, he was sometimes labeled arrogant. His friends, however, denied this. They said he was merely confident and that it was time someone challenged the foreigners who ruled them.

All his life there was to be this division of opinion about Jinnah. Some were to claim that he was self-centered, egotistical, aggressive. Others, that he was a man with a mission and the confidence to proclaim and support that sense of purpose. He was always a very controversial figure in India.

His political career began with his election in 1909 by the Moslems of Bombay to the Imperial Legislative Council, a lawmaking body. He was young for such a post, and was soon in the middle of controversies. Speaking on a resolution concerning indentured labor in Natal in Africa, he said that this was "a most painful question—a question which arouses the feeling of all classes in this country to the highest pitch of indignation and horror at the hard and cruel treatment . . . meted out to Indians in South Africa."

The President of the Legislative Council reprimanded him for the use of the word "cruel," pointing out that he was speaking of a friendly part of the Empire. Indians were not supposed to talk back, but Jinnah replied, "My lord, I should feel inclined to use much stronger language, but I am fully aware of the constitution of the Council and I do not want to trespass for one single moment; but I do say this, that the treatment that is meted out to Indians is the harshest that can be imagined and, as I said before, the feeling in this country is unanimous."

This was Jinnah the fighter speaking, and he would speak in similar tones upon many topics and on many occasions in the coming decades.

Meanwhile, the All-India Moslem League had been organized in 1906. Patterned somewhat after the All-India Congress, its chief aims were to foster loyalty to the British government, to protect and advance the political rights of Moslems, and to promote a feeling of brotherhood with other groups in India, provided this did not jeopardize the rights of Moslems. This was a sectarian group and Jinnah was no sectarian, so he did not join it.

He was active, however, in the All-India Congress, a movement aimed at obtaining more rights for Indians, with its membership drawn from all the religious groups—Hindus, Moslems, Sikhs, and Parsees, or Zoroastrians. In 1906 Jinnah attended their national congress, serving as secretary to the president, Dadabhai Naoroji, the Grand Old Man of Indian politics. This was a group with which he felt in sympathy, and he became active in it. As he saw India at that time, there was no need for people to separate according to their religions. There was one great cause they had in common— the ousting of the British and the winning of independence and self-government. On that they could all agree. On less important matters they could go their separate ways.

Jinnah was therefore elated when the Congress came out in 1908 in favor of independence and self-government within the British Empire, thereby abandoning its former more cautious policy on these twin goals.

During this period in his life he was also active in the Home Rule League, putting to use his ability as an organizer.

In 1913 one of India's great liberals and champions of freedom invited Jinnah to accompany him to England. He was Gopal Krishna Gokhale. Together they visited the hundreds of Indian students who were studying in the British Isles. Both men were disturbed by the divisions among these students based on castes, languages, and regional differences. Hoping to bind them together, they helped to organize the London Indian Association, which was open to all students from India.

Those months of association with Gokhale strengthened Jinnah's admiration for this older Hindu and Indian leader. He considered Gokhale one of the men who most directly influenced him. They had already worked together in an unsuccessful battle to achieve compulsory elementary education for all of India, and were to fight together on many occasions after that. Jinnah was so struck with Gokhale that he said his "one ambition (was) to become the Moslem Gokhale."

Two other Indians who left their mark upon Jinnah were Surendranath Banerjeq, a journalist and nationalist, and Iqbal, poet and philosopher. Iqbal's influence was perhaps the most powerful in Jinnah's decision to support the partition of India into two nations.

Two women also influenced him politically. One was Mrs. Naidu, an eminent poetess, who became the first woman governor of an Indian province after India won its independence. The other was Mrs. Besant, a leader in the Theosophist movement, an active politician, and the founder of the All-India Home Rule League.

Upon his return from England, Jinnah joined the Moslem League for the first time. He felt that this was possible now because the League had decided to take a firm stand in favor of an independent India, a position it had not been willing to take before. He had to be assured, however, that his membership would not be in conflict with his activities in the All-India Congress, which was still his first love.

He was elated in 1915 when the Congress and the Moslem League held their annual meetings concurrently in Bombay, and even more so in 1916, when these two groups met in Lucknow and made the famous Lucknow Pact. By this agreement the All-India Congress stated its willingness to have separate elections and voting organizations for the Moslems, and the All-India Moslem League, on its part, surrendered the right to vote in both the general and separate elections. This was a decisive step in the direction of collaboration between the two groups.

At this Lucknow meeting Jinnah had been elected president of the Moslem League, and nothing could have pleased him more than this joint action between the two groups in which he was active. Actually this was to be the high point in Moslem-Hindu co-operation. He was led to comment about the future in these words:

> Hindus and Moslems, united and firm, the voices of three hundred millions of people vibrating throughout the length and breadth of the country, will produce a force which no power on earth can resist. India has, I believe, turned a corner. She has passed through great sufferings and borne them patiently for centuries. There is now a bright and a great future in front of her. We are on a straight road; the promised land is in sight. "Forward" is the motto and clear course for young India. But in the onward march we must be circumspect and never lose sight of the true perspective before us. And wisdom and caution should be our watchwords.

It was also at the Lucknow meeting that two other great Indian leaders first met, Nehru and Gandhi. From then on, Gandhi was to be the personal force in the movement for independence, and non-violence, or soul force, was to be the accepted method for achieving this goal. Nehru became Gandhi's favorite, and those who opposed Gandhi's leadership and methods were to be in a minority from then on, and would have some crucial decisions to make.

An open clash of ideas as to the means of achieving independence came in 1920, when the Congress and the Moslem League met simultaneously. A large majority of the Congress and many of the Moslem League supported Gandhi. Jinnah was one of the few men who openly opposed him. It was not a popular stand for him to take. Jinnah's opposition was based on several counts. One was that the masses of India were untrained and undisciplined in non-violent methods and it would be difficult if not impossible to train them. Second, Jinnah felt that Gandhi's approach was a religious one, based largely on Hindu and to some extent Christian thinking. This made it a divisive rather than a unifying movement. In the third place, Jinnah was afraid of the outcome of non-violence.

Two years before this clash between Gandhi and Jinnah took place, another important event had occurred in Jinnah's personal life. As a young boy of fifteen he had been married to a bride selected by his family. She had died soon after their marriage, and for all this time he had been alone. One of his best friends was Sir Dinshaw Petit, a prosperous businessman in Bombay, and a Parsee, or member of the Zoroastrian religion. Jinnah was attracted to Petit's young daughter, Ruttenbai, and despite her father's opposition, he married her in 1918. She was then eighteen and he was forty-one. Ruttenbai had been a Parsee, but she now became a Moslem.

One child, Dina, was born to them on August 15, 1919. This event brought them tremendous happiness, but it was not to last long. The great disparity in their ages and differences in their temperaments caused a rift in their marriage. Within a few months Ruttenbai took Dina and returned to her people. In 1929, she died.

The failure of this marriage added a crushing personal blow to the political rebuffs Jinnah had recently experienced. During the decade of the 1920s, Gandhi's star was on the rise; Jinnah's was on the wane.

Jinnah was an intellectual, and his appeal was largely to the small group of middle-class men which was developing on the Indian subcontinent. He could be charming, courteous, and gracious in company, but he was reserved, dignified, and even brusque with all but a few close friends and associates. His speeches were logically organized and presented like a lawyer's briefs. But he could not unbend and identify himself with the common people. In fact, he could not even speak the language of the people well. English was his first language, and this was not a language they understood.

Gandhi was different. He was a spiritual giant and a political genius. He was a man of ideas but also of emotions and a person whom others could revere and love. He seemed to emerge from the masses of India even though he was in many ways far above them. He understood them and could communicate with them. He had an unusual knack for finding symbols which the common people could understand. As he sat at his spinning wheel making cloth, people began to understand that this was a protest against the shipping of raw materials to England for processing into cloth which would then be shipped back to India at exorbitant prices. His simple white cap made of homespun cloth became a symbol of the Gandhi non-violent revolution, and people everywhere began to wear it. When he made his famous march to the sea and defied the British government by making salt, millions of Indians understood this simple yet symbolic act of protest against a British monopoly.

The Indian independence movement was changing in character. It was no longer the province of a few. Now it was a mass movement with millions of men and women taking part in it. Now Gandhi was its leader, and in popular appeal Jinnah was no match for this man.

In England there was a growing awareness of what was happening in India, and when the Labour party came into power under Ramsay MacDonald, a Round Table Conference was called in London attended by fifty-eight delegates from India, representing all the important groups there. Jinnah was selected as one of these delegates. In the first of these Round Table Conferences he felt that some progress was made, but in the second little was accomplished. In this meeting he was overshadowed by Gandhi and by the Aga Khan as leader of the Moslems.

Finally the meetings broke up without reaching any agreement and the British made their own plans for India's future, embodied in the Government of India Act of 1935.

Jinnah was crushed. To one of the men who was to become his biographer, he said:

> But what is to be done? The Hindus are short-sighted and, I think, incorrigible. The Moslem camp is full of those spineless people who, whatever they may say to me, consult the Deputy Commissioner about what they should do. Where is any place for me between these two groups?

He was discouraged, depressed, and disillusioned. Two decades of work as the ambassador of Hindu-Moslem unity seemed to have slipped away. His personal life had been a failure; his political life had collapsed. What a sad day this was for him. This was the great watershed of Jinnah's life: the great dividing line.

He went to London, took up the practice of law, and considered the idea of settling permanently in England. His work in India was over. He had done what he could to promote Hindu-Moslem unity and Indian independence. He had failed. Even for a strong man like Jinnah this was hard to take.

In India the Moslem League had reached an all-time low in membership and in morale. Yet there were those who had not given up hope for its restoration. One of these was a young man named Liaquat Ali Khan, a graduate of both the Moslem University at Aligarh and of Oxford, a man with a winning personality and organizational ability. In 1933 he went to London and pleaded with Jinnah to return to India. Others bombarded Jinnah with similar appeals.

Finally in 1934 Jinnah did go back to India and traveled throughout the land, taking the pulse of his beloved country. Everywhere he went he talked to students, met with Moslem leaders, tried to close the breaches between the various factions in the Moslem League. Then, in 1935, he was elected president of the League. The English had meanwhile given the voting franchise to more people in India. Now new tactics for winning independence seemed necessary. So Jinnah and his colleagues started to reorganize the Moslem League to make it a more democratic, more dynamic movement.

Meanwhile Jinnah had been mulling over the place which the Moslems should take in an independent India. His old dream of a united nation had been shattered. Gradually he replaced it with the dream of a separate land for the Moslems, to be called Pakistan. For this new idea he was indebted to the poet and philosopher Iqbal, the Shakespeare, Goethe, or Dante of the modern Moslem world. Jinnah had seen much of Iqbal in London and had been greatly influenced by him. The seed of Pakistan was planted in Jinnah's mind as early as 1930, but it did not begin to grow until years later.

Speaking at Lahore in March 1940, Jinnah declared:

It is extremely difficult to appreciate why our Hindu friends fail to understand the real nature of Islam and Hinduism. They are not religions in the strict sense of the word, but are, in fact, quite different and distinct social orders, and it is a dream that the Hindus and Moslems can ever evolve a common nationality, and this misconception of one Indian nation has gone far beyond the limits and is the cause of most of our troubles and will lead India to destruction if we fail to revive our nations in time. The Hindus and Moslems belong to two different religious philosophies, social customs, literatures. They neither intermarry nor interdine, and, indeed, they belong to two different civilizations which are based on conflicting ideas and conceptions.

This was a new Jinnah speaking. It was a statement of his new philosophy. It is hard to believe that such a change could have taken place in him. And it had certainly been difficult for him to move in this new direction.

But he had moved, and the Moslem League moved with him. At Lahore they adopted what became known as the Pakistan Resolution, demanding a separate state for Moslems.

What had caused such a drastic shift in Jinnah's views? At the heart of the shift was his fear that the Moslems were losing out and that they would have to exist as a submerged minority in any new country which would be formed. This had come about, Jinnah felt, because of the stubbornness of the Hindus and particularly of Gandhi and Nehru. Coupled with this was his feeling that the All-India Congress had now become a political party of the Hindus, under the dominant leadership of Gandhi and Nehru. There might also have been a tinge of personal jealousy and rivalry between Gandhi and Nehru on one side and Jinnah on the other, over the leadership of the independence movement.

Throughout these many years of battle for the independence of India, Jinnah's chief support had come from the Moslems, but they had by no means been united in their support of him. Many had followed Gandhi; some had followed neither of them. In July 1943, a Moslem who had been opposed to Jinnah's leadership entered his office on the pretext of having a conference with him and drew a knife to kill him. Jinnah was then sixty-seven years old, but he was alert and agile and he parried the blow of his would-be assassin.

In September 1944, Gandhi and Jinnah met in the latter's home in Bombay and spent several days together trying to reconcile their differences. Gandhi was willing to concede partial autonomy to a Moslem state, but his terms were so demanding that Jinnah could not accept them. Gandhi wanted, for example, to win Indian independence as a united state before there was any division, and even then to have shared control of such matters as foreign affairs, defense, taxes, commerce, and internal communication.

Then came the end of World War II and elections in India, in which the candidates of the All-India Moslem League were very successful. Jinnah was overjoyed. "No power on earth can prevent Pakistan," he proclaimed.

In 1947, Lord Mountbatten was sent to India to provide for the departure of the British and the advent of independence for India. In the negotiations that took place in that interval, Jinnah represented the interests of the Moslems, demanding a separate state, and Nehru the interests of the much larger community of Hindus, Moslems, Sikhs, and others which was to become the gigantic modern state of India. Nehru was fifty-seven; Lord Mountbatten forty-six—and Jinnah seventy. Yet with his excellent mind and singleness of purpose Jinnah was able to hold his own in the company of younger men. When he was reminded that if there was to be a nation known as Pakistan, large sections of the Punjab and Bengal would have to be divided, Jinnah retorted, "Better a moth-eaten Pakistan than no Pakistan at all."

Meanwhile, hatred and bitterness between the various religious communities in the subcontinent were unleashed in full force. Rioting took place in many parts of India, with tremendous losses of life and heavy destruction of property. Finally Gandhi and Jinnah were prevailed upon to issue a joint statement calling for the cessation of such hostilities. This Peace Appeal was printed in the papers, plastered on the walls in giant broadsides, and shown in the movie theaters throughout the land. But it did not stop the fratricide.

Amost in desperation Mountbatten was recalled to London and a final settlement decided upon by the British cabinet, over which there was to be no wrangling, no haggling, no negotiations. It conceded the right of the Pakistanis to a separate country, with the right to decide whether they would stay in the Commonwealth or not. But the Punjab and Bengal were to be divided, parts going to each of the new nations. Under considerable pressure from Lord Mountbatten, Jinnah conceded, trying to the last minute to win time to consult the Moslem League.

On June 3, 1947, the plan for the independence of India and its partition into the two countries of India and Pakistan was announced by the Viceroy over the All-India Radio, followed by brief talks by Nehru and Jinnah. A few days later the Congress and the Moslem League ratified the plan.

With his sister and a small party of his associates, Jinnah climbed into a Dakota plane and left India at once for Karachi, the capital of the new country of Pakistan. Rawalpindi in the north had been suggested by some as the capital, but it was inaccessible compared to Karachi. Others had hoped that Lahore, the cultural center of that part of the world, would be selected, but it was very near the Indian border, had been the center of Hindu-Moslem outbreaks, and it was not a port city or on the main international air routes. Jinnah felt it was important that a new nation have as its capital a city which was well known and which would be easy to reach from other countries. His choice of Karachi was accepted largely on these grounds.

It was rumored in some areas that Lord Mountbatten would be invited to serve for a time as the Governor General of India and of Pakistan. But this did not happen. He was invited to become the Governor General of India, but Jinnah was selected as the Governor General of Pakistan. Some commentators on Pakistan politics say that Mountbatten was deeply offended by this move, and they attribute many of Pakistan's early difficulties to his bitter disappointment.

To most informed Pakistanis the combination of Jinnah as Governor General and Liaquat Ali Khan as Prime Minister was a happy one. Jinnah could help determine policies and lend his prestige and power to the new government without being burdened with the details of administration, while Liaquat Ali Khan could use his talents as an organizer to form the new government. In this respect it looked as if Pakistan was off to a good start.

On August 14, 1947, Jinnah was installed as Governor General, and on the following day Pakistan came into existence as a new country. This new nation had been created at a great price and it had been created largely by the efforts of one man—Mohammed Ali Jinnah.

With close to eighty million people, it became the sixth largest country in the world in population, following China, India, the Soviet Union, the United States, and Japan.

The problems which faced the officials of the new government were staggering.

First of all its geographical situation was very unfortunate. The eastern and western parts of the country were separated by a thousand miles of Indian territory. In the eastern sector there were approximately forty-five million persons, and in the western part thirty-five million. To unite these two areas or even to communicate between them was an enormous undertaking.

Next, there was the language problem. In the east almost everyone spoke Bengali, but in the west almost no one spoke that tongue. They spoke Urdu, or one of the provincial languages such as Punjabi, Sindhi, Pushtu, or Baluchistani. So temporarily the government resorted to English as a common working language.

Then there was the problem of Moslem refugees, with millions of them pouring across the borders from India, fearing that they would be attacked by the Sikhs or the Hindus. And in the opposite direction, millions of Hindus were escaping into India for fear of attack by the Moslems. Altogether over fourteen million persons left their homes in India and Pakistan, the largest mass migration within such a short period in the history of the world. Many of these people fled with only a few possessions, so there were the problems of feeding, clothing, and housing, as well as finding jobs for them. This would have been a staggering task for a well-established government. It was an overwhelming assignment for a new country.

Adding to the confusion was the enormous job of creating a new government for a nation of eighty million persons. It was possible to retain some of the structure left by the British, but even then there was plenty to do to set up the organization of the Pakistan state. Since the British had ruled the entire subcontinent primarily from the cities of what was now India, there were no desks, no chairs, no typewriters, no supplies for most of the officials of the new government of Pakistan. In the first few weeks they had to function in bare rooms or under the trees in makeshift offices.

There were also economic problems. East Pakistan was the center of the world's jute supply; but all the processing factories were located in what was now India, so it was decided to construct new factories as quickly as possible in East Pakistan. Dams needed to be built, irrigation systems constructed, spinning mills developed, and a master plan drafted for the economic survival and growth of this new nation.

Added to all this was the problem of uncertain boundaries. The people of Pakistan had assumed that the northern area known as Kashmir would join them because of its large Moslem majority. They were incensed when the Hindu head of that territory declared for India. Large numbers of Pathans from the Northwest Frontier Province of Pakistan felt that this was a gross injustice, so they banded together and entered Kashmir to protect their Moslem friends. They were met there by Indian troops trying to protect the new acquisition to India. Only the entrance of the United Nations into this struggle prevented an intense and costly civil war. For years this controversy was to continue, with the United Nations policing an uneasy truce.

These were only a few of the major problems confronting Pakistan. There were many others, especially in the areas of education and social welfare. Then there were the inevitable problems of bribery and corruption, black marketing, and nepotism to contend with, and the problem of economic control which was in the hands of a few prominent families, most of them large holders of land. Pakistan had other important decisions to make about national defense and its role in world affairs in these first few months.

Jinnah probably did not know that he would have just thirteen months to help launch this new state, although he must have known that he was not well when he became Governor General. However, he was determined to do all he could and he set out on a tour of the Punjab region, Baluchistan, the Northwest Frontier Province, the tribal areas, and East Pakistan, trying to infuse a spirit of sacrifice and constructive planning into the people, to care for the refugees, to quiet the communal riots, and to set up some semblance of local, regional, and federal governments. He could not do it all himself, and he was very fortunate in having Liaquat Ali Khan as Prime Minister.

Several subjects were especially dear to him, and he spoke frequently on them in this early period of Pakistan's history. One of them was the place of women in a new nation. On this he said:

> In the great task of building the nation and maintaining its solidarity, women have a most valuable part to play. They are the prime architects of the character of youth who constitute the backbone of the state. I know that in the long struggles for the achievement of Pakistan, Moslem women have stood solidly

behind their men. In the bitter struggle for the building up of Pakistan that lies ahead, let it not be said that the women of Pakistan lagged behind or failed in their duty.

He was well aware of the need for sacrifice, reminding the Pakistanis that they must:

Keep together, put up with inconveniences, sufferings, and sacrifices for the collective good of our people. No amount of trouble or sacrifice is to be shirked if you individually and collectively make a contribution for the collective good of your nation and your state.

The importance of industrialization was also on his mind.

If Pakistan is to play its proper role in the world, to which its size, manpower, and resources entitle it, it must develop its industrial potentialities side by side with its agriculture and give its economy an industrial bias. . . . By industrializing our State we shall decrease our dependence on the outside world for the necessities of life, give some employment to our people, and also increase the resources of the State. Nature has blessed us with a good many raw materials. . . .

He could not forget the wrangles which had already started between the various regions of Pakistan and constantly reminded his hearers:

If you want to build yourself into a nation, give up provincialism, because as long as you allow this poison to remain in the body politic of Pakistan, you will never be a strong nation. . . .

Much of his social life had come to an end with the breakdown of his home, and he had long ago given up his favorite pastimes, billiards and bridge. But throughout his life he continued to enjoy the theater and small dinner parties with after-dinner conversation. In the summers he went to Kashmir or to some of the "hill stations" of Pakistan, where he enjoyed riding and reading in the cooler weather which these mountain spots offered. His reading consisted of plays, history, biography, and politics.

For years Jinnah's physicians had urged him to work less and rest more. But he had been driven first by his passion to win independence and then by his desire to create a separate state of Pakistan. He could not afford to slacken the pace. The time came, however, when his body told him he must stop, even if his mind urged him to continue.

In the summer of 1948 he agreed to go to Ziarat in Baluchistan. There he lived in a small cottage, from which he had a peaceful view of miles of hills covered with juniper trees and, in the distance, more miles of hills which were almost completely bare. There were no people around to bring their problems to him, but there were problems galore in his mind and he could not free himself completely from them.

Physically, he was failing rapidly. He finally became very ill, and developed pneumonia. He was flown to a hospital in Karachi where he died on September 11, 1948. He was buried in the heart of Karachi, his birthplace and the capital of the country he had created.

Throughout this great man's life he had been called cold, austere, and dictatorial. His enemies had said that he was not really religious and had become a practicing Moslem for the sake of politics. Some said that he was ambitious and obstinate and that when he saw that he could not rule the All-India Congress or obtain the leadership of a united India, he had decided to create a new country which he could run.

But millions of Moslems saw him in a very different light. They point out that he had been called by many leading Hindus the Ambassador of Hindu-Moslem Unity and that he had struggled to protect their rights until he had reluctantly seen that this cause was hopeless. Only then had he been willing to support Iqbal's plan for a separate state of Pakistan. They made much of the fact that even if people disagreed with him, they could not challenge his integrity and his honesty. Futhermore, they pointed out, although Gandhi was a great man, he was a Hindu and could never have the same appeal for Moslems that he had for Hindus. Jinnah was the type of man the Moslems admired, and they lauded him because of his tenacity of purpose and his hard work in their behalf. He had removed this fear of remaining forever a minority group in a predominantly Hindu country and had won for them their own state.

To the Moslems of Pakistan, Jinnah would always be *Quaid-l-Azam*, The Great Leader, the man with a mission, the creator of their beloved country, Pakistan.

NEHRU
OF INDIA

In the drama of emerging nations in the twentieth century Jawaharlal Nehru was one of the leading actors. During his long and active life he played many outstanding roles. The first was in the fight for the independence of India, in which he co-starred with Gandhi. Then he became the leading figure in the establishment of democracy in India. A third role was that of spokesman for large parts of Asia in almost every major play on the international stage in recent times.

Yet he was not a universally applauded man. Like other prominent actors, he had a large following of enthusiastic fans and many bitter critics.

His admirers said he was "one of the most remarkable men in the twentieth century," "an almost perfect blend of East and West," "America's best friend in Asia," "a world-wide symbol of freedom and justice," "a man for the ages."

His critics referred to him as "India's Hamlet," "Napoleon," "Red," and "promoter of brown colonialism."

Certainly he was one of the most complex and controversial figures in modern times.

Jawaharlal Nehru had a good start in life by being born into the Nehru family on November 14, 1889, in Allahabad, India. The Nehrus were one of the "best" families in all of India—wealthy, socially prominent, and much respected for their integrity and charity. They were originally from Kashmir, the beautiful northern section of India, and they were

of the Brahmin caste, the highest-ranking group among approximately four hundred million Indians.

His great-grandfather and his grandfather had both served as officials under the Mogul emperors, and his father was a brilliant lawyer. He was a lucky boy and could go far if such a family background did not spoil him.

As a child Jawaharlal spent most of his time in the women's section of the Nehru home, which was presided over by his mother. She was a small, slender, dainty person with a gentle disposition. To Jawaharlal she was especially dear as a refuge from the wrath of his father.

In those early years Jawaharlal did not see much of his father, for Motilal Nehru was busy building a fine reputation as a lawyer. But the boy looked forward to the evenings when his father entertained their relatives, business associates, and friends. Then he would laugh his infectious laugh and enjoy good living. Jawaharlal was proud of his father's appearance, for he was handsome and carried himself with the air of a Roman patrician. The boy also learned to calculate his father's moods, for the older man had a fierce temper and strong opinions and did not like to be crossed.

Eleven years after Jawaharlal's birth a sister named Swarup was born, and some years after that a second sister, Krishna, the last of the Nehru children.

Much of the time Jawaharlal was a lonely boy. There were several cousins in the Nehru home, but they were older than Jawaharlal, and his sisters were much younger. He did not even have the companionship of school friends, for he worked at home with a tutor. Little wonder that he was "shy and sensitive," as his sister Krishna has pointed out.

However, there were many good times, such as the holidays and the trips to other parts of India for the elaborate weddings of relatives. And when he was ten the family moved into a large house with a wide veranda, a beautiful lawn, a tennis court, and a swimming pool. The new home was known as Anand Bhawan, or The Abode of Happiness.

When he was eleven a new influence came into Jawaharlal's life in the person of his twenty-six-year-old tutor, Ferdinand Brooks. Brooks had traveled widely, read a great deal, and was of a philosophical and religious turn of mind. He whetted and fed Jawaharlal's appetite for science and literature and aroused in him an interest in philosophy and religion.

Together they read and relished the great epics of Indian literature, contained in the ancient Vedas, or scriptures, and the best of English literature, especially English poetry. For three years Brooks lived with the Nehrus and he left a lasting impression on the future Prime Minister of India.

When Jawaharlal was fifteen he was sent to England to study. There he entered Harrow, a famous private school founded in 1572. His time there was profitable, but he was still lonely. He was an Indian and therefore a foreigner, and a colonial. Futhermore, he was more interested in books than were most of the boys. And he was especially keen on current events, following the defeat of Russia by Japan in 1905 with intense interest, and reading with excitement about the clashes in India between his people and the British. Yet he had no one with whom he could discuss these events, except on rare trips away from the school when he met other Indians studying or living in England.

At Harrow he took part in sports, enjoyed the school songs, and did especially well as a student. One of the prizes he won was a volume of Trevelyan's account of the Italian military and political leader, Garibaldi. Nehru read this volume and later purchased the other two in the series. As he read them, he compared India and Italy and wondered why his country could not become united and free.

In 1907 he entered Trinity College, Cambridge University. He was now a slim, somewhat shy, handsome eighteen-year-old, with a narrow, sharply chiseled face, dark hair, and beautiful piercing eyes.

He did well in his major fields of chemistry, geology, and botany, and took a quiet part in campus life. Most of the time he seemed to be a reserved youth, even paying the required fines in the debating society rather than speaking. With a small group of friends he was much more outgoing, and joined them in the fun and pranks of college students.

Even more important to him in his development than his studies were the lectures he heard, the reading he did, and the discussions in which he took part. Several intellectual giants in England in those days were stirring people with new ideas. They were men like Bertrand Russell, the mathematician, philosopher, and free thinker; John Maynard Keynes, the economist; Bernard Shaw, the playwright and socialist. Nehru heard these men speak and began to think about what they said. Their ideas were interesting to think and talk about, but he had no plans for acting upon them. He did take a trip to Ireland to see what the men in the Sinn Fein movement for Irish independence were doing, but for the most part his thinking was very academic.

After completing his work at Cambridge, Nehru moved to London and spent the next two years studying for the bar exams. He worked and played hard during those years. Nehru returned to India in 1912. He had been away from home seven years. There are always adjustments to make when one has been away from one's family and country; they were even greater than usual in the case of Nehru. When he had left India he had been an adolescent. Now he was a man, and yet he had to live again in the family home and adjust himself to the role of his strong-minded father. He had spent seven years in England speaking its language, reading its history and literature, imbibing its ideals and ways of thinking. He now returned to India, and he was not sure whether he was Indian or English. "I had become a queer mixture of the East and the West— out of place everywhere, at home nowhere," he said later in discussing this conflict in his mind. Futhermore, he and his father did not think alike about the events of the day. Naturally, the son was more radical than the older man.

The next few years were years of mental unrest for Nehru. He joined the moderates in the Congress party, and yet he was dissatisfied with their endless discussions and their lack of action. He joined the Home Rule League and the All-India Home Rule League. He devoted considerable time to the latter movement, in which he still felt more at home.

He was a young man in search of a mission and in search of methods which he could honestly and sincerely employ.

Meanwhile, in 1916, he was married to an attractive young girl of seventeen named Kamala. They spent their honeymoon in Kashmir, where they reveled in the lakes, valleys, and mountains of the land which had been the ancestral home of both their families.

Their marriage had been arranged by their families, with Jawaharlal giving his consent, but they did not really know each other, so the first few months were spent in becoming acquainted. They were both sensitive, proud, high-spirited, and strong in their likes and dislikes, so there were many misunderstandings and quarrels. But a strong bond developed between them, and Kamala became a wonderful helpmate to her husband. In 1917 a daughter was born to them, whom they named Indira. The girl was one day to follow her father as Prime Minister of India.

When World War I broke out in 1914, the British demanded Indian troops to help them in their fight against the Germans and their allies. This was bitterly resented in India, for the Indians argued that if they were good enough to fight they were good enough to govern themselves.

Thousands of Indians were ready for strong action against the British, but they were divided into several groups and lacked top leadership in their struggle. They were also divided in their strategy against the power and might of the British Empire. What they needed was a powerful, persuasive leader and a method of attack.

They found their man in Mahatma Gandhi and their method in non-violent resistance. Nehru has described Gandhi's effect on the situation in these words:

> And then Gandhi came. He was like a powerful current of fresh air that made us stretch ourselves and take deep breaths; like a beam of light that pierced the darkness and removed the scales from our eyes; like a whirlwind that upset many things, but most of all the working of people's minds. He did not descend from the top; he seemed to emerge from the millions of India. . . . The essence of his teaching was fearlessness and truth, and action allied to these, always keeping the welfare of the masses in view.

Gandhi was like a magnet drawing thousands and then millions of men and women to him. He pulled the Nehrus, too. He attracted the father through his sincerity and his program of action. But his emphasis upon the simple life, upon civil disobedience, and upon spiritual discipline was terribly demanding for a lawyer who lived in comparative luxury, believed in the importance of legal processes, and was not a deeply spiritual person.

Gandhi's pull upon the son was much stronger. Jawaharlal's respect for him grew into admiration and then deepened into something akin to love for this great man.

In Nehru's words, "I was simply bowled over by Gandhi."

The conflict between father and son deepened for a time, and it was only Gandhi's counsel of caution to Jawaharlal that prevented an open break between the two Nehrus. Gandhi wanted both of them in his movement and he was willing to wait until that was possible, convinced that the father would eventually join. And he was right. By the end of 1920 Motilal and Jawaharlal both joined Gandhi for the great fight that lay ahead.

This move meant tremendous changes and terrific sacrifices for the Nehrus. Motilal dismissed most of the servants, sold the horses and carriages, disposed of the Dresden china and Venetian glass, and gave up his law practice. It was like conversion to a new religion, demanding everything.

These three men were to make a powerful impact upon India in the years ahead. Jawaharlal said, "It was a triangle: Mr. Gandhi, my father, and myself, each influencing the other to some extent. . . ." They were somewhat irreverently referred to as Father, Son, and Holy Ghost!

The younger Nehru knew that if he were to be of any real help to the movement he had joined, he must know far more about India than he had yet learned. So he set out to educate himself, crossing and criss-crossing the entire Indian subcontinent, discovering for the first time the land in which he lived.

He found over four hundred million people living in unparalleled poverty, disease, and ignorance. He learned that three-fourths of the babies died at birth or within a few months. He discovered that to live on an income of about forty dollars per person per year meant bad housing, lack of clothing, polluted water, lack of education, and general misery. In terms of communication, he found out what it means to have twelve or fifteen major languages and hundreds of dialects. He saw for himself the divisions and hostility between persons of the Hindu and Moslem faiths.

Futhermore, he saw the effects of the caste system, developed centuries before as a means of dividing the labor of India's villages but now deteriorated into a horrible system of class discrimination. He realized that India was a giant pyramid with a few rich princes and landlords on top and the mass of the people at the bottom. These discoveries shocked and repelled him. He described his feelings in this statement:

> Looking at them and their misery and overflowing gratitude, I was filled with shame and sorrow—shame at my own easygoing and comfortable life and our petty politics of the city, which ignored this vast multitude of semi-naked sons and daughters of India, sorrow at the degradation and overwhelming poverty of India. A new picture of India seemed to rise before me, naked, starved, crushed, and utterly miserable. And their faith in us, casual visitors from the distant city, embarrassed me and filled me with a new responsibility that frightened me.

There was another side to the picture he was getting of India. He visited the old monuments and ruins, reread the stories of the wonderful reigns of Asoka and Akbar, and delved into the epic poetry and folklore of ancient India which he had first learned as a boy from his mother

Yes, this was a great people to be welded into a nation based on the firm foundations of the past but modernized in keeping with the changes which the centuries had wrought. He realized that:

> . . . our main purpose was to raise the whole level of the Indian people, psychologically and spiritually, and, of course, politically and economically. It was the building up of that real inner strength of the people that we were after, knowing that the rest would inevitably follow.

There were many points on which Nehru could not agree with Gandhi. He could not don the homespun clothes Gandhi wore. He did not agree with him on his emphasis upon the spinning wheel and the importance of local handicrafts. He was unable to fast or conduct public prayer meetings or live the life of a saint, as Gandhi did.

But there was a place for Nehru in the non-violent movement led by Gandhi. Nehru's brilliant mind, his winning personality, his ability to plan and organize, and his talents as a speaker and writer would be invaluable. And his father's decision to join Gandhi would attract other intellectuals to this movement.

During the 1920s Jawaharlal Nehru was active as secretary of the All-India Congress, as an official in the local government for a short time, and as a speaker and organizer for the political party known as the All-India Congress. Two years of that period were also spent in Europe, where he took his wife with the hope of improving her health.

While in Europe he attended the Congress of Oppressed Nationalities held in Berlin, in company with such men and women as Albert Einstein, Madame Sun Yat-sen, Ho Chi Minh, Romain Rolland, and others. There he began to see freedom in a large frame, something for the whole world.

On returning to India in 1928 he again became secretary of the Congress, at the same time that his father was its president. The next year he was selected as president, when Gandhi and his father both declined to serve in that post.

Already the movement for a greater degree of self-government for the Indians had begun to spread like a prairie fire, provoking many clashes between the Indians and the British. As a dramatic method of showing their displeasure with the British and of exerting economic pressure on them, Gandhi and many of his followers began to spin their own cloth rather than wear the clothes made in England. The little white homespun cotton caps which they made for themselves became the symbol of the Gandhi movement.

It was not easy to carry out the idea of non-violence

when the horses of the British soldiers charged through a crowd, or to remain passive when you were struck with bamboo sticks wielded by the police. Nor was it easy to lie down in the street to block the passage of troops. This was a new way of waging war, with weapons of the spirit rather than with firearms. Many people could not meet the demands of this non-violent movement, but thousands and then millions joined Gandhi in his epic-making attempt to win a greater degree of self-government for India.

In the 1929 Congress it was decided to declare India independent. In his presidential address Nehru said:

> We are now in an open conspiracy to free this country from foreign rule, and you, my comrades, and all our countrymen and countrywomen, are invited to join it. The rewards that are in store for you are suffering and prison and, it may be, death. But you shall have the satisfaction that you have done your bit for India . . . and have helped a little in the liberation of humanity from its present bondage. . . .

January 26, 1930 was declared Independence Day by the All-India Congress, and demonstrations for freedom were held throughout the length and breadth of the land.

Then, on April 6, Gandhi and a small band of followers marched to the sea and began the process of making salt by evaporating the water. The production of salt was a government monopoly, and the salt was subject to high taxes when purchased by the Indians. The making of salt by private individuals was a symbol of defiance and of independence. It was also the sign for a nation-wide campaign of civil disobedience.

On April 14, 1930, Nehru was arrested for conspiracy against the government and placed in solitary confinement. He had been in prison before, but this was to be the first of a long series of imprisonments which were to keep him in jail for a total of ten years between that time and the granting of real independence in 1947.

Writing about that period, he has said:

> The years I have spent in prison! Sitting alone, wrapped in my thoughts, how many seasons I have seen go by, following each other into oblivion. How many moons I have watched wax and wane, and the pageant of the stars moving along inexorably and majestically! How many yesterdays of my youth lie buried there; and sometimes I see the ghosts of these dead yesterdays rise up, bringing poignant memories, and whispering to me, "Was it worth-while?" There is no hesitation about the answer. If I were to go through life again, with my present knowledge and experience added, I would no doubt try to make many changes in my personal life: I would endeavor to improve in many ways on what I had previously done, but my major decisions in public affairs would remain untouched. Indeed, I could not vary them, for they were stronger than myself, and a force beyond my control drove me to them.

Sometimes he was in solitary confinement; sometimes he was allowed the company of fellow "conspirators." During these periods together, they talked, planned, and studied. Nehru could not help in the education of his daughter while he was in prison, but he was allowed to write letters to her, so in scores of long letters he told her the history of the world. Later these letters were gathered together and published in a book called *Glimpses of World History,* a fascinating volume. During another period in prison he wrote his autobiography.

Nehru's father also suffered imprisonment, and his life was shortened by this experience. When he died in 1931, nearly a hundred thousand people gathered on the banks of the Ganges River to witness the cremation of his body.

Not long after that Jawaharlal's wife Kamala died, and two years later, his mother. Both of these women had shared in the work of organizing the women of India, and both had undergone imprisonment for their beliefs. On the day of Kamala's funeral someone handed Nehru a red rose to wear, and for the rest of his life he wore a red rose in her memory.

The decade of the 1930s passed slowly for Nehru. Much of it was spent in prison. Each day of freedom was precious to him, for he never knew when he would be arrested again. He paid a visit to Spain, hopeful that the liberal forces there would win against Franco and the Fascists, for he saw in Spain the world-wide struggle against Fascism in miniature. He visited Burma and Malaya. He visited China, at that time still under the control of Chiang Kai-shek.

Then came World War II, and India became part of the Allied effort not through any decision of the Indian people but through an announcement from London.

These were trying times for all Indians and for the All-India Congress.

Gandhi reluctantly said that he would be willing to aid the British in return for a promise of independence. He insisted, however, that such aid be non-violent. Nehru was prepared to take part in other forms of support. There were weeks of negotiation as to war aims and India's future. Finally, in August 1942, the Congress passed the famous Quit India Resolution demanding the end of British rule. A nation-wide passive resistance campaign was launched. Thousands of Indians were imprisoned and upward of ten thousand killed.

Nehru had already been removed from circulation. In 1940 he had been tried and had made an eloquent statement in his own defense. His plea should become a classic in the literature of mankind:

> I stand before you, sir, as an individual being tried for certain offenses against the State. But I am something more than an individual; I, too, am a symbol . . . a symbol of Indian national-

ism, resolved to break away from the British Empire and achieve the independence of India. It is not I that you are seeking to condemn, but rather the hundreds of millions of the people of India, and that is a large task even for a proud Empire. Perhaps it may be that, though I am standing before you on trial, it is the British Empire itself that is on trial before the bar of the world. There are more powerful forces at work in the world today than courts of law; there are elemental urges for freedom and food and security which are moving masses of people, and history is being molded by them. The future recorder of history might well say that in the hour of supreme trial, the government of Britain and the British people failed because they could not adapt themselves to a changing world.

After the Quit India Resolution, he was again imprisoned, this time for the longest period of all, for he was not to be free again until June 15, 1945. In the intervening months the war had worn on and India had become a great armed camp under the control of its Viceroy, an army general. Despite the philosophy of non-violence, there had been strikes and riots and bloodshed. And there had been widespread famine, as the rice supply from Burma and other countries was cut off by the Japanese conquest of Southeast Asia.

On May 8, 1945, V-E Day was celebrated in England, and shortly after that important event an election was held in which Churchill's party lost, and Clement Attlee and the Laborites came to power. This was good news for India. Soon Attlee proclaimed that "India will be given self-government, and the people of India themselves will decide what kind of government they want."

Rear Admiral Viscount Mountbatten was sent to India to prepare the ground for independence. He was an excellent choice; and when he left India a short time later, there was an unexpected degree of friendliness between the two countries, toward which he had contributed immeasurably.

Arrangements had been made to grant independence in August 1948, but the date was advanced to August 15, 1947.

The biggest decision to be reached before that time was whether India should become one country or two. Economically, the subcontinent belonged together. Its partition would probably mean a division into two armed camps, with money spent on defense rather than on bettering the life of the people.

But the Moslems maintained that they had a separate religion and a separate culture, and that they could not afford to live forever as a minority in India. Therefore they demanded partition, with a large section in the west and another in the east comprising the new nation, and a corridor connecting the two parts.

Gandhi adamantly opposed the idea of partition. Nehru and most of the others reluctantly agreed to it, although they would not agree to the idea that a corridor of land connecting the two areas should be carved out of India.

But partition was not achieved without a torrent of hatred and bitterness between Sikhs and Hindus on the one side and Moslems on the other. Riots broke out in many places and murders were not uncommon. Millions of people fled from their homes and crossed the borders between what was to be India and Pakistan. Eventually over fourteen million people moved from India to Pakistan or from Pakistan to India—the largest short-term mass migration in the history of the world. An estimated two hundred thousand lost their lives in this gruesome two-way trek. The fight for freedom had been won, but at a ghastly price.

Independence came to India at midnight on August 14, 1947, and as the clock struck twelve, Nehru rose in the Constituent Assembly and declared:

> Long years ago we made a tryst with destiny and now the time comes when we shall redeem our pledge, not wholly or in

full measure, but substantially. At the stroke of the midnight hour when the world sleeps, India will awake to life and freedom. A moment comes, which comes but rarely in history, when we step out from the old to the new, when an age ends, and when the soul of a nation, long suppressed, finds utterance. It is fitting that at this solemn moment we take a pledge of dedication to the service of India and to her people and to the still larger cause of humanity. . . . That future is not one of ease or resting, but of incessant striving so that we might fulfill the pledges we have so often taken and the one we shall take today. The service of India means the service of the millions who suffer. It means the ending of poverty and ignorance and disease and inequality of opportunity.

It was a great speech from a great man in a great cause for a great country.

Scarcely had Nehru begun the mammoth task of organizing the new government and plotting its course for the next few years, than another tragedy befell the new nation. Grieved and troubled by the communal rioting between Moslems and Sikhs and Hindus, Gandhi had set out to visit many of the villages and cities where the riots were taking place, to persuade people to desist from such fraternal attacks and abuse. His efforts had been successful, in most instances, and he had returned to his home, only to learn that riots had broken out again in other places. This time he announced a fast unto death unless the riots stopped. It was the most dangerous of his many fasts, for he was now old and weak and the doctors said he could probably last only six days.

After five days the results of his fast began to show, and he decided to terminate it. He left his house to attend the evening prayer meeting in his *ashram,* or settlement. On his way he was killed by a Hindu extremist. The great apostle of non-violence, of passive resistance, of civil disobedience, had been shot by an assassin.

In a radio address to the Indian people, Nehru told them of the tragedy:

> The light has gone out of our lives and there is darkness everywhere. I do not know what to tell you and how to say it. Our beloved leader, Bapu as we called him, the father of the nation, is no more. . . . The light has gone out, I said, and yet I was wrong. For the light that shone in this country was no ordinary light. The light that illumined this country for these many, many years will illumine this country for many more years, and a thousand years later that light will still be seen in this country and the world will see it and it will give solace to innumerable hearts.

Of the nearly one million people who came to the cremation ceremony, none mourned the loss of Gandhi more than Nehru, for Gandhi not only had been his political mentor and friend but, in the years since his father's death, had become like a father to him.

More lonely, more sober, more determined than ever before, Nehru set about creating a country out of the 370 million men, women, and children who then comprised the new India. It was a gigantic task. It was not always easy to find the proper methods of achieving what he wanted, but his goals were certainly clear. He wanted:

A democratic India. At the local level this meant the strengthening of the *panchayat,* or local councils, which have existed for centuries in India but had lost most of their power and vitality under foreign rule. At the state or regional level it meant the abolition of more than five hundred princely states and eighteen regional units and the creation of twenty-six states with their own governors and legislative bodies. At the national level it meant the formation of a system of government based on both the British and American models, with a President, a Prime Minister, a House of the People, or Lower House, and a Council of

States, or Upper House. In this new republic, all men and
women over twenty-one were given the vote, and communal
voting, or voting by religious groups, was abolished. In 1951
and 1952 this meant that the national elections had to be
held over a period of months, because of geographical and
climatic conditions, and that a system of voting by party
symbols had to be instituted to protect the votes of millions
of illiterates. In this aspect of its development India had
made amazing progress.

An India with improved village life. Nehru was well
aware of the fact that India has been and will long remain
a nation of villages. Altogether there are at least five hundred thousand such units, consisting of fifty to one hundred
or more families each, living in mud or thatch houses, drinking water from a village well which is often contaminated,
lacking schools and health facilities, and scratching out a
meager existence on poor soil divided into very small plots
of ground.

He knew that Gandhi had said that such villages were
"dung heaps," and he was determined to do as much as
possible to implement Gandhi's dream of making them little
"Gardens of Eden," each with a good school, library, theater,
co-operative industries, a just land system, improved agricultural techniques, and self-governing councils.

To improve life at the village level India has undertaken
the most ambitious community development program of any
country in the world. Young men and women were placed
in charge of a wide variety of projects in a cluster of
villages. Their task was to encourage people locally to discover their needs and to help them in every way possible
to meet those needs, whether this involved better seeds,
irrigation, a cleaner water supply, a new school, a new road,
or some other much needed improvement.

Soon after this enormous program was launched, Nehru
said:

At the present moment I attach more importance in India to what we call our community projects than even to our major industrial or river-valley schemes which are very big and impressive.

Even though the training of these community development workers was a staggering assignment, India was able by 1958 to provide such leadership to approximately half of its villages.

An India with more food for more people. The job of feeding 380 million people is colossal. It becomes even greater when one realizes that each year there are approximately twelve million more mouths to feed.

One way of doing this has been to build more dams and to irrigate more land. Several large dams have already been built, such as the mammoth Bhakra-Nangal and Damodar Valley structures, plus more than a hundred smaller irrigation schemes and forty-three power projects. Now irrigation covers 20 per cent of the cultivated land areas.

In addition, much attention has been given to the use of fertilizer, improvement of methods and implements, and changes in the land tenure laws. The demand for fertilizers has increased by thousands of tons each year.

There has been considerable progress in this highly important aspect of Indian life, but the resistance to land reform has hindered the program and the ability of India to feed her new population as well as to improve the food supply has not been as great as it should be. Fortunately, Indian agriculture is highly diversified. India grows rice, wheat, sugar cane, cotton, jute, tea, coffee, rubber, spices, and many fruits.

An industrialized India. In the first Five-Year Plan of India, launched in 1951, the emphasis was on agriculture and community development. In the second plan, the emphasis was on industrialization. As Nehru and others thought about the economic development of their country, they saw the need for heavy machinery and heavy industry such as steel mills, fertilizer factories, plants for the production of farm implements, mining equipment, and electric power. India also needs many scientific research centers and trained technicians if she is to bring about a better life for her people and take her place in the international community of our day. In this area she has made much progress since independence, building thirteen such laboratories plus many technological institutes which are already yielding dividends.

Nehru himself showed a keen interest in the possibilities of atomic energy and even retained for himself the post of Minister of Atomic Energy. The ministry started several plants for the development of atomic energy for peaceful purposes. For one, aid was received from Canada. Another, a smaller "swimming pool" type of reactor was built by India on its own.

A united India. The task of building a united nation has not been an easy one either, despite the prodigious efforts of Nehru and his colleagues.

The first blow came in the partitioning of the country into Pakistan and India. Since that time the problem of communalism has been eased tremendously, and the forty million Moslems in the country are living happily, for the most part.

Then came the problem of Kashmir, a territory which is highly prized by both India and Pakistan. It is a beautiful country, full of historical signifiance to all people in that part of the world. It is the source of water for Pakistan and for large parts of northern India. Futhermore, the Kashmir Valley is productive, even though most of the rest of Kashmir is not particularly useful economically. In addition, Kashmir had a special significance to Nehru as his ancestral home.

Consequently, both Pakistan and India would like to have Kashmir, and both claim it as part of their countries. The

Pakistanis maintain that it is predominantly Moslem and that they must control this area in order to protect their water supply. Furthermore, they claim that the original decision of the Maharajah to permit Kashmir to become part of India was carried out by trickery. They further point out that India has blocked all attempts on the part of the United Nations to hold a plebiscite in Kashmir to decide its future.

On the other hand, India claims that the decision of the Maharajah to cede Kashmir to India was in accordance with the agreement reached at the time of partition and that the invasion of the Pathans from Pakistan was an act of war. They point out that Kashmir's adherence to India would in no way prevent Pakistan from using her share of the water under just agreements mutually arrived at.

Another problem which has stirred India since independence has been that of language. Nehru and others hoped to make Hindi the national language, to replace the thirteen or fourteen major tongues and the nearly seven hundred dialects of India, since it is the language spoken by the largest group and one with a rich literature. But there have been strong and even violent objections to making Hindi the national language.

As soon as independence came, several groups began pressing for states based on major languages. One such request was granted, and the state of Andhra was established for those persons speaking Telegu. Immediately others used this as a precedent and started demanding similar language states.

This controversy has not been resolved, and language still continues to plague the leaders of India.

Many Indians also feel that the Communists are a source of national disunity. Although Nehru felt that they could not and should not be outlawed in a democratic nation which guarantees freedom of thought and action, he nevertheless denounced them on three major counts. One of these is the fact that they are not Indian nationalists, despite claims to the contrary, since they are beholden to Russia and act upon the advice of their fellow Communists there. Speaking in 1958 on the other two charges against them, he said:

> I am unconcerned with Communist economics. But politically I dislike it for two reasons. First, it is too strongly linked with violence. Second, it has not shown due regard for standards I should like to see observed. Its philosophy is violent, and I do not like that. My own political philosophy is social democracy—socialism, if you like—plus the democratic structure of the state.

Despite these and other problems, India has nevertheless achieved a remarkable sense of national unity. More than anyone else or any other single force, Nehru served as a symbol of this unity.

A healthier and better-educated India. India's average life span being twenty-five years and its illiteracy rate being somewhere between 80 and 85 per cent, Nehru and the Indian people were confronted with a staggering job in the fields of health and education.

Great progress was made in both of these basic areas. Perhaps the most noticeable step forward in health was made as a result of a nation-wide attack upon malaria, which claimed a million lives each year directly and another million indirectly. With help from the United States government, the incidence of malaria was drastically reduced.

With similar help from the World Health Organization and the United Nations Children's Fund, an intensive campaign was waged against tuberculosis.

In the establishment of health clinics and hospitals and in the training of doctors, nurses, and midwives, India has also made notable strides.

In education the gains at many levels were tremendous. India undertook an extensive program of adult education and built thousands of schools and trained thousands of teachers. Yet even now the tasks which remain are staggering. Most of the vast population is still illiterate.

An India free from outside interference. Nehru did not let himself become so preoccupied with his own country that he could not be concerned about the world. In fact it was largely his keen interest in world affairs that catapulted India into a position just short of that of a world power.

To understand his general orientation on world affairs, it is important to keep several points in mind. One was that India was for so long a colonial power. Another was that Indians are Asians and as such have experienced discrimination on the basis of color for centuries. A third was India's geographical position in relation to Russia and China. Another was India's fear of the future if the United States and Russia should tangle with each other in nuclear warfare. Still another was Nehru's deep and abiding faith that people of different opinions can live together, despite ideological differences.

Upon one occasion he spoke on some of these points.

I do not know if it is adequately realized in many Western countries, or in America, how strongly we feel on the question of colonialism. It is in our blood. We have suffered from it. It is no good somebody telling us, oh yes, you are right, but wait, there are other difficult problems. This is a vital and important problem for us. Colonialism and racism, these two things are vital in the Asian countries. And whatever our differences may be, we meet together, as in Bandung, and we are all one in this.

All these factors combined to make Nehru the leading champion in the world of what some people call a "Neutralist" policy. He himself did not like that word, for he was the leader of the world's largest democracy and said he was not neutral. He much preferred to be known as an "independent" in international relations.

Although friendly to the United States, he was critical at times of its foreign policy, pointing to its preoccupation with Communism to the exclusion of other important issues, its lack of insight into the reasons for the growth of Communism in Asia and Africa, its ill-timed and ill-spoken support of Portuguese claims to Goa on the Indian subcontinent (Indian forces seized Goa in 1961), the lack of official support in the United States for revolutionary groups such as those in Algeria, and the frequent insistence of Americans on attaching strings to their foreign aid. Nehru's policy of independence from foreign involvement was badly strained when China attacked the Indian border in 1962. However, Indian troops repulsed the attack.

In the early years of the struggle for independence in India, Nehru was in favor of complete independence, but when the time came for a decision as to her status as a new nation he supported her membership in the British Commonwealth, largely because of the economic advantages it would bring.

Nehru believed in some kind of world government as a necessity. He stated his belief upon many occasions, saying once:

> Some kind of world government is bound to come either in our generation or in the next. Otherwise, the world tends to commit suicide. In what shape or how it will come about is difficult to say. It has to grow through the good will of peoples.

And always in the forefront of his thinking about world affairs was his belief that "the Pacific is likely to take the place of the Atlantic in the future as the nerve center of the world."

Nehru was not without faults. He found it difficult to delegate responsibility. Many believed he underestimated the aggressive nature of Communism. He failed to build up a strong group of younger leaders to succeed him. He sometimes seemed to have a compulsion for moralizing, for telling others what to do, whether he followed his own advice or not.

But his many virtues offset these shortcomings. He had great vision and great dedication. He poured out his life for the independence and development of India. He provided the one rallying point for the divergent groups within this vast country. His sincerity and integrity were never questioned. He had tremendous energy and lived for years on five hours of sleep in order to devote himself to his lifetime goals. He was a good speaker and a brilliant writer.

As one Indian historian said, "If Gandhi is the soul of India, Nehru is her mind and will." Or, as another compatriot wrote, "Nehru is proof that East and West have already met. He is the synthesis of East and West. In him the best of both cultures are fused in the coming world type—the man of the future."

For over seventy years Nehru lived a vigorous and highly useful life. There was genuine and universal mourning not only within India but throughout the free world when this great man died in 1964. The man who succeeded him as Prime Minister died rather soon, to be followed by Nehru's daughter, Indira Gandhi. In a message to the United States, his daughter echoed the spirit and convictions of her father:

> What we need, above all, is that larger sympathy and understanding which recognizes that it is possible to approach the same ends through differing means; for America and India have a future to share.

U NU
OF BURMA

To the east of the Bay of Bengal in Southeast Asia is the beautiful country of Burma. Sometimes it is called the Golden Land, the Golden Earth, the Golden Peninsula, the Land of Golden Pagodas, or some similarly flattering name.

Burma is wedged in between two of the most populous land areas of the world, China and India. To each of these nations it owes much culturally. Especially important to the Burmese people is the Buddhist religion, which was brought to Burma by the Indians centuries ago.

Burma is a little larger than France and a little smaller than Texas. In this area there are over twenty million people. They come from many ethnic backgrounds and speak eleven major languages and over one hundred dialects. But the country has taken its name from the largest group, the Burmans, and today three-fourths of the people speak Burmese.

Fortunately, Burma is not a poor country. Through the center of the northern part the Irrawaddy River and its largest tributary flow for more than nine hundred miles, as the Mississippi-Missouri flows through the heart of the United States. The wide delta of this major river has very rich soil and it is one of the best rice-growing areas in the world.

In the mountains, there are rich deposits of gold, silver, copper, zinc, nickel, tungsten, tin, rubies, sapphires, and jade.

These and other resources have never been fully developed, but Burma is potentially a rich country, and until fairly recent times there has been enough rice for the people and enough left over to export to other parts of the world.

The inhabitants of this seemingly pleasant country are

mostly short in stature and light brown in color. More important, they have been such a friendly, generous, gentle, and happy people that Burma has sometimes been called the Land of Laughter.

But underneath this surface of calm and happiness, there has been a great deal of struggle and strife and sometimes suffering. Some of this has been the result of Burma's attempts in the past century to free itself from foreign domination by Britain, which helped itself to slices of Burma in 1825, 1852, and 1865, to add to its Indian empire.

Burma won a small measure of self-government in 1937, when it was separated from India and given its own legislature, with a British governor, and many of the Burmese thought they would gain still more freedom when the Japanese arrived in 1942 during World War II. But the Burmese soon discovered that they had less rather than more freedom under these invaders.

Even after they won their independence from Britain in 1948, there was an almost constant struggle to defeat rebel and guerilla fighters and to bring peace, order, and stability to the land.

In Burma's modern history one name stands out, that of U Nu.

That is about as short a name as a person could have. U is the Burmese equivalent of Mr. or sir. That means that his name is really Nu—which means soft, green, or tender. But Mr. Tender can be firm, hard, and even tough at times, and there were occasions when he had to make full use of those qualities.

Nu may not look like our idea of a ruler of twenty million people, like a man who fought off rebels and Communists and guerilla bands to achieve peace in his home country, or like a top-notch politician. But in his active days he was all these and much more. As a leader he ranked with Nehru of

India and Mao Tse-tung of China as one of the three most
important figures in Asia. One American commentator said
of him, "I know of no one in Asia who matches him in the
combination of humanity, adroitness, and social force."

How he became an internationally famous politician instead of following his natural bents toward philosophy and
playwriting is a drama in itself.

Act One opened on May 25, 1907, with the birth of a boy
in the home of a middle-class family in Wakema, a small
village of approximately four hundred persons in the Myaung-
mya district of Burma in the midst of meandering rivers and
rich rice paddies. The boy's father was a lower-middle-
class merchant, selling silk and other textiles in a stall in
the local market. He earned a meager living, carried on the
Buddhist rites at the temple, took part in the many festivals
which enliven the monotony of day-to-day living in Burma,
and paid taxes to the British. The only person of prominence
in the family was an uncle, who was a teacher and later a
lawyer.

In most respects Nu was a normal Burmese boy, going to
school, helping his father in the market, and playing with the
other boys of the neighborhood. But he was a lively fellow,
full of ideas, and a little hard to control. He was especially
gifted at getting into trouble, and drinking became his chief
sport. Many times between the ages of nine and twelve he
had to be brought home by his friends, too intoxicated to
make his way himself.

This would have been disgraceful in almost any family
anywhere, but it was especially disgraceful to a Buddhist
family, for to a Buddhist drinking liquor is one of the deadly
sins. So his father banished Nu for a time, and he had to fend
for himself in a hut on the edge of the paddy fields.

But he was a smart boy and was able to complete his work
in school and go to the Myoma National High School in

Rangoon. This was probably the most famous secondary school in the country. It had been started by Burmese nationalists, and admission to it was a coveted prize. But even though he was bright enough to do his work and do it well, he failed in some of his subjects.

Here Act One ended. It wasn't a very promising opening, and failure seemed to loom ahead.

Act Two opened on young Nu walking alone at night in Rangoon, wrestling with his personal problem. He could not sleep, so he had gone out in the moonlight to walk alone. His failure had shocked and "haunted" him. He had, as he later said, "a deep sense of shame."

Asked about this part of his life, he told an inquiring reporter, "Some people have wondered if I didn't have a feeling that I was a man of destiny and that great forces were at work on me. No, I never had that feeling. I was ashamed. I wanted to do what was good rather than what was bad. I had started drinking at the age of nine and from thirteen or fourteen to eighteen I drank much more heavily than other students of my age. Now I had failed. If I gave up drinking, I thought to myself, I could pass. At that moment, I made a vow not to touch wine for five years. Actually I did not touch it for seven years, from eighteen to twenty-five."

It was also about that time that he started to write. When he saw the moon, heard good music, looked at beautiful flowers, he wanted to express his feelings. He had the urge to write and he began putting his thoughts on paper.

He stayed on in Rangoon until he finished the work for his B.A. degree at the university. Then he became superintendent of the National High School at Pantanaw.

While at Pantanaw he married Daw Mya Yee, whose name means "Madame Loving Emerald." Her father had been on the management committee of the school where Nu taught and she had been expected to marry Nu's boss, but Nu won in this particular contest. In the years ahead his wife was of great help to Nu in performing the functions expected of a Prime Minister's wife and maintaining a happy home.

During this period of his life Nu took his first step in politics by joining an organization called the Do Bama Asiayon, or "We Burmans." This was a group of nationalists committed to the eventual expulsion of the British from Burma.

Then Nu returned to Rangoon, this time to study law. The nationalist movement had made considerable headway. The biggest center of opposition to the British was probably in the student body of the university.

Nu helped to earn his way in those years by running a bookstore. There most of the young leaders of Burma gathered. These young men were students of history, and as they read about the French and American revolutions and more recent nationalist uprisings, they wondered how the same uprisings against oppression might be brought about in Burma. They knew their Burmese history, too, and realized that Burma had not always been under foreign rule. In fact, there were people still alive in Burma who had lived under the old Burmese monarchy, for Mandalay had not become British until 1886. The students thought and talked about how the former glory of their people could be regained.

They read whatever current news they could get and talked to visitors, especially to people who knew Gandhi and the Gandhi movement in neighboring India. And they read the writings of political scientists and political philosophers, particularly Karl Marx. Many of them were interested in what happened in the Soviet Union since World War I and some of them were impressed with the doctrines of Communism, or at least with its economic accomplishments. In these student groups the seeds of Burmese independence were being sown.

In 1934 Nu became vice-president of the powerful University Students' Union, and during the period of 1935–36 he was president of the Union.

He was older than some of the students and that was in his favor, for age is highly respected in Burma. But it was not age alone that won him the respect and affection of most of them. He was a gifted speaker and was fearless in his attacks on the university administration. His comments became so barbed that the officials finally suspended him and a couple of his friends, one of whom had written an account in the student paper about the treasurer of the university, whom he called "Hellhound at Large." About seven hundred of the two thousand members of the student body struck in protest. Eventually the university officials reinstated Nu and his friends.

Commenting upon this period in his life, U Nu has said,

> I am not exaggerating when I say that I cannot stand injustice. For instance, while I was in the University College, I was incensed whenever I saw the British authorities deal unjustly with students. For example, many students saluted the principal and the teachers. I thought that was a humiliating thing to do and rebelled against it. I urged the students not to salute and openly denounced those who did. I advised them merely to say "Good morning" and "Hello." Saluting, I said, was done by inferiors to superiors.

That he sometimes overdid his opposition to these British officials, U Nu admitted at least tacitly when on one of his trips to England he visited the former president of the University of Rangoon to apologize for some of his actions.

But the fact remains that these were British officials in Burma. The young nationalists resented their presence and took every opportunity to impress their position on the British—and on the Burmese.

By now there were two major interests in U Nu's life. One was writing; the other was politics. Which would it be? Here Act Two ended, with the major decision of his life to be made.

Act Three found U Nu in prison in Mandalay. He was there because of his leadership in an organization known as Bama Let Yon Tat, an anti-imperialist and anti-British organization which was feared by the British as war between the Allies and the Japanese became inevitable.

During his year and a half in jail Nu wrote five plays and two novels to add to the long list of works he had already written and published since leaving the university. Several of these were translations into Burmese of books published in England by liberal groups. One was a volume on Chiang Kai-shek's China, lauding the Generalissimo. This was written after a trip to China in 1939. Curiously enough, one was a translation of Karl Marx's *Das Kapital* and another Dale Carnegie's *How to Win Friends and Influence People*.

Nu's prison experience was a rough one. In a filthy cell built for twenty, there were two hundred. Then came an outbreak of cholera. Finally, as the Japanese began to bomb Mandalay, the guards fled, leaving the prisoners with nothing to eat but dried peas.

While in prison the young political leaders drafted a resolution which read in part:

> The English proclaim that they entered this great war to protect small countries and to defend their independence against oppressors. Burma is a small country. Why not begin by giving it independence? If you cannot grant independence now, promise to grant it as soon as the war is over. If you proclaim this now, we will help the English side against the Fascist brigades who threaten the independence of small nations. If you do not make this proclamation, we will do all we can to hinder your war effort in whatever way we can.

The prisoners were released, but their request was not granted. Now they were faced with a dilemma. There were thousands of Burmese who looked to the Japanese as their saviors. The Japanese had proved by their defeat of Russia in 1905 that Asians could beat Westerners, using the tactics they had learned from the West. Now the Japanese had launched a movement advocating "Asia for the Asians," and many Burmese believed them sincere. But most of the young leaders of the Burmese independence movement knew better. They had not been taken in by the Japanese slogans. On the other hand, the British had let them down. Thus they were caught in the middle of a world-wide struggle.

The Japanese invasion of Burma came early in 1942; and on August 1, 1943, the Japanese granted independence to the Burmese, asking them to set up their own government. U Nu became Foreign Minister and, later, Minister of Information.

But this was a puppet government, with the Japanese really in control. When U Nu described his work later, he referred to the Foreign Office as the "Telegraph Office," since all they seemed to do was to send telegrams of congratulation to the Axis leaders!

By 1944 the Burmese nationalists were able to contact the Allied Command, and by early 1945 the Burmese Army and the underground organizations had begun open resistance to the Japanese. By the fall of 1945 the Japanese had been driven out of Burma.

The British took over command of the government at that point, and U Nu was free to return to his home town of Wakema to write. Within a few months he had prepared a volume titled, in its English edition, *Burma Under the Japanese*. One brief selection gives the feeling of the book:

> I have been a puppet myself during the Japanese regime as a puppet minister and I know what it means. . . . How we detested those days.

The Burmese had hoped that with the return of the British they would gain at least partial freedom. Actually, they had less liberty than they had had just before the invasion of the Japanese.

Months of pressure and negotiation and a change of governments in England finally brought the Burmese to their desired goal, and in January 1947, the British agreed to "a free and independent Burma, whether within or without the British Empire."

Plans were soon laid to elect a Constituent Assembly which would frame a constitution for the new nation. But to the entreaties of friends to run for a seat in this Assembly, U Nu continued to say no. He had been vice-president in recent months of the Anti-Fascist People's Freedom League, but had not taken an active part in politics.

Finally, upon the death of one of the men who had been elected to the Assembly, U Nu was persuaded to run for the vacant seat in a by-election. He was elected, and at the first meeting of the Assembly was elected Speaker.

Then came July 19, 1947. On that fateful day, General Aung San, six members of his cabinet, and two other men were assassinated by members of the right-wing opposition. Aung San, a brilliant young general, had been the leader of the Burmese resistance movement which had co-operated with the British during the war and helped them to reconquer Burma in the spring of 1945.

At this point the curtain closed on Act Three in the life of U Nu.

Act Four commenced at 4:20 on the morning of January 4, 1948. That was the time picked by the astrologers as most auspicious for the independence of Burma. The capital city of Rangoon was alive with people shouting and singing. In the background were fireworks. In the middle of the crowd was U Nu, the head of the new government whose beginning was being celebrated. But he and his advisers had serious problems to face. Uppermost in their minds were the revolts taking place in many parts of Burma. Some areas were held by Communists, some by members of the People's Volunteer Organization, and others were controlled by guerillas and bandits. In still other sections there were uprisings of the Karens, an ethnic group which the British had favored and some of whose members now wanted a separate state or nation for their people.

Had all these anti-government groups united, they could easily have taken over the country. But fortunately for Burma, they were not united.

Believing that Burma needed all these groups, U Nu set out to win their support for the new government. The Karens were given a state of their own in southeastern Burma, with a high degree of self-government. However, some of the Karens still contended that their state was not large enough, and they continued to oppose the national government. Overtures were made to the Communists and the members of the People's Volunteer Organization but they were interested only in total control. When Nu found that he could not win their support, he declared the Communist party illegal.

These anti-government forces were so strong and their control of territory so widespread in the early part of 1949 that U Nu's government held little more than Rangoon and Mandalay. Even in the capital city, there were strikes, barricaded streets, and fighting.

This was a tough problem for Burma. Until peace and stability were restored, people would not move back to the villages or plant their crops. River, road, rail, and air transportation was curtailed, and plans for new facilities lay useless in the government's files. Dams could not be built while the rivers were controlled by bandits. Not even the mapping of mineral resources, let alone their development, could be undertaken, while such unrest existed. But at last, through a policy combining courage, firmness, and friendliness, U Nu and his colleagues were able to make substantial progress against the various rebel groups.

World War II had left Burma in a terrible condition economically. One writer has said that the destruction was greater in that nation "than . . . in any other country of the world except perhaps Greece." It is estimated that one-third of the country's capital was destroyed and almost half of the agricultural land neglected or left idle during those many years of warfare.

In order to recoup these losses and move ahead to a better life for all the Burmese, the government launched an ambitious program which came to be known as Pyidantha. That term can be translated as "Happy Land" or as "The Welfare State," depending upon one's point of view. In the words of U Nu, its purpose was to make the Burmese people "healthier, wealthier, and happier, and our country a pleasanter place to live in."

Although Pyidantha was a term used originally for only a part of the economic and social development of Burma, it came to be applied to almost all of the projects in which the government was engaged. The phrase caught the imagination of the people and became very popular. The basic plans for it filled a book of over eight hundred pages.

The major goal of Pyidantha was that by 1959–60 the inhabitants of Burma should be producing nearly a third more than they had produced just before the war. That would mean better agriculture, better industry, better education, better health, and better local government.

To help the farmers, a program was launched whereby the national government would limit the size of farms to twenty-five or fifty acres, depending upon local circumstances. The land that was thus released was to be bought by the government and redistributed to the people. In order to save the farmers from paying extremely high rents to landowners, a ceiling was placed on the interest rates paid on borrowed money. Aid was also given them in learning newer and better ways of farming, especially in the production of rice, the biggest crop of Burma.

Since the government wanted to encourage the building of village wells, roads, schools, bridges, and ponds for local water supplies, it developed the idea of "grants-in-aid," usually matching the funds which the local people were willing to put up for these projects.

Over the centuries the people of Burma have built thousands of Buddhist pagodas. They have felt that by such acts of faith they earned merit in a future life. Now the government tried to encourage the people to develop the same feeling toward the building of a school, a road, a well, or some other much needed project. This combination of government aid and wise use of a tradition resulted in hundreds of projects undertaken locally by the Burmese people.

Similarly, the government encouraged the development of industry. Among the plants constructed after the war were a steel factory, a jute plant for making bags and twine, a silk plant, a sugar and alcohol factory, and a tea plant—to mention only a few projects.

In the field of transportation the most ambitious undertaking was the construction of a modern airport at Rangoon, with a modern air-conditioned terminal building.

To improve the nation's health a program was established with emphasis upon conquering malaria, tuberculosis, and venereal diseases. In this aspect of Pyidantha, Burma had the help of the World Health Organization and the United Nations Children's Fund. To provide the necessary doctors for such a nation-wide program, the University of Rangoon Medical School increased the number of students admitted annually from thirty to two hundred fifty. Burma, like all new nations, is still far from having filled the need for such technically trained people.

Even more staggering was the increase in the number of children in school. Before independence, the elementary schools enrolled 153,000 children. By 1957 that number had increased to 1,500,000, or nearly ten times the original figure, and it is still growing. The fact that many of these children drop out after a year or two of schooling is disheartening, but there have been gains. When Burma obtained independence there was not one government-operated middle school (approximately equivalent to an American junior high school). By 1957, 453 such schools had been established.

Similarly striking progress was made in technical education, in the training of teachers, and in an adult mass education movement.

Especially dear to the heart of U Nu was the founding of the Burma Translation Society, whose purpose was to translate English textbooks into Burmese, to encourage young Burmese writers, and to produce inexpensive "readers" for adults on everything from ways to improve farming to venereal diseases. Hundreds of thousands of copies of those publications are issued monthly.

Pyidantha was conceived as a broad attack upon the internal problems of Burma. It was comprehensive and extremely ambitious, especially in view of the internal problems of that land. There was much to be done, but the original plans had to be trimmed to manageable proportions. This occurred in 1957, when a more realistic Four-Year Plan was announced.

Originally it was planned to leave much of the agricultural and industrial development in the hands of the government. Burma was to be a socialist state. But here again plans were changed. With characteristic frankness, U Nu declared in June 1957: "From practical experience, I no longer like to see the government's finger in all sorts of economic pies. If it is allowed to go on unchecked, then, because of lack of proper supervision and efficient management, state enterprises will sooner or later only line the pockets of thieves and pilferers. In the circumstances, from now onward the government will concentrate on key economic projects."

An English commentator on Pyidantha has said that "there is little doubt that [it] has attracted the popular imagination, and in promoting the cause none has been so enthusiastic, none has set such an example as U Nu."

Meanwhile the new government of Burma was faced with external as well as internal problems.

First it was faced with the decision whether to remain in the British Commonwealth or not. On that issue, Burma decided not to join this group of nations. Thus it took a stand that, of all the nations which have won their independence from England, only Ireland and the United States have taken. Why? This is what U Nu himself said about it:

We wanted to be independent. Not that the others which remained in the Commonwealth weren't independent, but we thought we could be *more* independent outside than inside that group. Besides we were not connected with the British racially, religiously, or culturally. Moreover, if we had stayed in the Commonwealth, the Communists in Burma would have said, "See, we are not really free." We emphasized this point with the British and they listened and did not press us as they could have done, realizing that our struggle with the Communists was much greater in Burma than in Pakistan, India, or Ceylon.

There was another important factor in the decision of the government, and that was the character of the men who made the decision. They were not men who had studied in England as many of the leaders of India, Pakistan, and Africa had. And they were younger men than the leaders of the three countries just mentioned. They were probably more radical in their outlook and possibly less aware of the economic advantages of membership in the Commonwealth.

U Nu and his friends also had to make a decision as to their relations with China. As they argued about recognizing the Communist regime there, they were always aware of the fact that Burma has a thousand-mile border with this giant neighbor. Eventually, in 1949, they decided to recognize the Communist regime of Mao Tse-tung.

Meanwhile, the Burmese fought the Communists within their own borders and outlawed the party. U Nu spoke his mind freely on the Communists in his country, saying:

> The demand of the Communists to give full democratic rights to the people is like a thief shouting, "Thief!" The whole country knows only too well what type of democracy exists in those areas over which Communists dominate. . . .

Another issue involving China was even more delicate to handle. Several thousand Chinese had supported President Chiang Kai-shek until he had been forced by the Communist opposition to flee to Formosa with his Nationalist China government. Then many of his followers had moved across the border from China into Burma, where they had caused trouble for months. Finally, satisfied that the problem could not be settled quietly, Burma took its case against these Chinese groups to the United Nations, charging that they were fomenting trouble in Burma and using their new land as a base for operations against Mao Tse-tung. An agreement was finally reached whereby the United States flew hundreds of these Nationalist Chinese to Formosa, although some of them stayed on in Burma and continued to give trouble.

Another potentially explosive situation in foreign relations occurred in 1953 when Burmese planes dropped bombs on several villages in Thailand during their attack on the Chinese Nationalists. In retaliation, the Thais sent anti-aircraft units to the Burmese border. In an effort to prevent further trouble U Nu went to Thailand, publicly offered his apologies for the action of the Burmese Air Force, and offered compensation for the damage. This compensation was returned by the Thais and was eventually used by the Burmese themselves in Thailand for special works of merit there.

U Nu had been aware for years of the importance of co-operation with other Asian nations and was one of the men responsible for calling the Afro-Asian Conference at Bandung, Indonesia, in April 1955. In one of the best speeches made at the conference, he declared that "for the first time in over a century, the peoples of Asia and Africa have begun to live, not merely to exist. . . ." Then, in a typical statement of his Buddhist philosophy applied to international relations, he said:

> Mistrust begets mistrust and suspicion begets suspicion. It may have been permissible in the days of conventional weapons for nations to live in a perpetual atmosphere of suspicion and mistrust. But in the nuclear age such a concept is obsolete. We cannot afford to live in mistrust of our neighbors. We have to learn to live with them in mutual trust and confidence, and where this happy state of affairs has not existed in the past, someone has to break the ice. For trust also begets trust and confidence begets confidence.

He then went on to cite the restoration of friendship between Thailand and Burma as a good example of the application of this philosophy.

In 1955 Nu undertook an ambitious world tour, visiting Israel, Yugoslavia, Britain, the United States, and Japan. It was an interesting selection of countries. Israel was undoubtedly chosen because of U Nu's interest in her technical progress as a new nation. Out of the visit came an agreement by which Israel furnished Burma with considerable economic assistance, especially technical personnel. Yugoslavia was probably selected because of its "independent" policy in international relations, even though it was a Communist country, and because it resembled Burma in its multiracial, multireligious population, as well as in its topography.

During his stay in the United States, Nu toured the Tennessee Valley area, visited the Grand Canyon, went through an automobile factory in Detroit, attended a baseball game, and gave many talks. Stopping in Philadelphia, he visited Independence Hall on July 3. A brief excerpt from his remarks there reveals something of this Burmese statesman.

> The ideas and ideals, the ringing words and slogans of the American Revolution, have a tremendous importance to all men who struggle for liberty. In all parts of the world where men live under tyranny, or under foreign domination, or in feudal bondage, those who dream and plot and fight for freedom do so in the name of the eternal principles for which your Revolution was fought. In those parts of the world, the ideas of the American Revolution are today the most explosive of all forces, more explosive in their capacity to change the world than B-52s or even atomic bombs.

Behind all the statements and actions of U Nu was his basic belief in the principles of Buddhism. There were those who said that his interest in Buddhism was solely or essentially for political purposes. Certainly he valued Buddhism as a unifying factor in Burma. But his interest in Buddhism went much deeper than that, for his Buddhist convictions were much more than political. He had a shrine in his own home and started the day very early with prayers and meditations. Frequently he went on pilgrimages. Much of his reading was in the history and philosophy of his religion, and in 1960, Nu was ordained a Buddhist priest and took the name U Dhamme Dasa.

In spite of the relative success of the programs outlined above, Nu's career was reaching the close of its final phase. In June 1956, Nu resigned as Prime Minister to reorganize his Anti-Fascist People's Freedom League. He became Prime Minister again in 1957.

Just before the curtain fell on Act Four, U Nu became embroiled in a bitter fight within his own party, the Anti-Fascist People's Freedom League. In order to win more votes in Parliament, he accepted the support of some of the radical, or left-wing, groups in June 1958, and agreed to a split in the AFPFL.

It began to look as if he had moved too far to the left and that these groups would take over the government. To avoid a civil war, Nu called upon General Ne Win, the commander-in-chief of the armed forces and a staunch anti-Communist, to take over the government in October 1958. Had the invitation not been forthcoming, Ne Win would have staged a coup and won control anyway. Prime Minister Ne Win permitted the Parliament to continue to sit and consulted it frequently. In time, Parliament held free elections to determine who Win's civil successor would be. Although the army was opposed to him, Nu won the election and returned to the office of Prime Minister in April 1960. He remained in power less than two years. In 1962, Shan tribesmen threatened to secede from Burma unless they were given more independence from the central government. General Ne Win staged a coup and took over in an attempt to hold the nation together. Now he became violently undemocratic. He suspended the Assembly, abandoned the constitution, enforced strict censorship, and placed U Nu under house arrest. In the years that followed Ne Win abolished free enterprise in Burma, nationalizing petroleum and mining, banks, transportation, and even retail shops. The result of this last was that thousands of Indian shopkeepers, many of them Burmese-born, left Burma to go to India.

Under the new government, educational standards dropped. University education is offered free to anyone with minimal qualifications, but overcrowding, low quality of education, and poor teaching have resulted. In 1963 Ne Win closed Burma's three universities, believing them to be breeding grounds of Communism.

In October 1966, U Nu was unconditionally released from prison by Ne Win. The former Prime Minister was free to go to his "hearth and home," the General promised. "Had I known his viewpoint two minutes before he staged the coup, the course of events would have turned out quite differently," U Nu said, after he had spent an hour with the General before his release.

The democratic government which U Nu envisioned for Burma has largely disappeared. In 1964, all parties except the official Burma Socialist Program Party were banned. It may be a long time before Pyidantha reappears in Burma. But thoughtful observers are optimistic in their belief that popular government will come again to Burma. History, they say, is on the side of free peoples. With this U Nu would doubtless agree, for he is, above all, a philosopher, with a philosopher's dreams for his people.

RAHMAN
OF MALAYSIA

It was two minutes before midnight on August 31, 1957, and thousands of people were gathered on the parade grounds in the center of the city of Kuala Lumpur in Malaya. As the lights were dimmed, an expectant hush swept over the crowd. A band struck up "God Save the Queen," and the Union Jack was slowly lowered from the place it had occupied for many years. Then suddenly the music changed. This time the new Malayan national anthem echoed across the parade grounds, and the new flag of Malaya rose triumphantly in front of the government secretariat. The design of the new flag was meaningful. Six red strips and five white stripes represented the nine Malay states and the two former British settlements, and an eleven-pointed star and a yellow crescent against a blue background represented Islam.

Their new flag symbolized for the people of Malaya the end of centuries of foreign rule by the Portuguese, the Dutch, the British, and, for a period during World War II, the Japanese. The flag meant freedom. It meant independence. It meant Malaya. At the stroke of midnight, the throng of people chanted together seven times the word *merdeka,* freedom.

Then Tunku (Prince) Abdul Rahman, the Prime Minister of the new nation, rose and spoke to the crowd with deep feeling.

A new star rises in the eastern sky—a star of freedom for yet another Asian people. . . . There shall be freedom of worship, freedom of speech, freedom from want, freedom of association, freedom of assembly, and freedom of movement . . . in this newly born country.

It was a great occasion. That night there were fireworks and dancing and singing in many parts of Kuala Lumpur and throughout the Malayan peninsula.

The next morning thousands wended their way to the new Merdeka stadium for the official ceremonies. There the Duke of Gloucester, official representative of Queen Elizabeth II, handed over the papers ending British rule in Malaya.

After the reading of a moving message from Her Majesty the Queen, and the comments of the Duke, the Prime Minister again addressed the crowds in the stadium:

> Today a new page is turned and Malaya steps forward to take her rightful place as a free and independent partner in the great community of nations—a new nation is born, and though we fully realize that difficulties and problems lie ahead we are confident that, with the blessing of God, these difficulties will be overcome and that today's events, down the avenues of history, will be our inspiration and guide.

He recalled the "comradeship" of Malaya and Great Britain, especially during two world wars, and paid tribute to Britain's officials for their legacy of justice before the law, an efficient public service, and the highest standard of living in Asia. Then he turned to the future, calling upon the Malayan people to dedicate themselves to the onerous tasks ahead.

After the ceremonies, a mammoth parade was formed. Malay troops dressed smartly in their green *songkoks,* or Moslem hats, white tunics, and green sarongs marched past the reviewing stand and saluted the three officials there— the Duke of Gloucester, the Tunku, and Sir Abdul Rahman, the recently elected Paramount Ruler of the Federation—a man with the same name as the Prime Minister, but not a relative.

In a lighter mood later that day the Tunku said he felt "as enthusiastic and excited as a child being given a new toy." But if he was receiving a new toy, it was a very complicated one in this first year of independence.

Jutting south from the mainland of Asia is a long, narrow peninsula which looks like a drumstick, the pedal of a piano, or the foot of a giant. The land formerly known as Malaya is the southernmost part of that peninsula and is about the size of Florida, shaped a little like a diamond. To the north is Thailand, and to the south and west is the island of Sumatra, a part of the Indonesian Republic. These are Malaya's only near neighbors. To the east is the China Sea and to the west the Straits of Malacca. Much further away in the Indian Ocean. Because of its location, Malaya has approximately a thousand miles of coastline.

At her extreme southern tip is the very small but highly important island of Singapore, connected with Malaya by a causeway.

Three-fourths of Malaya is jungle, with the trees making a solid, skyless roof. The lush growth is due to Malaya's location near the equator and to the heavy rainfall.

The people of Malaya are as varied as those of any country in the world. About one-half of them are Malays, whose ancestors came there thousands of years ago. In the past they were tremendously influenced by the Indian culture in architecture, painting, dancing, and music. But much of that influence was lost over the years. They did, however, retain the Moslem faith which they adopted hundreds of years ago.

The majority of the Malays live in villages, or *kampongs*. They lead a quiet, leisurely life, raising rice on small plots of ground and fishing, often with traps. They speak Malay, which has become the national language of Malaya.

The second largest group of Malayans is the Chinese, about 37 per cent. The ancestors of a few of them came from China centuries ago; these people no longer look to China as their home, as the more recent immigrants do. Nevertheless, for a variety of reasons, most of the Chinese tended to stay apart from other groups in Malaya in order to preserve their own way of life. About half of them live in the cities and carry on retail trade, or work in mills, factories, sawmills, and banks. Many of them came in the early days of tin mining and are still engaged in that work.

The third group, made up of Indians and Pakistanis, is an important segment of the population of Malaya, despite the fact that it numbers only about 10 per cent. Some of them can trace their roots in Malaya through centuries. The ancestors of others came to the country around 1870 to work on the coffee plantations and the rubber estates.

The balance of the population of Malaya is composed of Europeans, Eurasians, and others from abroad.

The standard of living of the Malayans before independence was not high, but far higher than that of most Asians. Malaya has rich deposits of tin, and leads the world in the output of that product. She also has thousands of acres of rubber trees, and was at the time of independence second to Indonesia in production of that important crop. When the prices of these two products were high on the world market, the Malayans prospered. But when the prices of rubber and tin dropped, there was suffering in the land.

This, then, was Malaya—a relatively rich, stable land with all kinds of possibilities for the future. This was the land that won its independence on August 31, 1957. This was the territory ruled by Prime Minister Abdul Rahman, or the Tunku, as he is familiarly called, a genial, kind-hearted, and warmly human man.

The Tunku's full name is Tunku Abdul Rahman Ibni Almarhum Sultan Abdul Hamid Halim Shah, which means simply Prince Abdul Rahman, son of the late Sultan Abdul Hamid Halim Shah.

A foreigner meeting him for the first time would probably notice his clothes first, for they are unusual and very attractive. In place of a shirt he would be wearing a *baju,* or loose-fitting jacket made of silk, with the collar attached, but with gold braids instead of buttons, and no tie. Over pants called *seluar* would be wrapped a sarong, often in a contrasting color. He would have shoes or sandals on his feet, but possibly no socks. On his head would be a *songkok,* or black hat with no brim and no adornments of any kind. This is the general Malay costume worn by middle- and upper-class people. It is very colorful and suitable to a warm climate.

Rahman is a large man by Malayan standards, nearly six feet tall.

Right away you would be struck by his friendliness. He would be easy to talk with and would seem intensely interested in you, as he is in most people he meets. He gives the impression of enjoying life, of being glad to be alive. This attitude was reflected in the comments he once made at a dinner given by the Press Club of Malaya:

> Why should anybody have to fight in this country in order to live? Let us all be happy and make merry while life lasts. I be-lieve we can achieve our goals by laughing and treading our way happily toward them.

Those are not the words that you expect to hear from a serious statesmen, but they help to explain the Tunku.

And they explain also a good part of his success as a politician and leader in the fight for independence, for it is his friendliness, his joviality, his interest in people that have helped so much in bridging the chasms between the various groups that make up Malaya—the Chinese, the Indians and Pakistanis, and the Malays.

It this were just a pose, it would not work. But people recognize that Rahman is sincere and genuine, and they trust him. This is especially true of the minority groups, for they would not have agreed to co-operate in achieving independence and establishing the new government if they had not trusted the man who would become its head.

The Tunku likes to take trips into the country, whether to open schools and to dedicate mosques, or even, in earlier days, to clear an area of rebel forces and declare it free from terrorists.

But no one should be deceived into thinking that the Tunku is a light, frivolous person interested only in fun. On the surface he is gentle and soft-spoken, but underneath there is firmness. On some things he is immovable. He can be determined, stubborn, and frank. He can even be ironic and sarcastic. He often chides people, and he is not afraid to tell other political leaders, "Hold your tongue," when he thinks they are saying things that are not good for the country.

Although he is a prince, he has lived most of his life with the common people and knows pretty well how they think and feel. This is a rare quality in a prince and has stood him in good stead on many occasions. Some people refer to it as an intuitive ability, but it is certainly based in part on long years of association with the people of Malaya. One of the Tunku's strengths is that he comes from a prominent family and is a prince. This is a very important prestige factor in Malaya and one of the reasons for his rise to power.

Like most of the other leaders of new nations, the Tunku is not a brilliant administrator, but he has had the good sense to draw around him several able men. And he usually lets people alone so that they can carry out their tasks without his interference.

Nor is he a scholar. But he has the ability to persuade people to work with him and for him—which is one type of greatness.

Almost everyone who knows him well talks about his common sense. He seems to have a flair for simplifying matters, for getting to the root of a situation, seeing it quickly, and stating it simply. This quality is especially valuable to him in the assessment of long-range problems, at which he is very acute. And he is a hard worker.

Finally, he has patience. He knew how much needed to be done in Malaya, but he also knew that he could not push people too hard or too fast. As he said at the time of independence:

> Give us a chance. We have just been born. Surely nobody expects us to be able to run all at once. Some people think that as soon as you plant a tree, it must bear fruit. We must allow it to grow a bit.

The Tunku's story is that of a prince and playboy who became the father of his country's freedom. It is the story of a man's gradual achievement of a position of leadership, without any dramatic or sudden changes in his character.

The Tunku was born February 8, 1903, in the town of Alor Star. His father was Sultan Abdul Hamid Halim Shah, the chief religious officer of the state of Kedah, and his mother was Mak Check. She was a rare person, fair in her coloration, beautiful, and strong-willed. She was half Burmese and half Siamese, and although she had not been born into a Moslem family she was brought up as a Moslem. She was also a very good businesswoman and owned a good deal of property.

As a boy Abdul was not strong, and he was something of an "ugly duckling." His early years were largely un-eventful. He grew up under the care of his mother and his Siamese nurse and learned to fly kites, spin tops, and play marbles, like boys all over the world. When he wandered away from the house he could always be found in some home in the village, for he liked to visit his less fortunate friends, even though he was a prince.

When he was four his formal education began. He first went to a school where Malay was spoken in the mornings and English in the afternoons. Then, when he was seven he went to the English school in Alor Star, known as the Sultan Abdul Hamid College.

At ten he was sent off to Siam (now Thailand) to live with his brother, who had just returned from Rugby and the Royal Military Academy in England. In Bangkok he attended a Siamese school, but this was relatively easy for him as he had spoken Siamese with his mother and his nurse from the time he began to talk. Within a year, however, his brother died, and Abdul went to Penang to continue his studies.

At the age of sixteen he set off for England, where he studied with a tutor for a time and then entered St. Catherine's College, Cambridge. There he met with racial discrimination for the first time, when he was told that the college had been built for English students and that he could not be given a room in the regular dormitory. The Tunku, greatly offended, reported this to the higher officials and was offered a room immediately, but he refused to accept it.

Futhermore, though he was a very good soccer player, he was barred from the freshman team because of his color.

He studied history and law in Cambridge, but he did not worry too much about his academic record. He was more interested in having good times on weekends, made possible by a generous allowance from home. A long list of traffic offenses testifies to the fact that he enjoyed driving his Riley sports car and ignored traffic regulations rather frequently.

But the car was put to good use during the British national elections, when he drove some of his Welsh friends to political meetings and helped them to get voters to the polls on election day. This was his introduction to politics and one of the most practical lessons he learned in his years in England.

In 1928 he returned for a short visit to Malaya and was feted and honored as the first Malay student to graduate from a great British university. Unfortunately this turned his head a bit, and when he went back to England he did very poorly in his law examinations. Finally, he returned to Malaya, but without having been admitted to the bar. He had, however, helped to found the Malay Society for students from that part of the world in England and had served as its secretary. During a later period in England, he became its president.

Upon his return to Malaya in 1932 he married. His first child was a daughter. But not long after the birth of the second child, a son, his wife, Che Meriam, contracted malaria and died. Her death occurred in one of the outlying provinces where the Tunku had been assigned as a district officer. It was a terrible loss to him, and he was infuriated because he considered it needless. Immediately he plunged into an anti-malaria campaign, determined to bring this dread disease under control in his district.

The Tunku's second wife was a European whom he had known in his Cambridge days. Her difficulty in adjusting to life in Malaya and the disdainful attitude of the Europeans toward her Malayan marriage made their life together an unhappy one, and she returned to England. In 1939 the Tunku married his present wife, a quiet, friendly woman named Che Sherifah Rodziah. They have not had children of their own but adopted several Chinese children because of their interest in better race relations in their country.

After several assignments as an officer in the Civil Service, the Tunku returned to England to continue his studies. But when World War II broke out, he hurried back to Malaya.

Soon the Japanese landed in northern Malaya and moved on to the east and west coasts. The British felt it was needful to evacuate their high officials and certain important Malay leaders. The Tunku's father was one of the men to be taken to Penang for protection. But the Tunku decided that Penang was not a safe place because of the danger of air raids and that his father should remain with his people during these troubled times. Discovering the route the British officials would take to evacuate his father, the Tunku hurried there and "kidnapped" his father, taking him eventually back to his home town of Alor Star.

During the early months of the war the Tunku had taken a leading part in storing rice and in planning evacuation centers. People had criticized him for these actions, saying that he was only stirring up fear and panic among the populace. But he nevertheless persisted in his efforts, and eventually the people were grateful for his foresight.

When the Japanese arrived, the Tunku was kept on as district officer in Kulim. He worked hard to maintain law and order and to provide sufficient food for the people. But he was not too co-operative in the eyes of the Japanese officers and was soon demoted, first to state auditor of the Alor Star region and then to superintendent of education.

Throughout these war years he was very close to the common people, spending almost all of his time with them. He was their protector and friend and his popularity increased greatly. On one occasion he risked his life for them by taking the responsibility for the fact that some of his men refused to hand over their arms to the Japanese.

In this period he was also active in founding a welfare organization to aid the refugees who had escaped from forced labor on the railroad being built between Burma and Siam.

Those were sad days in Malaya, for the people were divided in their attitude toward their invaders. Some were willing to collaborate with the Japanese, hoping thereby to win their independence at the end of the war if the Japanese were the victors. Some were willing to co-operate with the Japanese while they planned and plotted for the return of the British. Some felt that they could not co-operate with any group from outside their country but must organize against all foreigners.

Life was especially hard for the Chinese in Malaya. They were the real foes of the Japanese. Hundreds of them were tortured and killed and thousands suffered from lack of food. Many of them eventually fled to the hills and joined various resistance groups. The largest of these was controlled by the Malayan Communist party, which was very effective in its opposition to the Japanese in that period.

Meanwhile, the Japanese relied heavily upon the Malay police force to keep order and to suppress the Chinese. The bitterness and hatred between these two major racial groups were long felt in the new nation.

Finally, in the fall of 1945, British troops replaced the Japanese and a military administration was established. The following year, civil government was restored and the eleven major areas of Malaya were organized into the Malayan Union.

Many Malayans were already pressing for greater local control or for independence. But the British were not fully aware of the political consciousness which had developed during the years of Japanese occupation. They were absorbed in defeating the rebels who were still holding out in the mountains, in restoring the tin and rubber industries which yielded Britain much-needed dollars in world trade, and in providing an adequate food supply for the people. In addition, the British felt that the bitterness between the racial groups would make self-government impossible.

Many of the upper-class Malays decided that they needed a political organization to fight for freedom, and the United Malay National Organization was founded in 1946 by Dato Onn and his friends. A somewhat similar group had been formed the year before by some of the leading Chinese intellectuals, who called their group the Malayan Democratic Union.

These and other groups brought enough pressure to bear so that in 1948 the British took one more step toward granting eventual independence by giving the Malayans more power in a Malaya Federation. This included all the area of the former Malayan Union, plus Singapore.

Meanwhile, the Tunku had decided that he would complete his preparation for a legal career. In 1947 he returned to England and stayed there until 1949, when he was admitted to the bar, twenty-one years after he had originally tried to pass the examinations.

In 1949 he returned to Malaya. He was now quite a different person from the one he had been upon his return in 1932. The years had mellowed him, and he was a much wiser man. Soon he was to become the leader in Malaya's fight for independence and to serve as its first Prime Minister.

Looking back over his life, it is easy now to see some of the factors which had made him the potential leader of his country. First, there had been the influence of his mother. The fact that she was half Burmese and half Siamese made racial understanding easier for her son. During his school years in England he had learned something about racial discrimination and had been greatly impressed with the need for tolerance and understanding. He had also learned something in England about democratic ideals and practices as well as about practical politics. On the boat trip back from England he had met Eugene Chen, the Foreign Minister of China at that time, and had been much influenced by him.

In looking at the neighbors of Malaya, he had observed that the Siamese had been free for centuries.

The war years under the Japanese had given him much administrative experience and brought him close to the people of Malaya, thus democratizing him. His decision as a middle-aged man to return to England to complete his work in law reflected his growing maturity and determination. He was no longer the playboy prince. Now he was a potential worker toward independence and Prime Minister.

In the years since the founding of the United Malay National Organization there had been a great deal of dissension in that party. Its founder, Dato Onn, had become disgusted with the leadership of the group and had now decided to form his own Independence of Malaya party. The UMNO was really on the wane, and several people declined the presidency when it was offered to them in 1951.

Finally they turned to Rahman. He was an able organizer, a prince who understood the common people, and a man with a winning personality. Perhaps he could restore the party to its former popularity.

Against the advice of many of his friends, Rahman accepted this post and set out immediately to rebuild the UMNO. This work took him to all parts of the country, where he met not only the politicians but also the people. Everywhere he went he was asked to speak. Rahman is not a gifted orator, but his charm, his earnestness, and his obvious knowledge are persuasive.

His efforts to revive the UMNO were successful, and in the municipal elections held in 1952 in Kuala Lumpur and two other towns it won twenty-four out of forty-three seats. This would not have been possible, however, except for the Tunku's insistence on an alliance with the Malayan Chinese Association. In its early days the UMNO had flirted with the idea of co-operation with the Chinese, but Dato Onn had eventually decided against this before forming his Independence of Malaya party. But the Tunku felt that collaboration was essential for the party and also for the future of Malaya, and his counsel won. To those who wanted the Malays to remain separate he spoke harshly, declaring:

> To advocate such intolerance is highly dangerous. It is so vicious and potentially explosive that it must be stopped. I intend to stop it. We don't want religious warfare.

In the 1955 federal elections he went even farther, joining with the Malayan Indian Congress as well as with the Malayan Chinese Association. This alliance gained fifty-one out of the fifty-two seats in the federal legislature and the Tunku was chosen Chief Minister and Minister of Home Affairs.

Independence was on its way, and in January 1956 the Tunku went to London, on what was known as the Merdeka Mission, to arrange for complete self-government and the establishment of Malaya as a new nation, as well as to obtain a loan and grant for the Development Plan for the new country which was now emerging.

Then on August 31, 1957 came independence. There had been no war. There had not even been a civil disobedience movement, as in India. Some of the credit goes to the British for this gradual transferal of power to the Malayans. Much of the credit also belongs to Rahman, for he had been one who believed in persuasion rather than belligerency as a method of achieving one's desired goals.

When the Tunku took over the reins of government as the first Prime Minister of Malaya, he was confronted with many problems. The top ten goals of his government were probably these:

1. Internal security
2. Harmony among the various racial groups
3. Economic development
4. Adequate capital
5. Improvement in educational facilities
6. Solution of the language problem
7. Improvement and diversification of agriculture
8. Improvement of health
9. Successful foreign relations
10. Improved relations with Singapore

At the close of World War II the Communists were a powerful group in Malaya. Since they were hiding out in the hills and were dependent upon nearby villages for their food supply, the British took drastic measures and moved nearly five hundred thousand people into compounds surrounded by barbed wire. The people were required to eat together so that the food supplies could be controlled and kept from the Communists. These and other measures were extremely successful and helped to break the backbone of the Communist forces.

The winning of independence and the growing opposition of the populace to terrorism also made the task of crushing the Communists easier, but there were still several hundred of them in hiding when the Tunku took over in 1957. He used psychological warfare against them and also dispatched troops to the mountains to ferret out the remaining rebels.

The Tunku was a determined fighter against Communism. He has said:

> I know from the experience of other countries that Communists can never co-exist with any government. They drove the Nationalist government out of China. They tried to drive the Nationalist Korean government out of Korea and the Nationalist government from Vietnam. I would be deceiving myself if I were to think that they are going to treat us differently.

To promote unity among the non-Communist Malayans Rahman lent his personal prestige to fostering better race relations. To his first cabinet he appointed three Chinese and an Indian. It was his hope that eventually the people would think of themselves as Malayans rather than as Malays, Chinese, Indians, and Pakistanis.

Malaya had been a relatively prosperous country, but it was far too dependent upon tin and rubber for its wealth. In 1957 the Federal Legislative Council approved an ambitious Five-Year Plan which would cost about $500,000,000. This included a wide range of plans, from the building of secondary industries to the replanting of many thousand acres of land with higher-yielding rubber trees, in order to compete on the world market with the new synthetic rubber. Considerable progress was made on this comprehensive plan, although it was hampered by the drop in rubber and tin prices and by the fact that money which should have been available for financing this Five-Year Plan had to be diverted for many months to fighting the rebels.

At the time of independence about 60 per cent of Malaya's citizens were literate, which is a high degree of literacy for a new nation. But there is a vast difference between people who are able to read and write a little in some language and an educated populace.

Between the years 1941 and 1956 the number of children in Malayan schools rose from 263,000 to 950,000, and continued to increase rapidly. But with 62 per cent of her population under eighteen years of age, this was an enormous number of children to provide for. Finding and training teachers and providing buildings was in itself a tremendous undertaking as well as an expensive one.

Unfortunately, Malaya raised only about half of the rice she needed to feed her people and was dependent upon outside sources for this and other foodstuffs. The government concentrated upon the improvement of methods of cultivation and marketing in an attempt to increase and improve the food supply. It tried to improve fishing methods and to increase the supply of livestock. A Rural and Industrial Development Authority was created to administer these improvements.

Considerable progress was made in improving health, especially in freeing the country of plague, cholera, smallpox, and malaria. Malayans are very proud of the fact that in the resettlement of five hundred thousand persons there were no major epidemics. The development of a strong Rural Health Service with mobile trucks, boats, and airplanes brought results.

The Tunku has a strong interest in foreign relations, due in part to his extensive travels and partly to his realizations of Malaya's dependence economically on the rest of the world. As soon as Malaya won its independence, it became a part of the British Commonwealth and also of the United Nations. At the same time it recognized the Soviet Union.

Rahman was especially interested in closer relations between the nations of what he calls "the sarong belt." He felt that the peoples of Southeast Asia needed to support each other more fully instead of "dancing to the tune of bigger nations." He especially advocated a mutual aid plan in winning the support of private investors for this part of the world.

In 1961 plans began to be formulated, under Rahman's leadership, for a federation of states in Malaya's corner of the world. In 1963, the Malaysian Federation came into being. It consisted of Malaya, Singapore, Sarawak, and Sabah, the last two being part of the Island of Borneo. The population of Malaysia is about ten and a half million, whose governing body is a federal parliament. Rahman became Prime Minister of Malaysia. President Sukarno of Indonesia was violently opposed to the Federation, claiming that it was a British scheme for keeping power in Southeast Asia. For over three years he conducted an annoying but unsuccessful military "confrontation" against Malaysia. In 1966, with Sukarno's power rapidly disappearing, the new government of Indonesia signed a peace agreement with Malaysia and the undeclared war ended.

Rahman, the liberal leader, who plays a powerful role in his country without being a dictator, has high ambitions for Malaysia. He is trying to bring the Malayans more prominently into the economic life of their country, whose rubber and tin industries have heretofore been dominated by the British and Chinese. The Rural and Industrial Development Authority promotes projects in areas where the natives live and tries to improve rural living conditions. Rahman is also raising educational quality and opportunity in Malaysia. About two million children attend the government-sponsored schools in Malaysia, a big advance in recent years.

Rahman recognizes the importance of education in the national language for creating unity among the diverse peoples of his country. Religion and related customs, as well as language, have been a barrier to unity between the Chinese and the Malayans. The Chinese fear that the Malay majority may someday force them to leave the country. Rahman knows that a common education for the two groups will help to break down mutual suspicion and mistrust without interfering with religious and traditional loyalties.

Largely because of animosity between the Chinese and the Malayans, Singapore seceded from the Federation in 1965. This was unfortunate, because Singapore is valuable. It has one of the greatest ports in the world. The Chinese, who make up over half the population, operate most of the industries, and agricultural and business enterprises. Among the successful industries is the largest tin-smelting plant in the world. The native Malayans are for the most part engaged in fishing, which is also one of Singapore's economic assets, and hold most of the government posts.

Despite this loss, on balance the outlook for the Malaysian Federation is good. It survived Indonesia's attempt to destroy it. In fact, the struggle bound the people more closely together in a common cause. The flow of foreign capital into the country is healthy. With an able, liberal leader such as Rahman, Malaysia is one bright spot in Southeast Asia.

SUKARNO
OF INDONESIA

April 18, 1955 had finally arrived, and in Bandung, Indonesia, it was going to be quite a day! For weeks the people had been preparing for it. They had scrubbed and whitewashed their homes, renovated and refurnished the hotels, repaired the streets, even erected new street lights. Nothing like this impending conference of Asians and Africans had ever taken place in the history of the world, and Bandung had outdone itself to give its visitors a warm welcome and a good impression of their city.

Before dawn the people of Bandung had begun to line the streets, waiting patiently to catch a glimpse of the leaders of Asia and Africa who would arrive for the opening session of the Bandung Conference. Occasionally they glanced at the flags of the twenty-nine nations to be represented here. Or they stared at the bright posters welcoming the delegations to this mountain city of eight hundred thousand persons. But mostly they sat or stood as quietly as only an Asian crowd can.

Suddenly the sirens sounded, and the big, sleek cars began to arrive in front of the Gedung Merdeka, an imposing building in the center of Bandung which had once been a clubhouse of the Dutch rulers of Indonesia. Tiny flags were waved, flashbulbs popped, cameras clicked, and the schoolchildren surged toward the cars, hoping to get the autographs of the visitors if the short, squat soldiers with their white helmets and Sten guns would let them get near the delegates.

The people in the streets did not know much about the

men who arrived, but they did know that they were important. They knew that they represented the colored peoples of the world—the black people, the brown people, the yellow people. They knew that these men represented men and women like themselves who had fought against colonial rule and had won independence, as they had done in Indonesia. They knew that these leaders represented over half of the world's population, coming from big countries like China and India and little countries whose names they had heard but had forgotten.

One by one the leaders arrived and were applauded. Among them were Chou En-lai of China, Pandit Nehru of India, Prince Wan of Thailand and Prince Sihanouk of Cambodia, Gamal Nasser of Egypt, Mohammed Ali of Pakistan, Carlos Romulo of the Philippines, Sir John Kotelawala of Ceylon, and others.

Inside the auditorium the conference was called to order, and a small brown man, nattily dressed in a white uniform with a black velvet hat, stepped to the podium to give the welcoming address.

This man was Sukarno, leader of the Indonesian fight for independence from the Dutch, President of the Republic of Indonesia (one of the five nations which had convened the Bandung Conference), and Asia's outstanding orator.

After a few opening remarks, he plunged into his address with the reminder that, "This is the first intercontinental conference of colored peoples in the history of mankind!"

And what kind of a world were they meeting in? This is how he described it:

> . . . We are living in a world of fear. The life of man today
> is corroded and made bitter by fear. Fear of the future, fear
> of the hydrogen bomb, fear of ideologies. Perhaps this fear is
> a greater danger than the danger itself, because it is fear which
> drives men to act foolishly, to act thoughtlessly, to act dan-

gerously. . . . And do not think that the oceans and the seas will protect us. The food we eat, the water we drink, yes, even the very air that we breathe can be contaminated by poisons originating from thousands of miles away. And it could be that, even if we ourselves escaped lightly, the unborn generations of our children would bear on their distorted bodies the marks of our failure to control the forces which have been released on the world.

He then paid tribute to all those who had taken part in the struggles for freedom in Asia and Africa, reminding his hearers that:

For many generations our peoples have been the voiceless ones in the world. We have been the unregarded, the peoples for whom decisions were made by others whose interests were paramount, the peoples who lived in poverty and humiliation.

Then he briefly outlined the struggles for independence in the past era, pointing out that:

Today in this hall are gathered together the leaders of those same peoples. They are no longer the victims of colonialism. They are no longer the tools of others and the playthings of forces they cannot influence. Today, you are the representatives of free peoples, peoples of a different stature and standing in the world.

Sukarno pointed out that the differences among them were great—differences of color, of social background, of cultural pattern, of religion. Nevertheless, he said:

We are united by our common detestation of colonialism in whatever form it appears. We are united by a common detestation of racialism. And we are united by our common determination to preserve and stabilize peace in the world.

He spoke at length on colonialism, and moved on to paint a dark picture of the current arms buildup. Then he asked

what the representatives of Asia and Africa could do in
such a world when their economic strength was so meager
and their political power so puny. His answer was this:

> We can inject the voice of reason into world affairs. We can
> mobilize all the spiritual, all the moral, all the political strength
> of Asia and Africa on the side of peace. We, the peoples of
> Asia and Africa, 1,400,000,000 strong . . . can mobilize what I
> have called the Moral Violence of Nations in favor of peace.

He asserted that this was possible, as had been proved
on such occasions as the meeting in New Delhi of a previous
small conference on Asian and African nations which had
strengthened the hand of the Indonesians in their fight for
independence and in the work of the five sponsoring nations
of the Bandung Conference in bringing a halt to the hostilities in Indochina.

Pointing out the great diversity of religions in the vast
area the delegates represented, he pleaded for a policy of
"live and let live," of mutual tolerance and understanding
by the people of so many different faiths. He urged those
present to give guidance to mankind in its search for security
and peace, showing the world that "a New Asia and a
New Africa have been born."

In his closing comments he championed the rights of other
emerging nations to independence.

> Let us remember that no blessing of God is so sweet as life
> and liberty. Let us remember that the stature of all mankind
> is diminished so long as nations or parts of nations are still un-
> free. Let us remember that the highest purpose of man is the
> liberation of man from his bonds of fear, his bonds of human
> degradation, his bonds of poverty—the liberation of man from
> the physical, spiritual, and intellectual bonds which for too
> long stunted the development of mankind's majority.

His speech was greeted with tumultuous applause. It had summarized the feelings of millions of the world's peoples and had been presented brilliantly. It was evidence of Sukarno's power as a speaker—a power which had won him the affection of millions of Indonesians and the title of Bung (Brother) Karno, or Su (Supreme) Karno, from the masses of men, women, and children in his homeland. The speech had reflected his bitter hatred of colonialism, his consciousness of color, his awareness of the power of religions, and his hope for the unity of the peoples of Asia and Africa.

He had not outlined specific proposals which he hoped the conference would consider, for this was a keynote speech, and such details must be left to the delegates. Neither had he stressed the important economic and social issues which plagued all of the nations represented at Bandung, probably because his primary interest had always been in politics rather than in economics or sociology.

But this speech had set the stage for one of the most important conferences in world history, and that was what he had intended to do.

On that day and on the days that followed, Sukarno basked in the spotlight of the conference. In the months ahead he would be engrossed in a civil war and his stature as a world statesman would be somewhat diminished, but now he was enjoying the culmination of fifty-three years of a rich, full, exciting life.

If he had had time to think about it, he might have marveled at how far he had come in those fifty-three years, for no one could possibly have predicted such a rise for the baby who was born in Surabaja in East Java on June 6, 1901. That child was born into a good family, but hardly one from which to expect a future leader of the entire area of Indonesia.

His father was a schoolteacher from Java and a Moslem,

while his mother was a Balinese dancer. She had been reared as a Hindu but had been converted to Islam. They were both intelligent people, saturated in the history and folklore of these two islands and these two faiths, so that their son was able to learn much from them and to profit by this wide and rich background. They were also anxious for their boy to obtain a good education, which was difficult in those days for an Indonesian. All these factors helped to give him a better than average start in life.

Like other small boys, he played around the thatch and wattle house and in the *kampong*, the cluster of houses where the neighbors lived. Then in the evenings he would often go with his parents to see the shadow plays or the puppetry for which Indonesia is famous. The shows would often start late in the evening and continue until dawn, and he would fall asleep in his mother's arms. But he saw enough to learn about Bima and Gatutkatja and the other legendary figures represented by the fascinating puppets made of dried buffalo skin.

At other times he went with his parents to the local dances and watched the rhythmic posturing of the men and women who had spent many years learning how to use their bodies gracefully and symbolically.

He also enjoyed the music of the gamelan orchestras made up of xylophones, two- and three-string violins, flutes, cymbals, and other instruments.

Through these rich and varied media, the boy learned a great deal of history and folklore which had been passed down for centuries from the remarkable Indian legends of the past.

Sometimes the children imitated their elders in their play, making their own crude puppets and giving shows, playing their own homemade instruments, and dancing as they had seen the adults do. Or they told each other the stories which they had heard the storytellers narrate so vividly.

All of this rich cultural background left a strong impression on Sukarno and in later years he became a patron of the arts, buying the paintings of young Indonesian artists and hanging them on the walls of the presidential palace, holding musicales, dances, and shadow plays in his home, and getting small groups together to sing Western or Indonesian folk songs. This not only gave him personal pleasure but was a way of encouraging the artistic side of Indonesian life.

Most Indonesian children in those days never went to school. Education was the privilege of Dutch children and the children of the wealthy. But Sukarno's father was a schoolteacher and he was determined that his boy should receive a good education. So at the age of six, Sukarno started to school in his home town.

In his studies he did not distinguish himself, but outside the classroom he was a favorite. He could climb higher than the other boys and beat them in running and jumping. Soon he was a leader among them, starting on the long career that was eventually to make him leader of eighty-five million people.

He was a handsome boy, somewhat precocious and a little spoiled. Some called him Djago, which meant the rooster, or the champion.

When he was twelve, he entered the local Dutch elementary school. There he had to work harder and there he began to take more interest in his studies. He even took French lessons outside of school hours. By the time he was fourteen he had completed the work in that school and passed his "Klein Ambtenaars Examen." This was a diploma which meant that he could work as a minor clerk in the Dutch government. He now had far more education than most Indonesians, but his father was still not satisfied and arranged for Sukarno to live in the home of a friend named H. O. S. Tjokroaminoto in Surabaja and to attend the Hooger Burger School, a kind of high school attended mostly by Dutch children and the children of high Indonesian officials. For five years Sukarno studied there, completing his work in 1920.

Tjokroaminoto was a leading religious and political leader and the founder of a group known as the Sarekat Islam. This group was interested in Indonesian independence and was willing to try to obtain it by force if necessary, which was the most radical approach that had been taken up to that time in Indonesia.

Many of the meetings of this group were held in the home where Sukarno was living, and he often listened to the leaders talk about their aims, their strategy, and their organizational problems. Little did he realize then that he was receiving a marvelous education—one which would enable him to become the future leader of his land. Undoubtedly what he learned in the home of Tjokroaminoto was the most influential factor shaping his later life.

Soon Sukarno was committed to the ideal of independence and joined a junior group which came to be known as Young Java. In this group he became a forceful speaker, a capable organizer, and an outstanding writer. Many of the editorials in the party newspaper *Utusan Hindia* were written by him and signed "Bima," after the hero in the puppet shows he enjoyed in his boyhood.

He was not yet involved deeply in politics, and his formal education was still not complete. He moved to the city of Bandung to become one of the first eleven students in a Dutch technical college. He did excellent work, and was called by one professor "the most promising student we ever had." Despite his concentration on his studies, he seemed to have plenty of time for politics. Hour upon hour he read the biographies of famous figures in history and all he could find on politics and history. He spent a great deal of time talking to the political leaders in Bandung and often spoke on politics to student groups or clubs in that city.

One of his speeches created such a stir that the Chief Commissioner of Police in Bandung ordered Sukarno off the platform and closed the meeting for fear of what the crowd might do after they had been whipped up by this young orator. From that time on Sukarno was hailed as "The Lion of the Platform" and was much sought after as a speaker.

For five years Sukarno studied at the technical college. He completed his work in 1925, with a thesis on harbor construction.

After his graduation as an engineer he turned to politics full-time and successively organized a study club of young intellectuals, an Indonesian Nationalist Organization, and finally the Partai Nasional Indonesia, or Idonesian Nationalist party. His ideas had changed considerably since the evenings he had spent in the home of Tjokroaminoto. He was now advocating independence for all of the islands, trying to broaden the base of this movement by including the masses as well as the educated classes, and urging non-co-operation with the Dutch as a means of gaining more freedom and eventual independence.

Obviously Sukarno was a "troublemaker" who needed watching. The Dutch kept their eye on him and on December 29, 1929, arrested him and three other leaders. Eventually they were tried and Sukarno was sentenced to four years' imprisonment on the charge that he was plotting a rebellion which was to take place early in 1930.

The trial of these revolutionary leaders dragged on for four months. It was marked by one of Sukarno's greatest speeches, "Indonesia *menggugat,*" or "Indonesia accuses." In it, Sukarno brought charge after charge against the Dutch for more than three centuries of misrule, pointing out the poverty, the misery, the humiliation of the Indonesians and contrasting these with the great wealth the Dutch had acquired from Indonesia. Following this speech, he was sentenced to prison by the Dutch court. After two years he was released. He returned immediately to politics. But he discovered that during his imprisonment the Nationalist party had split into a moderate and a radical group. He tried for a time to unite these two factions, but finally saw that it could not be done. He then joined the radical group and was made its chairman. Mohammed Hatta was serving as the leader of the moderates.

Sukarno and Mohammed Hatta were to be closely linked in the years ahead. In many ways they were contrasting figures, complementing each other in their backgrounds, their training, and their philosophies. Hatta was born in 1902, a year later than Sukarno, on the island of Sumatra, whereas Sukarno was born in Java. Hatta studied in Indonesia and then went to the Netherlands to continue his education, majoring in economics. Sukarno, on the other hand, was one of the first revolutionary leaders to obtain all his education in his native land. As a result, he never saw the Dutch or other Westerners except as colonialists and oppressors and he never came in contact with the strong liberal movements of Western Europe. Sukarno was also very weak in his grasp of economics, the field in which Hatta had concentrated in the Netherlands.

Hatta was a scholarly, sober-minded, religious man who appealed to the intellectuals and was very wary of the Communists. He had the respect but not the passionate devotion of the masses. Sukarno, on the other hand, was a buoyant, dynamic person with a great gift in public speaking and an ability to reach the masses.

He was more radical in his thinking, less closely identified with the Moslem faith and willing to work with the Communists to promote his political aims.

Although the two men worked together during the fight for independence and for the first few years of the new government, one writer has said that the history of Indonesia is largely the history of quarrels and reconciliations between the two leaders.

Within a few months after Sukarno's prison term ended, his group of radicals had grown to twenty thousand, largely as a result of his oratory and his organizational prowess, while Hatta's group had only about a thousand members.

Sukarno's success angered the Dutch, and on August 1, 1933 he was arrested again and sent with his family first to the Flores Islands and later to Bengkulu in South Sumatra.

From 1933 until 1942 he was either in prison or exile, like other leaders of new nations. Commenting upon those years Sukarno has said:

> Sometimes people have sympathized with me because long years of my life were spent in jail and in exile. Well, those years . . . were a mixed experience. I hated them because they separated me from the dearest thing in the world—the struggle of my people for rebirth. At the same time, they were a blessing because I had what is so rare in this world, the opportunity of thinking about basic issues, the opportunity of examining afresh the beliefs I held.

When the Japanese began to take over Indonesia during World War II, the Dutch took Sukarno to Padang, where he stayed until the Japanese took him to Djakarta a short time later.

When he and other leaders were freed by the Japanese, they had to decide what their attitude would be toward their so-called liberators. Several sessions were held with the top leaders of all independence groups present. At that time Sukarno and Hatta felt that the Axis powers would win the war, and they were willing to work with the Japanese at the price of a promise of independence at the end of the war. The socialist leader, Sjahrir, believed the Allies would win and was not willing to collaborate at all. So it was decided that Sukarno and Hatta and others would co-operate with the Japanese and attempt to wring whatever advantages they could from them. Meanwhile, Sjahrir would develop an underground independence movement. And they would all keep in touch with one another.

It was a risky arrangement, but the times seemed to demand it. All of them were playing for high stakes and they must be ready to risk everything for eventual independence.

At first many Indonesians looked upon the Japanese as their liberators and friends. But they soon began to turn against them. The Dutch had been harsh and arrogant at times, but they had seldom been cruel. The Japanese introduced forced labor, terrorized the people, commandeered their scanty food supplies, and treated them brutally.

By March 1943, the Japanese permitted the establishment of a Center of People's Power group with Sukarno as chairman and Hatta as vice-chairman, and that fall set up a Central Consultative Body which was supposed to advise the Japanese on legislation for the islands. Then, in the spring of 1944, the Center of People's Services was organized to consolidate the entire war effort, with Sukarno again as chairman.

Sukarno used these posts to remind the people of the promise of eventual independence and to urge their co-operation with the Japanese toward that end. He spoke frequently to millions of Indonesians over the radios set up in the village squares, becoming a master at "double talk" so that the people would know how far they should go in yielding to the demands of their new invader "friends."

With the Dutch gone, the local Indonesians were recruited for higher posts in the government and were thereby able to gain experience which had been denied them up until that time. This training was to be invaluable to them once they obtained their independence.

The Japanese badly needed recruits for their army, too, and so they recruited nearly twenty thousand Indonesians and trained them. This was another type of training which had been denied them by the Dutch, who had used their own troops to maintain order rather than risk training the Indonesians for the army.

By the summer of 1944 the Japanese were beginning to lose ground in the Pacific and the Indonesians were growing more bold in their refusal to co-operate with their new foreign rulers. The red and white flag of independence was seen more often, the stirring music of "Indonesia Raja," the anthem of the independence movement, was sung more openly, and the Japanese were being attacked by the Indonesians more frequently all over the islands.

Finally there was a revolt among the Indonesian troops. Many of them were sentenced to death, but obviously the Japanese control of the islands was slipping and they began to cast about for ways to bolster their waning power. The most fruitful was to give the Indonesians still further power in the government and to recognize their insistent demands for independence. So the Japanese permitted the establishment of a Preparatory Committee for Independence, with Sukarno and Hatta as chairman and vice-chairman, respectively.

It was to this committee that Sukarno spoke on June 1, 1945, outlining the five principles on which the independence of Indonesia must be built. It was a short, concise statement, simple enough for the people to understand and couched in terms which would appeal to them. In brief this is what Sukarno said:

1. *Nationalism:* Indonesian nationalism in the fullest sense [is] neither Javanese nationalism nor Sumatran nationalism, not the nationalism of Borneo, the Celebes, Bali, nor any other, but Indonesian nationalism.

2. *Internationalism:* We should not only establish the free state of Indonesia, but we should also aim at making one family of all nations. Nationalism cannot flower if it does not grow in the garden of internationalism.

3. *Representative Government:* I am convinced that the necessary condition for the strength of the Indonesian state is . . . representative government. . . . There is not one state truly alive if it is not as if a caldron burns and boils in its representative body, and if there is no clash of convictions in it.

4. *Social Justice:* Do we want a free Indonesia where capitalists do as they wish or where the entire people prosper? Do not imagine . . . that as soon as the people's representative body comes into being we shall automatically achieve prosperity. We have seen that in the states of Europe there are representative bodies, there is parliamentary democracy. But is it not so that in Europe the capitalists are in control?

5. *Belief in God:* Let us observe, let us practice religion, whether Islam or Christianity, in a civilized way. What is that civilized way? It is the way of mutual respect.

He concluded by saying that the winning of independence would involve risks, likening it to the risks involved in diving for pearls in the ocean—a figure of speech which was quite clear to these island people.

It looked as if independence might be just over the horizon, and on August 8, Sukarno and Hatta were flown to Indochina to perfect plans for a Declaration of Independence which the Japanese Emperor would release when Russia entered the war in the Pacific against Japan.

Meanwhile, on August 6 the atomic bomb had been dropped on Hiroshima and on Nagasaki on August 9. On August 14 the Japanese surrendered.

All this had happened much more suddenly than anyone had expected, and the Indonesian people were jubilant. Many of them could already taste the sweetness of revenge against the Japanese.

Sukarno and Hatta were not so jubilant. They were wary about declaring independence and fanning the flames of revenge, for they feared a blood bath all over Indonesia. At this point a group of young nationalists kidnapped Sukarno and Hatta and pressured them into preparing a statement of independence at once. This they did, and on August 17, 1945, Sukarno read the following brief declaration signed by Hatta and himself.

Proclamation

We, the people of Indonesia,
herewith proclaim the independence of Indonesia.
All matters pertaining to the transfer
of power, etc., will be carried out effectively
and in the shortest possible time.

Djakarta, August 17, 1945
On behalf of the Indonesian people

Sukarno—Hatta

It was not a ringing document, beautifully phrased, as one might have expected, but it meant that more than three centuries of Dutch rule and three and a half years of Japanese occupation were over. At least that is what the Indonesians hoped it meant.

That same day, August 17, 1945, Sukarno was elected unanimously as the first President of the Republic of Indonesia.

But the Dutch did not give up easily. They were determined to hold on to this rich colonial empire with its rubber, oil, tin, bauxite, and other valuable resources. They had suffered greatly from the German occupation during World War II and they were not able to return immediately to Indonesia. But they would be back! In the meantime British forces were dispatched to the islands to round up the Japanese, to end the war in that part of the world, and to hold the fort until the Dutch could return.

In Indonesia the new government was faced with many problems. The most urgent was to wrest their country from the Japanese troops who were still there. This was not an easy task, but Sukarno's government was in control of most of the country by the time the British troops arrived in September 1945.

The new government was also plagued by internal dissension, with the extremists staging a coup d'état in July 1946, kidnapping Prime Minister Sjahrir as part of their plot. Their attempt to take over the government was unsuccessful, however, and the Sukarno government easily withstood this attack.

Gradually the Dutch reappeared, taking over one part of the islands after another, including the strategic port cities in Java and Sumatra. This show of strength made it easier for them to negotiate with the new government of Indonesia which had been formed in their absence. These negotiations were long and involved, but finally a formula was found upon which both parties could agree, even if reluctantly. This compromise involved the formation of a loose confederation of three parts. One would be the new Republic, which would be limited to Java and Sumatra. The second would be Borneo and the third would be East Indonesia. Over these last two parts of Indonesia the Dutch were to have partial control.

This arrangement meant the loss of large parts of Indonesia to the new Republic, and the Parliament was unwilling to yield to the Dutch demands but finally was persuaded to do so by Sukarno himself.

This new federation was established in 1947, but before long there was friction as to how much self-rule the Republic actually was to have. Sporadic fighting broke out and in July 1947, the Dutch launched a full-scale "police action" against Java and Sumatra.

The troubles in Indonesia had now become a cause for great concern among other nations of the world, for they feared that this small-scale war could eventually involve the world in another global fight. On August 1, 1947, the Security Council of the United Nations called for a cease-fire. in Indonesia and appointed a Committee of Good Offices to see what could be done to heal the breach between the Netherlands and Indonesia. Australia, Belgium, and the United States were appointed as the members of this committee.

An agreement was reached, but the conflict continued to break out in various parts of the islands. Determined to crush the new Republic, the Dutch launched a second major attack on Christmas Eve of 1948, capturing Sukarno and other members of his cabinet and exiling them from the capital.

World opinion was now beginning to side strongly with the Indonesians, and the United Nations took a much firmer stand than it had taken before. After intense and prolonged negotiations, the Dutch yielded and recognized the independence of Indonesia, transferring sovereignty to it on December 27, 1949.

Freedom had come at last, and the United States of Indonesia, with Sukarno as its President, was a full-fledged nation and a member of the United Nations.

This new country is one of the most curious in the world, for its three thousand islands are strung along the equator for a distance equal to the entire width of the United States. It can be compared to the United States if three-fourths of our country were flooded.

On these three thousand islands there are over 118 million people, making Indonesia the fifth largest country in the world. Fifty-five million of them live on the island of Java, where the capital, Djakarta, is located, and another twelve million or so are on Sumatra; the rest live on Celebes, Borneo, Timor, and other islands.

Potentially Indonesia is one of the richest countries of the world. It has more resources than any other nation except the United States and the Soviet Union. It produces approximately half of the world's rubber and much of the world's oil, and it has rich deposits of bauxite, manganese, sulfur, nickel, gold, silver, diamonds, copper, and zinc, plus plenty of copra from the coconut trees, sugar, pepper, cinchona for the making of quinine, and other valuable products. If these resources could be developed, Indonesia would have a high standard of living.

The problems Indonesia had to face after the Dutch finally withdrew were many and varied, causing continued conflict and lack of real solidarity and gains for this infant country.

First of all, there was the geography of Indonesia and the difficulties involved in administering a nation which spreads over such a large territory, with inadequate means of transportation and communication among the many islands.

Growing out of this unfortunate geographical fact and other factors were jealousy and rivalry between the islands. Of the exports of Indonesia, 70 per cent come from Sumatra and the other islands, and the people on these islands felt that their wealth was being used to support the poorer islands, rather than themselves.

A third handicap was the lack of trained administrators. Unfortunately, the Dutch did not leave a well-trained civil service, as the British did in most of their possessions, so Indonesia has suffered greatly from lack of men with experience in government.

Complicating the picture further was the low percentage of literacy. But Indonesia has made impressive gains in educational facilities. Under the Dutch, only about two million children attended primary schools and about 26,500, secondary schools. In 1960, over eight million children were in primary school and over 700,000 in secondary school.

Another disturbing and divisive factor in Indonesia's modern history, however, was the conflict among the various political parties. There were many such groups in Indonesia, but four were powerful and almost equally divided. In the 1955 general elections, for example, these four polled the following numbers of votes:

Nationalist Party (PNI)	8,075,362
Masjumi Party (Moslem)	7,852,519
Nahdatul Ulama (Orthodox Moslem)	6,450,691
Communist Party (PKI)	6,006,260

In the early years of independence Sukarno infuriated the Masjumi party as well as other Moslems by his insistence on a secular state rather than an Islamic state, which they wanted. Nevertheless, an uneasy alliance was formed between the Nationalists and the Masjumis, with Hatta serving as Vice-President of Indonesia and Sukarno as President.

As the years rolled along, the gap between Sukarno

and the Moslems widened and he turned more and more to the left-wing groups for support. In January 1956, he championed the inclusion of Communists in the government. The objection to this stand was so great, however, that he did not include them, although he did appoint some Communist sympathizers.

Then, in 1957, shortly after a trip to Communist China, he called for a change in the structure of the Indonesian government. He proceeded to appoint a National Council representing the various interests in Indonesia, such as business, labor, the professions, women, youth, and other groups. Included in this National Council were four or five Communists and a dozen or more representatives of left-wing groups.

To the people of Indonesia he explained that the type of democracy prevalent in Western Europe and in the United States would not work in Indonesia at this stage in their development. So, he said, they must seek a form which was suited to them. This new form of government he called "guided democracy."

Opposition to the direction in which Sukarno and his government were moving had been growing for months prior to his statement on "guided democracy." His statement was therefore the break in the dike, unloosing a flood of opposition. Hatta resigned as Vice-President and attacked Sukarno for his anti-democratic move. At the same time several generals announced their split with the central government, and an opposition government was established on the island of Sumatra.

These rebels said that they would not support the Sukarno regime until a new government was formed, with Hatta as Prime Minister. Furthermore, they demanded that there be no Communists in the government.

Throughout 1958 there was continued conflict between the Indonesian government and these opposition leaders. The central government was able to crush a part of the rebellion, but it was unable to bring the revolt to a successful conclusion.

For more than twenty years, Sukarno had been the leader of Indonesia. He had sacrificed much for his country, enduring long periods of exile, spent twelve years in jail, and risked death many times. He had survived five assassination attempts. But he had never wavered in his fight for the freedom of his people.

Like all men, Sukarno had his faults, and many of them were of the spectacular variety. He enjoyed the reputation he had gained, not without cause, as the "playboy of the Eastern world." He was often boastful and vain, and he loved ostentation. His critics sometimes said that he lived like an ancient oriental emperor. He was often devious and politically deceptive, cleverly playing off one element against another. This was his way of keeping, he hoped, everybody in hand and more or less contented. Furthermore, despite Indonesia's tremendous potential wealth, Sukarno seemed less concerned with saving the country's economy than with building prestige projects, which he did with the more than $1.5 billion in foreign aid which he secured from East and West.

A favorite joke in the capital was that the President's formula for government, "guided democracy," was neither guided nor democratic. Certainly he resented criticism and sometimes punished those who dared dispute him. In 1962, for example, he imprisoned one of Indonesia's wisest leaders, Sjahrir, the man who had been the first Prime Minister of the independent country. Sjahrir's offense had been to seek to establish a parliamentary democracy in the new nation. Sukarno was and wished to remain supreme, and in 1963 had himself appointed President for life, promising the people, "Follow my leadership. I devote my life to you, the Indonesian people."

What proved to be Sukarno's greatest mistake for himself and his country, however, was his pro-Communist policies. In the early 1950s he had been understandably resentful of the role of the American CIA in support of his political enemies, and became publicly anti-United States. Later, the United States, in a conciliatory move, helped him obtain West New Guinea, the last Dutch-held territory in Indonesia. But Sukarno continued to play East against West. In 1961 he is reported to have said to President Kennedy, "I am the best bulwark in Indonesia against Communism," but he gladly accepted aid from the Communist bloc.

It was probably under Peking influence that Sukarno, two years after the Chinese government took the same stand, expressed his violent opposition to the establishment of the Malaysian Federation. He labeled it an attempt by the British to control Malaya, Singapore, North Borneo, and Sarawak. The newly created Malaysia was uncomfortably close to Indonesia, and Sukarno threatened in 1964 to "crush Malaysia before the cock crows on New Year's Day." When Malaysia became a member of the UN Security Council, Sukarno, urged on by Peking, withdrew from the UN, thus making it the only country that has withdrawn from that world organization. Economically, this was almost a fatal blow for Indonesia, for it cut off two sources of financial aid, the International Monetary Fund and the International Bank for Reconstruction and Development, both UN agencies.

By this time, the Communist party in Indonesia numbered about three and a half million members, making it the third largest in any country, topped only by the Soviet Union and China. Again and again Sukarno followed the advice and granted the requests of the Communist leaders within his own country and sided with China in foreign affairs. The Moslems in Indonesia saw their religion threatened, and the army, the intellectuals, and the middle-class people of Indonesia became annoyed with their government's neglect of them and with the high-handed attitude of Communist leaders, who now controlled the Parliament and held most of the important offices.

By 1965, even Sukarno's friends began to have serious doubts about the wisdom of their President's policies. In October of that year, the gathering storm broke. The anti-Communists, including the military, seized power and began a purge of all the Communists they could find. General Suharto, with troops of his Strategic Reserve Command, captured the government radio station and announced that a Communist attempt to seize the government, which had been slated to take place that morning, had been thwarted by his troops. General Suharto assumed control of the government from Sukarno, thus bringing to a head a struggle between the President and military leaders that had been going on for months. During the weeks that followed, thousands of Communists were killed in what may be described as a horrible blood bath. The conditions under which most of the people were living almost defies description.

But still Sukarno did not change his ways. He dismissed his popular Minister of Defense, the anti-Communist General Nasution, and thereby set off violent demonstrations by large groups of students. Now it became necessary to place the palace where Sukarno lived under heavy armed guard. The student demonstrations continued for many months. They demanded that Parliament, which had become a rubber stamp for Communist decisions, assume its constitutional role and lead the country in true democratic fashion. In

March of 1966, Sukarno was forced to select a new cabinet, making General Suharto Minister of Defense. The General became, in effect, the new ruler of Indonesia.

Despite a carefree attitude and optimistic speeches to the press, Sukarno knew he was in trouble. In March, 1967, he lost his title of President and all his power in the country which he had saved but which he had brought to bankruptcy. Indonesia's debts to other countries were enormous, its transportation system was broken down so that goods could not be moved to markets, its staple food, rice, was scarce and high in price, and the general cost of living had risen more than 2000 per cent within a period of seven years. Even his undeclared war ("confrontation") against Malaysia had been unsuccessful. The Indonesian people were indifferent to it and the military discouraged by it. In August 1966, the new government of Indonesia signed a peace agreement with Malaysia, formally ending the futile war of three years. The island of Borneo had been a bone of contention. Sukarno claimed it for Indonesia, although the people of Sarawak and Sabah, two territories in Borneo, had joined the Malaysian Federation. Now they were to be given an opportunity to reaffirm their position through general elections.

In August of 1966 the new government of Indonesia informed the United Nations Educational, Scientific, and Cultural Organization that it wished to resume participation in that body. Later that year it was reinstated in the United Nations itself.

Despite his failures, many Indonesians have not forgotten that Sukarno brought them freedom, and that he risked everything, including his life, to do so. "He is the father of our country." "He is still loved in the countryside." "He held our country together." These are typical comments among his loyal supporters.

Sukarno's weaknesses brought his country to ruin, but he must be credited with winning the freedom of Indonesia. A younger generation may follow what was good in his leadership and profit from his errors to build a strong and democratic nation.

MAGSAYSAY
OF THE PHILIPPINES

It was a grueling day for Ramon Magsaysay. He wakened early that Saturday morning and, after a massage and shower, donned his gray pants and white *baralong* Tagalog shirt—the Philippine version of the sport shirt, with an open collar, short sleeves, and a beautifully embroidered front.

He did not awaken his wife, Luz, but breakfasted alone and then slipped off to see his parents in the Singalong section of Manila. He saw other people at the presidential palace later in the morning and lunched with his wife and their eldest daughter, Teresita, before setting off for the airport.

There he boarded the cigar-shaped presidential plane, *Mount Pinatubo,* a former U. S. Army C-47, named after the highest peak in Zambales Province, where he and his men had hidden and fought as guerillas during World War II against the Japanese.

Landing in the island of Cebu, he was greeted by local officials, a crowd of his ardent Filipino followers, and the twenty-one-gun salute accorded the President.

In quick succession he spoke at the airport, at the University of Visayas, the University of the Southern Philippines, the Southwestern University, and, later that evening, at the University of San Carlos, besides making several visits to prominent politicians on Cebu. It was ten o'clock before he and his party ate dinner. Even after that he attended the inauguration ceremonies of the Patria Recreation Hall. Brief stops at a dance and a housing project brought his crowded day to a close.

Just after one o'clock on Sunday morning, March 17, 1957, he and his party of aides and newspapermen taxied down the runway at the airport and set off for Manila.

The men in the Manila airport tower kept waiting for word from the plane. An hour passed and they had heard nothing. Two hours dragged by. Three. Four. Five. Six. Now the airport authorities were really alarmed. They sent out searching parties to try to locate the missing plane.

But it was not those men who found it. It was a twenty-nine-year-old shepherd who heard a deafening sound and had looked up to see flames on the mountainside. Hurriedly he wakened his son, called a cousin, the *barrio* lieutenant and his two sons. Together they clambered up the mountainside to investigate the big fire.

Just after six in the morning they found twenty-six charred bodies in the wreckage of a burning plane—and one survivor. He was a newspaperman who had been hurled to the side of the wreckage. The man was in need of immediate help, so some of them hurried to their *barrio*, or village, to get a hammock to carry him to safety and to tell the local officials what they had found.

By nine the news reached Manila, and within a few minutes it had been radioed and teletyped to the world. Magsaysay, the popular President of the Philippines, had been killed in an airplane crash. More slowly the word passed from person to person all over the hundreds of islands which comprise the Philippines. "The Guy is dead." "The Guy is gone."

Men and women wept openly, unashamed, for Magsaysay was their hero. He was one of them. He was a man of the masses. And high officials throughout the world scratched out messages of condolence to Magsaysay's family and the Filipino people, for this man had become a world figure during the past few years.

His rise to fame had been meteoric. He had blazed into the news of the world like a shooting star—and then even more suddenly disappeared.

The story behind his rise to fame in the Philippines and in the world is a thrilling one.

Since the close of the Spanish-American War in 1898, the Philippine Islands had been a territory of the United States, under a civil government. It was in Iba, about one hundred twenty-five miles from the territorial capital, Manila, that Magsaysay's life began. He was born on August 31, 1907 in a bamboo and *cogon* (grass) house, the second child and first son of Exequiel and Perfecta del Fierro Magsaysay.

The legend has already been started that the Magsaysays were a very poor family, even by Philippine standards, but the fact is that they were better off than most people of their day. The mother came from one of the leading families of the area, and the father was a teacher and skilled artisan who owned land near Iba.

When Ramon was a baby, Exequiel earned his livelihood as a teacher of carpentry in the local trade school. He was very proficient in his work, a strict disciplinarian, and scrupulously honest. To him everyone was to be treated alike— even the son of the superintendent of schools, who did so poorly that Señor Magsaysay flunked him.

There was pressure from the superintendent, but Señor Magsaysay refused to yield. The boy had flunked, and he would not give him a passing grade. The result was that Señor Magsaysay was fired.

What really hurt was the fact that the local people thought he had been foolish and ostracized the Magsaysay family. Why be so stiff-necked, they asked, when a job is at stake?

So the Magsaysays moved to Castillejos, nearer Manila, and opened a *sari-sari*, or general store. In most places the Chinese were the storekeepers and being keen traders, they were able to control the business, but there was no competition. However, it was difficult to make ends meet, so Ramon's mother worked in the store and his father opened a carpentry and blacksmith shop.

Meanwhile Ramon was growing up, eating his favorite dish—a stew made from tender cashew leaves and green vegetables boiled with tomatoes, and tiny shrimps and catfish from the nearby river—running errands for his parents, and swimming and fishing in his spare time.

By the time he was seven his father thought he was ready for real work, and at 3:30 each morning the two of them set off to work on the local roads, jogging off together on the family horse. At eight he was promoted to tending the *carabao*, or water buffalo, from which the family got its milk supply. Then he was allowed to help his father in the shop, blowing the bellows or turning the old-fashioned lathe on which his father welded the wagon wheels. In his spare time he tended the vegetable garden and cared for the fruit trees, selling some of the products and taking the rest home.

As he looked back later on his childhood, he said that the greatest need he had was for sleep. "We were too poor. Parents and children—we had little time for each other. We were always working, and when we were not working we would try to get some sleep. There was not much of that, either."

Then there was school—a dreary and monotonous duty for Ramon. He did well in his studies but found the day-to-day routine boring. Sometimes he would play hooky, going off to swim, fish, or hunt. One of his teachers says he was "a bright, obedient boy in the classroom, but a naughty and restless type outside."

He often read to his younger brothers and sisters and loved to discuss current events with anyone who would talk with him, which usually meant the adults. By 1922 he had finished the local elementary school, graduating second in his class.

Since there was no high school in his home town, he went to San Narciso, twelve miles away. To cut down on expenses, he lived alone in a house which was supposed to be haunted and therefore was very inexpensive to rent. He cooked his own meals and did the small amount of laundry he needed. On Friday afternoons he would climb on his bicycle and head homeward for the weekend, coming back Monday morning with a supply of food and clean clothes.

Then came a major event in his life. His mother thought that this bicycle trip was a long and hard one and decided to give him a Model T Ford. How Ramon loved that car! The radiator was burnished copper. No hot-rod owner today could be more proud of his automobile than Ramon was of this third-hand Ford.

The car was not intended for joy-riding, however. It was for transportation and for earning money. Soon he was carrying other students to school, running a kind of taxi for special parties, and making trips to the coast to buy fish, which he peddled in town.

Life was not easy, but school activities were fun, and there was even an occasional prank to relieve the monotony. One night Ramon climbed the belfry tower in the local church and tied a cord to the bell clapper. Then he took the cord and hid it as far in the bushes as it would reach. At midnight the bell began ringing and would not stop. The parish priest and the people threw on their clothes and hurried to the chapel—to find the bell ringing by itself. Those who were superstitious thought it was an evil omen. Others wondered about the cause of this mysterious action. Soon, however, the mystery was solved, for someone tripped over the cord and it broke, thus stopping the bell. In a burst of bad conscience, Ramon went to the priest the next day and confessed his "sin."

On another occasion the car was used for fun rather than to earn money. A special party was being given in San Narciso, and ice was ordered from a distance in order to refrigerate the ice cream, a rare treat. All this was stored under the home of one of the teachers. The boys found out about the ice cream and quietly pushed Ramon's car to the house so as not to disturb anyone. Then they piled the ice cream into the automobile and headed for the beach. By early morning they could hold no more and they returned to town to get other students to join them in devouring their stolen goods. This time no one confessed, and the disappearance of the ice cream remained a mystery for a long time.

Ramon had fun, too, playing his "bandolin" and singing. But he distinguished himself most as a debater. He was on the school debating team and president of the debating club. He even had the audacity to challenge the local priest to a debate on the topic of Philippine independence. He also challenged the local Congressman to debate the subject of taxing people for the local gin. Ramon himself did not drink, but he felt that this tax was an unjust one.

Having completed high school in three years instead of four, Ramon then moved to Manila to enter the University of the Philippines. He was twenty years old now, and quite certain that he must not take any more help from his family. After all, they did not have too much to begin with and there were eight brothers and sisters younger than he to make demands upon the family treasury.

He soon learned that working and going to school in Manila was not easy. The college work demanded more time, and the cost of living was much higher in the capital city than it had been in San Narciso.

Sometimes it seemed as if he spent most of his time as a student walking. He walked to the university from his living quarters, a distance of five miles. He walked from one part of the university to the other, another long distance, to save the cost of buses. Then he walked to work and back home again. No wonder he wore out the leather in his one pair of shoes and had to resort to cardboard to take the place of leather soles.

In his spare time he drove cars, washed cars, and repaired cars, saving every *centavo* that he could.

He was a strong young man, but four hours of sleep a night wasn't enough, even for him. He realized that he was on the verge of a breakdown and so withdrew from college. After he regained his health, he transferred to the José Rizal College where he majored in commerce. Life was still not easy, but it was a little better than before. Finally, in 1930, he graduated from college with the degree of Bachelor of Science.

His first full-time job was with the Try-Tran Company, a local transportation firm. He was a good mechanic and an honest employee, and was soon promoted to the position of shop superintendent. His discovery that some of the men were taking out the good parts of the cars and replacing them with poor parts endeared him to the management but aroused the hostility of some of the employees. Scouting for inexpensive spare parts was another way in which he saved the company money and helped to put it on its feet financially.

A repair shop is not the usual place to find a wife, but that is the place where Ramon first met Luz Banzon. She and a friend had come to collect money owed to the Banzons. By telling their chauffeur that the company would take them home, Ramon managed to drive Luz and her friend to the Instituto de Mujeres (Institute for Women), where they were students.

This was an exclusive girls' school and it was difficult for visitors to call, so Ramon decided to pose as Luz's brother in order to visit her during the special visiting hours on Sunday. He was eight years older than she, and he thought she was by far the most wonderful person he had ever met.

He faced a great obstacle in his plan to marry Luz, for she was from a wealthy and prominent family, with several suitors who drove Packards and Cadillacs rather than Fords. But he persisted, driving his old car a hundred miles each way from Manila in order to visit her on weekends, after the school year was completed.

This went on for two years before the family consented to their marriage, which took place on June 10, 1933. In time the family included Teresita, Milagros, and Ramon Jr., later known as "Jun."

Life was difficult for the Magsaysays, but there was fun, too. The father was proud of his beautiful, unpretentious wife, and of his three children. He would sing simple folk songs to the children in the Ilocano language which he had spoken as a boy, and play horse with his son as the rider. At work he was often impatient with people who talked incessantly but, like most fathers, he was patience personified when his children prattled on endlessly.

His first display of ability in handling people came with a bus strike in the Try-Tran Company, which he managed with great skill. It looked as if the Magsaysays were off to a good start in the quiet, uneventful life of a Filipino family.

Christmas, 1941, should have been a wonderful day for the Magsaysays. Their debts were now cleared and they had started to build a modest bungalow with their own hands. Ramon had a steady job which he liked. The future looked bright.

Then came Pearl Harbor and the Japanese invasion of the Philippines.

Magsaysay volunteered in the Philippine Army and was made a captain in charge of ten ambulances. Luz and the children headed for the hills, to spend the next months being passed from home to home by friends and comrades in the fight against the Japanese.

Meanwhile, Magsaysay was with the Zambales guerillas. He knew the area, and he knew the local language, Tagalog. He knew the people. At first he was put in charge of foraging for food, and earned the nickname "Chow."

But as the Japanese closed in on the area, he became their Public Enemy Number One, with a reward of 100,000 pesos on his head. He was too valuable a man to lose and could be of help elsewhere, so he was sent to Manila to collect supplies. He worked as a hack driver, and on his rounds spotted supplies that could be obtained for the guerilla army. Then he arranged for them to be picked up and stored or shipped to various parts of the Philippines. He lived during these months in many houses, lest he be caught as a spy and hung. He kept abreast of the latest developments in the war by way of a short-wave broadcasting set which he kept hidden under his bed. Sometimes his family sent him rice, which was becoming a very scarce and expensive item.

The war dragged on. The Philippine government under José Laurel was forced to collaborate with the Japanese, and many Filipinos became disheartened. The American Army under MacArthur had been gone from the islands for months, and it looked as if it would never return. Morale was low, especially among the guerillas. Jealousies broke out among the various leaders, and Magsaysay was asked to return to the Zambales Province to try to restore order and raise morale.

In this new assignment he was always on the go, a khaki-clad figure astride a big bay horse. He foraged for food, settled the feuds of the guerillas, collected supplies, and bolstered morale among the *barrio* people and soldiers—anything and everything which would help the war effort. Sometimes a collaborator was caught and the officers would press for the extreme punishment. But Magsaysay said no. He knew the Filipino people well enough to know that harm done to one person is considered harm done to the entire family, and he did not want to earn the hatred of the people for such acts. "Someday," he said, "we shall need their support in winning the war."

Finally on January 9, 1945, MacArthur and his troops landed at Lingayen Gulf and started their march to Manila. Between them and the capital city lay the San Marcelino airstrip, held by the Japanese.

Magsaysay was told to clear that airstrip. It was his toughest assignment of the war. It meant the evacuation of thousands of civilians, and many of them pleaded with him not to attack. They feared defeat and terrible reprisals to follow.

After hearing their pleas, he assembled as many of them as he could and told them why he must carry through his plan. But he promised them that "if, after attacking the Japanese, it is shown that I have brought disaster against my fellow citizens of Zambales, I want you to bring my wife and three children with me—if I am still alive—into the square before our Catholic church in Castillejos. Have a firing squad shoot us there."

Fortunately the maneuver was a success and the Magsaysays were spared. The Japanese were routed, and MacArthur and his men were able to land and push on until the Philippines were again under control of the American Army and the Filipinos.

A military governor was now needed for the province, and Magsaysay was appointed. On February 4, 1945, he was sworn in. With characteristic energy and enthusiasm, he set about providing medical help, food, and transportation facilities. He likewise made plans for the erection of homes in forest areas for war veterans.

When the time came for Magsaysay and his men to receive their back pay, he turned it down lest anyone think that he had taken part in the war to make money. When his men handed him an envelope with a generous sum of money collected for him as a sign of their loyalty and appreciation, he returned it to them, saying that their families needed their money much more than he did. Here again was the effect of the early training which his father had given him years ago in absolute honesty and absolute loyalty to a cause, without thought for any reward.

Magsaysay's discharge came in February 1946, and he and his family moved to their old home town. He was approached by Manuel Roxas, the man who was soon to become the first President of the Philippine Republic, to run for Congress on his party's ticket. But Magsaysay refused. He was not interested in politics and certainly not interested in the Liberal party platform.

Later he changed his mind and ran as an independent Liberal. He became an ardent campaigner, visiting every *barrio* he could, eating and sleeping in the huts of the common people, talking with them about their problems, shaking so many hands that people laughingly referred to "the Magsaysay stroke." Pitted against three other Liberal candidates and one member of the Nationalists, he won by the largest majority in the history of that province.

When the new Philippine Congress opened, he was made chairman of the Committee on National Defense, a very high honor for a newcomer.

As a Congressman Magsaysay did not fit into the old molds. He startled his party and the people by his independence. When one of his fellow party members was accused of graft, he was the only Congressman who sided with the opposition's charges, because he felt that his colleague was guilty. When the government red tape delayed the awarding of Quonset huts to the various Congressmen for use as schools, he cut the red tape by arranging a raid on the surplus materials depot. Called to the presidential palace, he defended himself by saying that the huts were needed for schools and the delay was senseless. When roads in his district needed repairing, or salaries were delayed, he would visit the proper officials himself to see that action was taken immediately.

These deeds made him popular with the people, but very unpopular with some politicians.

His post as chairman of the Committee on National Defense brought his appointment to a commission to go to Washington to intercede on behalf of the Filipinos who had taken part in World War II on the American side. They were anxious to have the hospitalization benefits of the G. I. Bill of Rights extended to them and to have a veterans' hospital built in the Philippine Islands. For a long time it looked as if the commission would be unsuccessful, despite the resort to every possible pressure on the part of the Filipinos, including the lobbying of Filipino taxicab drivers with their passengers, some of whom were Congressmen. But the measure, known as the Rogers Bill, was finally passed, and Magsaysay had a new feather in his cap.

Before he returned to Manila, he purchased a fine radio-phonograph and learned to dance—two items which had not been on the agenda of the commission. In the months ahead this hi-fi set was to be one of his rare means of relaxing. He loved music and had a large collection of records, which he kept under lock and key. He especially liked symphonic music. Later he bought a television set and enjoyed watching wrestling, boxing, and cowboy pictures. When he was in the presidential palace in years to come, he enjoyed movies, usually selected by his wife—ordinarily one cowboy picture and anything else which involved action. At other times he would shoot game and birds, go horseback riding or fishing. Another of his recreations as President was to take one of the cars from the palace garage, insisting on driving the car himself rather than letting a chauffeur take the wheel.

In 1949 he was re-elected to Congress by a vote of 19,000 to 12,000, carrying the other candidates of the Liberal party to victory with him.

While he had been in Washington President Roxas had died, and Elpidio Quirino had succeeded him. Quirino was not anxious to have Magsaysay as Secretary of National Defense but eventually yielded to pressures and appointed him to that post in the fall of 1950.

Once in that job, Magsaysay went to work to purge the army of incompetent and dishonest personnel, to replace expensive cars with jeeps, to put an end to gambling for high stakes, and to restore the reputation of the army, which had sunk to a low ebb in recent years.

One newspaper claimed: "In the first four months in office, Magsaysay did as much for the Department of National Defense as his predecessor had done in four years."

An even bigger problem was the Huks—bands of guerilla

fighters. Thousands of them were still carrying on warfare in various parts of the country. In some places they even controlled an entire area. Originally they had been an Army of the People to Fight the Japanese, known as the Hukbalahap movement. But at the close of the war they had refused to disband. Many of them were poor, confused, hungry farmers who saw in this movement their only hope for betterment. Some of them were disgruntled soldiers. Some were adventurers. Some were sincere Communists. It was this latter group which gained control of the Huks.

Magsaysay decided upon a two-pronged attack on them. He would grant clemency and help to those who yielded and crush those who refused to give up. He proceeded with extraordinary vigor, capturing or killing twelve thousand Huks within a few months and persuading ten thousand to surrender.

Realizing that many of them were farmers who were in debt or saw no hope for the future under existing conditions, he decided upon a bold plan. To each Huk who yielded he would offer six hundred to eight hundred acres, a house, farm implements, seeds, and buffalo on easy terms, with ten years to pay back the government loan.

In addition he offered large sums as rewards for the capture of the Huks, especially their leaders, and he made a concentrated effort to capture firearms and ammunition.

The fact that he dramatized all that he was doing was a tremendous help. He organized a Peace Fund to which people could contribute, to help pay for the rewards for the capture of Huks. He called the big offensive by special names such as "Plan Saber," "Operation Pick-up," and "Marblehead." He himself met the descendant of the greatest national hero of the Philippines, Rizal, and won him over to the side of the government. This flair for the dramatic was decried by his opponents, but it was a great help in breaking the back of the Huk movement.

His next big assignment was the policing of the elections in 1951. Everyone knew that the elections of 1949 had been very dishonest, at least in many places, and a national movement to guarantee free elections now had gathered momentum. There were instances again of dishonesty, but on the whole the 1951 voting was more widespread and more honest than in previous years. As a result, the Liberals suffered some setbacks, and Magsaysay was accused of betraying his own party. To such charges he countered, "I was not interested in which party was going to win the elections. It is beyond my comprehension why any man should get mad simply because we had a clean and honest election."

In June 1952, the Lions International was to hold a mammoth convention in Mexico City, and they invited Magsaysay to be the keynote speaker. President Quirino objected to the trip, largely because of his jealousy of Magsaysay's growing popularity, but was finally persuaded to let him go, chiefly as a result of the insistent demands of his own daughter, an ardent admirer of Magsaysay's.

To the Lions convention Magsaysay told the story of the attack on the Huks, saying:

> Our military offensive is indispensable, since force must be met by force. But our social offensive is the extra weapon which the enemy cannot produce. Here the enemy meets democracy's strongest element—the ability to realize and satisfy the needs of its people without taking from them their freedom and dignity as human beings.

Before he left the Lions convention he had been promised approximately two million dollars' worth of plows, tractors, disks, harrows, and other farm implements for the furtherance of the resettlement schemes in the Philippines.

From Mexico City he went to Washington, where he had a general physical checkup in the Walter Reed Hospital and met with Pentagon officials. Then he proceeded to New York City, where Fordham University awarded him an honorary Doctor of Laws degree.

Throughout the months when he had been Secretary of National Defense, relations between Magsaysay and President Quirino had been strained. Meanwhile, behind the scenes, a great deal of maneuvering had been going on. The Nationalist party wanted to win and they wanted Magsaysay as their candidate for President in the next election. So they persuaded the top leaders to step aside in order to permit the nomination of a candidate who was popular, new, young—Magsaysay.

The final break between the President and his Secretary of Defense came when reporters asked the President if Magsaysay would be his running mate as candidate for Vice-President. Quirino answered, "He knows nothing about affairs of state or how to conduct them. He is only good for killing Huks."

This was the tug which broke the thin thread between them. In a crisp letter Magsaysay offered his resignation, declaring that he could not just go on killing Huks. "You must realize," he said, "that we cannot solve the problem of dissidence simply by military measures. It would be futile to go on killing Huks while the administration continues to breed dissidence by neglecting the problems of our masses."

At the Nationalist party convention Magsaysay was overwhelmingly nominated and the campaign was on, with Quirino of the Liberal group pitted against him. Magsaysay started on a grueling round of visits to an estimated eleven hundred *barrios* for a total of three thousand hours of speaking. The opposition accused him of being a traitor, of being

supported by the Americans, of being an awkward, unedu-
cated mechanic.

Quirino was a tired, sick man. He underwent two operations
during the campaign. A third candidate was Carlos Romulo,
a prominent Filipino in international affairs but not as well
known or liked at home. He finally withdrew from the race
and supported Magsaysay.

On election day, nearly 80 per cent of the Filipinos voted,
an unusually large percentage there or anywhere in the
world. It is generally agreed that the election itself was fairly
clean. The final vote was Magsaysay: 2,912,992; Quirino:
1,313,991. The people had spoken. In the words of a popular
campaign slogan, they had said, "Magsaysay is my guy."

The old order had fallen; a new order had begun. An old,
sick, embittered leader had been retired. A young, energetic,
popular, idealistic leader was taking over.

The inauguration took place on December 30, 1953, in the
Luneta, a large public park in Manila where José Rizal, the
father of the Philippine nation, had been killed by a Spanish
firing squad on December 30, 1896.

Thousands of people came for the inaugural, and it took
Magsaysay thirty minutes to reach his Ford convertible,
twenty yards away from the speaker's stand, when the ceremonies were over.

Thousands more took him up on his campaign invitation to
"Come and see me any time," and made their way to the
Malacanan Palace. There the oath was administered to his
cabinet. Later that afternoon he dedicated an artesian well,
a symbol of his interest in social and economic progress in
the Philippines.

Again on New Year's Day crowds flocked to the palace.
There were bare feet in the palace that day—and on many
days thereafter. Like Andy Jackson in United States history,
Magsaysay had opened the doors of the "White House" to

THE PEOPLE, spelled in capital letters. He had said it would become the People's Palace, and he had kept his promise.

What did they see in this man? What made him so popular?

Physically he was impressive—nearly six feet tall, which is very tall for Filipinos, weighing around a hundred eighty pounds. He was broad-shouldered and handsome, more Malayan than Spanish in appearance, although he had some Spanish ancestors.

Their President also represented the qualities they admired. As one Filipino writer stated it:

> Every single Filipino will say that the reason he loved President Magsaysay is that he was "mabait." It is a favorite dialect adjective, both vague and meaningful, general and special. It covers humanity, gentleness, humility, and generosity, and is generally translated "good."

In a time and place where honesty was too seldom found in politicians, he was scrupulously honest. He issued orders that he would accept no presents at any time from anyone except his family. He refused to let his son drive a new car lest it be interpreted as a show of wealth. He canceled a government contract with a member of his family, even though he was the lowest bidder, lest this be considered as favoritism to his relatives. With his own funds he was extremely generous; with the public funds he was extraordinarily "tight."

Tremendous energy was another of his characteristics. He literally burned himself out for the people, installing three telephones on his desk to keep in touch with officials and the people.

Uppermost in his mind were the needs of the common people from whom he had sprung. He had a real compassion for them. During the campaign he promised that every complaint that they made would be heard and acted upon immediately; and as soon as he was elected, he established a Bureau of Complaints. To it anyone in the Philippine Republic could telegraph a brief message free of charge and within two or three hours get action.

He summarized his philosophy in this regard in an interview with an American journalist by saying:

> The mistake the world is making with the simple peoples is to try to hurry them into political concepts they don't understand and aren't prepared to cope with. I know. I am a peasant myself. When my people can raise their produce and get it to town on decent roads, when they can be cured of their illnesses and buses can take pregnant women to hospitals in a hurry, when they have the necessary water to grow rice so they don't have to import it, then we will think more of their political education. I say spit on the big, fancy schemes. I want all the little things first. Then perhaps we can get on to the bigger things.

He was not only concerned about the common people; he had confidence in them. He believed they were the foundation stones of the new Republic. He told them, for example:

> I believe that this epoch should be the epoch of the common man. This country is like a pyramid, like a tower. It is made up of millions of stones. The first stone on the top of the pyramid is the President of the Philippines. The stones below . . . are the cabinet ministers, the senators, the congressmen, the bureau directors, and everybody's schoolteachers. And the foundation stone of this pyramid is the common man. . . . We could not succeed in anything in this country unless we care for the masses of our people—the rural people, the *barrio* people. . . .

Magsaysay's histrionic gifts were also an asset. He dramatized and got the full effect from each important move. One biographer has said that "he had the stage actor's sense of the dramatic and the athlete's sense of timing."

He disliked making formal speeches but was superb in the short, extemporaneous talks he would give when he visited in the *barrios* with the people. They were full of emotional warmth, colored with personal anecdotes, and delivered with punch. He knew how to communicate.

At the same time he was impatient and impetuous. He could not brook delays and he was often critical of his colleagues and subordinates and a hard man to work for or with. "Action" was his motto, and "heads rolled" when there was no action or the action was delayed.

His lack of training in economics was a handicap. He recognized the simple things that needed to be done, like the building of artesian wells for a clean water supply and for irrigation, or the importance of a new school. He did not always see the larger issues or appreciate the necessity for long-time planning needed to achieve his goals.

Some felt that he had too little historical perspective. For instance, they charged him with winning the support of the Catholic Church in his campaign for the presidency, thus introducing religion as a factor in politics to an extent which had been unknown in the Philippines before.

Nor did he have a consistent group of advisers. He would select a man and then become impatient with him, removing him from a post or shifting him to another job. Often he made such moves hurriedly, later regretting his action. Then he would wait a while and appoint his friend to another important position.

His job as President was a most difficult one. He was faced with the devastation of war, danger from the Huks, and graft and corruption in the government. There were many immediate problems to be solved and much need of long-term planning.

For three years and three months he served as President of the Philippine Republic. What was he able to accomplish in that period? What problems did he leave unsolved? His own estimate of the achievements of his administration up to 1956 included ten gains. Briefly stated, they are as follows:

1. The holding of clean elections.
2. The restoration of peace and order.
3. The passage of the Land Tenure Act.
4. The establishment of agrarian courts.
5. The construction of feeder roads, artesian wells, and irrigation.
6. The restoration of government to the people.
7. The increase in foreign investments in the Philippines.
8. The revision of the Bell Trade Act with the United States.
9. The participation of the Philippines in the Bandung Conference.
10. The election of a Filipino to the Security Council of the United Nations.

This is a record of which anyone might be proud. But it is the statement of Magsaysay himself and therefore highly subjective. What do others who were less involved say about the progress and problems of the Philippines in that period?

There is no doubt that he strengthened the belief of the common people in their share in the government. During Magsaysay's period as President, the "little fellow" had the right to be heard. He created new hope for the future in himself and his country. This is essential in a democracy and was a great gain in the Philippines. People became really proud of being Filipinos.

He also intensified his campaign against the Huks and was able to destroy them as a major force· in the life of the nation. The most dramatic demonstration of this gain was the announcement on May 17, 1954, of the surrender of Luis Taruc, the number-one Communist in the Philippines. Small bands of Huks remained even after that, but the movement was no longer a major problem from then on.

Despite the firm opposition of the large landowners, a Land Reform Act was passed in 1955. This was the beginning of much-needed changes, but Magsaysay was never fully able to implement this Act, and land reform is still desperately needed in this island republic.

The army was not completely purified in this period, but it was changed for the better. Officers were educated to their constitutional responsibilities and a philosophy of concern for the ordinary citizen began to take hold. This was indeed a new military attitude.

There were likewise great gains in the development of co-operatives and credit unions, measures which Magsaysay felt would help the common man in his struggle for a better life, since these would mean lower prices and sound credit facilities at reasonable rates.

He appointed a vigorous Secretary of Labor, and the power of the labor unions grew tremendously in his administration. A Magna Carta for labor had been passed under the Quirino administration, with considerable pressure from the United States, as one condition for economic aid, and Magsaysay gave substance to this law.

In education there was steady growth, with the development of the Philippine Community School, an outstanding contribution to a more practical educational program throughout the islands. Great gains were also made in the mass education movement, aimed at teaching the illiterate farmers and other adults.

Yet many actions of his administration were open to question.

A Retail Nationalization Bill was passed which virtually turned over to the Filipinos the extensive retail trade which had been in the hands of the Chinese for many years. Magsaysay was critical of this measure and fearful lest it set a pattern for the nationalization of banks, printing, medicine, and other activities, but he yielded to the pressures of the people, who had long resented the economic hold the Chinese had gained.

The unemployment which had plagued the Philippines was not arrested, either. Strong measures based on a carefully thought-out program of economic planning for a long period of years would have had to be taken to correct this situation. Magsaysay had neither the training nor the inclination to tackle this tremendously complicated task, and unemployment is still a primary problem of the Philippines.

Magsaysay was bitterly attacked by many economists and other intellectuals who accused him of being a super-salesman, running a government by public relations. They said he raised false hopes based on temporary expedients, that he had no long-range plan for the improvement of the Philippine economy. Many of these men felt that further industrialization was one basic change which was needed, in order to draw men off the land, rather than to encourage them to settle on it.

Magsaysay's chief critic was Senator Claro Recto, a leading scholar and elder statesman whom Magsaysay admired personally and to whom he owed much politically before he broke with him.

One of the many points on which these two men disagreed was the desirable degree of co-operation with the United States. Magsaysay felt that the ties with the States should be strengthened, while Recto led the group which felt that the Philippines were much too dependent on, and much too closely allied with, their former rulers.

Magsaysay knew that his work had just begun, and he was aware of many of the problems which lay ahead. In his State of the Union address to Congress in 1957, he said:

Much remains to be done. We must continue our vigilance. Communism with its ever-shifting tactics remains a threat. We cannot afford to falter in our social justice problem. The masses of our people, the base of our democracy, will continue to be the beneficiaries of our special concern and our devotion. We must accelerate the pace of economic progress. Mindful of our duty to our people and determined in our goals, we must better our accomplishments of the past three years with a renewed dedication to the public welfare.

But the chance to foster further gains was not to be his. In the midst of his efforts, his life was cut short by the airplane accident on a Philippine hillside.

When they brought his body back from the mountains in a plane, five hundred thousand people waited to view the remains of their hero, their "guy." Two million people attended the funeral, lining the streets and perching on the rafters of unfinished buildings. These were his friends—the jeepney drivers, the mechanics, the *barrio* farmers and their wives and children, the keepers of *sari-saris*—the masses to whom he meant so much.

He was buried with a simple marker, with the dates of his birth and death, the years of his tenure as President, and the simple words, "President of the Philippines."

He had been a common man but an uncommon leader and a "wonderful guy" to the Filipinos.

INDEX

Abdullah, of Transjordan, 204, 205, 206, 207

Aborigines Rights Protection Society of the Gold Coast, 72

Achille, Louis T., 96

Aden, 158

African Scholarships Program of American Universities, 24–25

African Students Organization of America and Canada, 70

Afro-Asian Conference at Bandung, 286, 311–15

Aggrey, influence of, on Nkrumah, 68

Ailey, Alvin, dancers, 93

Akan tribe of Gold Coast, 65, 67

Akintolo, of Western Region of Nigeria, 62

Algeria, 149, 153–54, 158

Al-Kuwatly, Shukri, of Syria, 174

All-African Peoples' Conference, 88

All-India Congress, 228–29, 230, 231, 236, 238, 243, 254, 257

All-India Home Rule League, 230, 250

All-India Moslem League, *See* Moslem League of India

Anthologie de la nouvelle poésie nègre (Senghor), 103–4

Anti-Fascist People's Freedom League of Burma, 279, 288

"Application of John Mill's Arguments for Feminism as Applied to the Tribal Societies of Tanganyika, An" (Nyerere), 9

Arab Higher Committee for Palestine, 219

Arab League, 154

Arab Legion, 205, 212–13

Arab refugees from Palestine, 206

Arabs in Tanganyika, 8, 14

Arab Union, 158, 175, 218–19

Arafa, Moulay, of Morocco, 119, 121

Arden-Clarke, Sir Charles, in Gold Coast, 76

Aswan Dam project in Egypt, 167, 170–71, 176, 199

Ataturk, Kemal, of Turkey, 146

Atomic Energy Commission of Tunisia, 151

Attlee, Clement, 258

Aung San, of Burma, 279

Azikiwe, Nnamdi, influence of, on Nkrumak, 69

Baghdad Pact, 212

Balewa, Abubakar Tafawa, of Nigeria, 48–64; kidnapping and murder of, 49–50; Northern Region background of, 51; education of, 52; work of, for a united Nigeria, 53, 55; honors received by, on visit to Britain, 53; as Minister of Public Works, 53; as Minister of Transport, 54; visit to U.S. by, 54, 55–56; as Prime Minister of Education of Nigeria, 54; as Prime Minister of independent Nigeria, 55–56, 59, 60, 62–63; personal life of, 61–62; inaction of, at critical times, 62–63

Balfour Declaration of 1917, 159, 161, 186–87

Bama Let Yon Tat organization of Burma, 277

Bandung Conference, Afro-Asian, 286, 311–15

Banerjeq, Surendranath, of India, 230

Bedouins of Transjordan, 187, 211, 213, 221

Belgian explorers in Tanganyika, 8

ments of, 255–56, 257, 258; autobiography of, 256; and wearing
of a red rose, 257; visits of, to
Spain, Burma, Malaya, China,
257; on Britain and independence
of India, 257–58; on independence of India, 259–60; goals of,
for independent India, 261–67;
and Communism, 265–66, 268,
269; "Neutralist" policy of, 267;
as "independent" in international
relations, 268; faults and virtues
of, 269; as synthesis of East and
West, 269
Nehru, Motilal, 247, 251, 252, 254,
256
"Neo-colonialism" in Africa, 89
Neo-Destour party of Tunisia, 131,
134, 135, 137, 138, 140, 141,
149
Nepotism in African culture, 61
Ne Win, of Burma, 288–89
Ngengi, Kamau. See Kenyatta, Jomo,
of Kenya
Nigeria, 48–64; tribal and linguistic
divisions of, 50; geographical-po-
litical divisions of, 50–51; religious groups in, 51; becomes independent nation within British
Commonwealth, 51, 55, 57; resources of, 57, 60; educational
program in, 58, 59; fighting diseases in, 59; National Development Plan for 1962–68, 59–60;
disunity and discontent among
people of, 60–61; military take-
over of, after murder of Balewa,
63. See also Balewa, Abubakar
Tafawa
Nixon, Richard M., 83
Nkoku, Eni, of University of Lagos,
63
Nkrumah, Kwame, of Ghana, 65–91;
study and work in U.S., 65, 68,
70–71; as Prime Minister of
Ghana, 65; background of, 65–
67; early schooling of, 68–69; as

teacher, 69; study in England,
71–72; race prejudice, experience
with, in U.S. and England, 71,
72; activities of, in independence
movement, 73–82; imprisonment
of, 74, 75; as Prime Minister under British control, 76; power and
drive of, in rise to leadership, 76,
77–82; goals of, 77–79; as clever
strategist, 80; personality of, 81;
progress of Ghana under government of, 85–87; downfall of, 88–
91
Non-violent resistance: in Gold Coast,
75, 80; of Gandhi, 231–32, 233,
251, 254–55, 257
North African Federation, 153
Northern People's Congress (NPC),
52, 55
Nuwar, of Jordan, 213–15
Nyerere, Julius, of Tanzania, 3–28;
family background of, 4; boyhood
of, 4–5; education of, 5–6, 8–9;
name changed from Kamborage to
Julius, 6; teaching experience of,
9–11; as student at University of
Edinburgh, 10; as devout Roman
Catholic, 10; as orator, 12, 14;
work of, for independence of
Tanganyika, 12–17; attitude of
British government toward, 13;
as temporary member of Legislative Council, 13–14; visit to U.S.,
13, 16–17; factors in popularity
and political success of, 14–15;
as first Prime Minister of independent Tanganyika, 17; as President of Tanganyika, 22–27; self-
help program of, 23, 28; as
President of Tanzania, 27–28;
superior gifts of, 27–28; basic
objectives of, 28

Odinga, Oginga, of Kenya, 45
Okotie, Festus, of Nigeria, 61
On African Socialism (Senghor), 104
Onn, Dato, of Malaya, 302, 303, 304

ABOUT THE AUTHORS

LEONARD KENWORTHY has been interested in world affairs for many years. In 1940–41 he was director of the Quaker International Center in Berlin, where he worked in the interest of Allied prisoners of war and assisted Jewish refugees. He joined the staff of the United Nations Educational, Scientific, and Cultural Organization (UNESCO) in 1946, heading its section on education for international understanding.

For the past few years Dr. Kenworthy has been Professor of Education at Brooklyn College of the City University of New York, and has traveled extensively, having visited eighty-three countries and territories. In addition, he has served as curriculum consultant to many school systems and has written widely for people of all ages.

ERMA FERRARI grew up in northern Maine and was educated at Bates College.

Her writing credits include magazine articles and several books for young people. She lives in New York City and is on the staff of a publishing house.